Inside Today's Elementary Schools

James J. Dillon

Inside Today's Elementary Schools

A Psychologist's Perspective

James J. Dillon
Department of Psychology
University of West Georgia
Carrollton, GA, USA

ISBN 978-3-030-23346-4   ISBN 978-3-030-23347-1 (eBook)
https://doi.org/10.1007/978-3-030-23347-1

© The Editor(s) (if applicable) and The Author(s), under exclusive licence to Springer Nature Switzerland AG 2019
This work is subject to copyright. All rights are solely and exclusively licensed by the Publisher, whether the whole or part of the material is concerned, specifically the rights of translation, reprinting, reuse of illustrations, recitation, broadcasting, reproduction on microfilms or in any other physical way, and transmission or information storage and retrieval, electronic adaptation, computer software, or by similar or dissimilar methodology now known or hereafter developed.
The use of general descriptive names, registered names, trademarks, service marks, etc. in this publication does not imply, even in the absence of a specific statement, that such names are exempt from the relevant protective laws and regulations and therefore free for general use.
The publisher, the authors and the editors are safe to assume that the advice and information in this book are believed to be true and accurate at the date of publication. Neither the publisher nor the authors or the editors give a warranty, express or implied, with respect to the material contained herein or for any errors or omissions that may have been made. The publisher remains neutral with regard to jurisdictional claims in published maps and institutional affiliations.

Cover illustration: Monika Mlynek / Alamy Stock Photo

This Palgrave Macmillan imprint is published by the registered company Springer Nature Switzerland AG
The registered company address is: Gewerbestrasse 11, 6330 Cham, Switzerland

Acknowledgments

I would like to thank my elementary education professors, especially Ronald S. Reigner and Rosalind Duplechain. I am also grateful to all my supervising elementary teachers who opened their classroom doors to me and taught me more than they will ever know. I thank Andrea Laubstein and Isabel Tweedie who gave me countless hours of help researching this book. I also thank all those who read and commented on my work in its early drafts. I thank my wife Kaki and two children, Ben and Zoe, for helping me to appreciate what is important in life. Mostly, I want to thank all the little students I have had the pleasure of interviewing or teaching over these many years. They have taught me as much or more than I taught them.

Contents

Part I	Shortsighted Vision and Lopsided Staffing	1
1	**The House on Sleepy Hollow Road**	3
	Bridges and Potholes	6
	How the Book Is Organized	9
2	**So Many Girls…So Few Princes**	11
	Some Negative Effects of the Gender Staffing Imbalance	16
	References	24
3	**When Am I Ever Going to Use Any of This?**	27
	Adventure and High Purpose	29
	The Romantic Child	29
	Lessons from Harry Potter	31
	Industry Versus Inferiority	36
	The Zombie Apocalypse	38
	References	42
4	**"And Then God Made School Boards"**	45
	The Administration	48
	Total Management Mentality	53
	Adversarial Posture	55

	Who Becomes an Administrator?	56
	Toxic Culture	57
	The Good Ones	60
	References	63
5	**The Bottom of the Barrel?**	67
	Women's Work: The Mother	68
	Drill and Kill: The Sergeant	70
	Just Tell Me What to Do: The Sheep	72
	The Easiest Major: The Underachiever	73
	Teacher Training, Where It All Begins	76
	Why Should We Teach Anyway?	78
	References	82
6	**What to Do About These Four Things**	85
	Our Vision of Teachers and Schools	86
	Personnel Reform	95
	References	102

Part II	**The Wall of Separation, Administrative Bloat, and Boundless Accommodation**	103
7	**Platonic Curriculum; Epicurean Society**	105
	Who Formulates the Standards?	107
	What Are Standards Designed to Do?	109
	What Is the Nature of the Standards?	111
	Five Basic Problems with Current Elementary Standards	113
	Three Possible Solutions	119
	References	123
8	**Just Wastin' Time**	125
	The Different Kinds of Wasted Time	127
	Where Does the Time Go?	128

	Time-Off-Task	132
	Why Is so Much Time Lost?	134
	How Lost Time Negatively Impacts Teacher and Student	136
	References	138
9	**No Child Left Behind?**	143
	A Brief History of Standardized Tests	145
	Common Critiques	148
	The Real Reason Why NCLB Caused So Much Trouble	153
	Life After NCLB	158
	References	162
10	**I'm Five Teachers at Once!**	165
	What Is DI?	167
	A Sympathetic Critique of DI	168
	Less Noble Reasons for Using DI	178
	References	182
11	**The Incredible Bending School**	185
	Reasonable Special Education and Non-Academic Services	187
	Unreasonable Special Education and Non-Academic Services	189
	References	202
12	**Look Not to the Stars**	205
	A Picture of Contemporary Parental Engagement	207
	Barriers to Parental Engagement	209
	Why Parental Engagement Matters	210
	References	213
13	**What to Do About These Six Things**	215
	Wall of Separation	215
	Multiplying Diversions	228
	References	231

Part III What to Do About All Ten Things   235

14 A New Day   237
   Dealing with Fear   238
   Seeing Through Ideology   240
   Letting Go of the Need to Control   244
   Conclusion   252
   References   254

Index   257

PART I

Shortsighted Vision and Lopsided Staffing

CHAPTER 1

The House on Sleepy Hollow Road

When I was a child, there was a huge old house about a mile from mine. It sat, eerily enough, on a street called *Sleepy Hollow Road*. It was in a terrible state of disrepair. The lawn was never mowed and the shingles on the roof had seen better days, but it was older and statelier than the other houses in the neighborhood.

You could tell there was something important about this house, that it had a magnificent past. But there was a cast iron fence all around it. Nobody from the neighborhood had been inside. I do not ever recall seeing an actual person in or around that house. Of course, stories abounded among us kids about what went on in there. One friend heard a couple lived there who years ago killed and ate their children. Another was certain the house was owned by an old lady with 23 cats. Other friends advanced varieties of the "haunted house" theory. At some point, I probably believed all these stories. What is notable is that while nobody had ever been inside the house or met any of the people who lived there, *everyone* had a clear and strong view about what went on in that strange place.

Today's schools are a lot like that mysterious house on *Sleepy Hollow Road*. Our schools are perhaps not quite so spooky, but we drive or walk past them every day and speculate about what goes on inside. There are no large metal fences, but real barriers exist. We citizens, parents, politicians, and even educational researchers and administrators really know precious little about the inner life and daily rhythms of our schools since we see them mostly from the outside. But at the same time, most of us have strong views about what is wrong with the schools and how to fix them.

I want this book to crack open the creaky front gate of that old house on *Sleepy Hollow Road*. I want to summon up the courage to knock on the door and take a real look inside. This book will provide a tour of today's elementary schools. I will point out the important things I see in there, what I am proud of, and what I am worried about. You can tell me if you see the same things and feel the same way about them. Perhaps you will see and worry about different things.

The American public school system is the most radical and just social project in the history of the world. I will say that again: *in the history of the world*. Our system is better, kinder, fairer, and more ambitious than any other country's on the planet. We should all be supremely proud of it. But our system is a work in progress, a bold idea trying to realize itself and failing to do so in many important ways. For it to have a chance of success, we must all involve ourselves much more in the life of the elementary school than we currently do. We cannot allow our schools to be that scary house on *Sleepy Holly Road* that we have never been in but have strong opinions about. Let us go inside!

I want you to imagine making a visit to a public elementary school. Perhaps it is the school you attended as a child. Perhaps it is the school you have kids in now or is the one your kids used to attend. Perhaps it is the one your kids will attend someday. The important thing is to visualize right now an actual elementary school building. Imagine getting into your car or taking the bus to this school. Your tour begins at 8:00 on a Monday morning. You have arranged your tour with the principal, so they are expecting you. You will spend the day inside of a second-grade classroom. If you are driving a car, it may be hard to find a parking spot at this time of the morning. But after circling around several times, you eventually see one. You park your car, get out, and make your way to the front office. You notice a few small jitters in your stomach as you press a button near the door to be buzzed in. After a little waiting, the door clicks open and you step inside.

Before we go in, let me say a few things about myself, your tour guide. I have spent the past 25 years studying the way elementary-aged children learn and grow. I have talked with them, observed them, tested them, analyzed their artwork, and interviewed their parents and teachers. For much of my career, I have worked as a college professor. I have researched children, published my findings, and taught adults how to understand, parent, and teach young people. I have also been a Cub and Boy Scout leader for the past ten years where I have mentored hundreds of young children. I have two children of my own who went through the public elementary schools. My brother has been a fifth-grade teacher for the past 25 years. My wife is an elementary paraprofessional of six years. And my mother-in-law taught elementary school for almost 40 years. Many of my friends are public elementary school teachers. Education is in my blood.

About seven years ago, following a lifelong dream, I decided I wanted not just to study children's learning but to teach children myself in my very own classroom. So I went back to school to earn my state teaching certificate, a gray-haired man in his late 40s amidst the millennial generation's earbuds and smartphones. Though I had a doctorate in child psychology, I returned to classes to take about 60 hours of undergraduate courses, which were required to become a certified, public elementary school teacher.

In addition to the coursework, teachers-in-training must get hands-on experience by doing practicum work in real elementary classrooms. I had the opportunity to work at four different public elementary schools over a three-year period. Two were poor and two were affluent. These field placements involved me in almost 1000 hours of supervised experience in elementary classrooms at almost every grade level. Four hundred of my supervised hours involved full-time student teaching in a second-grade classroom. In 2014, I finished my coursework and passed the state licensing exam in Georgia. For this book, I have interviewed 18 elementary school teachers and over 30 elementary school students from across the country.

Much of what I experienced about the way teachers are trained and what really goes on in elementary school classrooms inspired me. Other things surprised me. Perhaps the most surprising thing of all was how different the world of the elementary school is from almost anywhere else in the world. It has its own rhythms, tone, and rules. Most of the time I felt like I was living a double life: there was my neighbor-father-husband life at home and there was my teacher life at the elementary school. The closest analogy I can draw to describe this situation is the military. When soldiers return from battle or from an extended stay on a military base, they often need time to adjust to the vast differences between these two worlds. During my classes and field experiences, I would often ask myself, "I wonder what the parents of these children would say if they could see this?" or "If the governor or my congressman could just sit with me for an hour in this classroom and watch what really goes on, I wonder how they would think about their policies when they returned to the legislature?" I would come home at night after spending all day in an elementary classroom and it felt like I was returning from another planet.

BRIDGES AND POTHOLES

While politicians and administrators are responsible for funding, managing, and supervising the educational system, it is not clear to me how much time they have spent in actual classrooms, much less teaching a classroom themselves. Yes, they visit occasionally and even read a story to a pre-selected group of kids in the library, but anyone who has spent more than a few hours in a real classroom quickly realizes that when most politicians and administrators talk, they sound like people who know almost nothing about education. They speak passionately about schools and teachers using words like "accountability," "testing," "standards," and "merit pay," but almost all teachers know politicians and administrators are not talking about things that will really make things better for students. Administrators roll out new plans and initiatives with great fanfare every two or three years, but teachers have seen this dog and pony show before. Most of them will simply roll their eyes and yawn, knowing when the initiative fails or runs out of funding in a few years, they will be left all alone with their students once again.

A good education is the key to a successful life, especially in today's "information economy." Nobody wants their kids "left behind" and people are terrified it will happen to them. Teachers know that politicians and administrators respond mostly to the fears and ignorance of parents, not the daily rhythms of the classroom and the needs of real students. But fear and ignorance are not the soundest foundation upon which to build an educational system. The gap between those who work with elementary children all day and those who do not is alarmingly large.

When parents ask their kids how things are going at school, the most many get is a "fine." Yes, there are carefully staged visits for "curriculum night" or to chaperone a field trip, but these glimpses do not give them anything close to a sense of what really goes on in there. Most of us parents have no clue what goes on inside our kids' classrooms. This book is my attempt to build a bridge between these two worlds, to give people who are not a daily part of elementary education a sense of what really goes on there. Harkening to Dr. Seuss' "Thing 1" and "Thing 2," the book reveals ten surprising and even worrisome Things in our elementary schools and then considers what to do about them.

I offer one cautionary note before I return to our tour. There are a few areas of life I think of as "potholes." These are not actual gashes in the road, but potentially disastrous topics that you steer clear of in polite conversation. Politics can be a pothole. So is religion, parenting, nutrition, and exercise. We can get extremely emotional about these topics when they are discussed in public. We can become rigid and defensive, closed to different points of view. It seems these days there is less and less space to talk rationally and to deliberate together about controversial topics. Education is a pothole as well. Think of the last time the plight of the schools came up over Thanksgiving dinner. How did that go? So, another way to think of this book is that I am driving straight into a big pothole!

Given the emotional attachment we all have to issues of education, some things I say might at first seem uninformed by the latest theory or research. They might even seem ignorant, or worse, crazy, sexist, or as though Western civilization itself will collapse if they are implemented. These are the kinds of reactions that come up when people talk about education. Please trust that I care very much about all children and their development. I am a fierce supporter of public schools and the teachers who work in them. My point is not to advance an ideology, or dismantle one, but simply to share what I see and think in an open space where hopefully we can talk together about important matters. So before I advance specific ideas in this book, it is important to first establish a rational, deliberative space where we can reflect calmly on the state of contemporary public elementary education from a teacher's perspective. All of what follows cannot sink in if this zone is not first opened. I hope you will give me this space as a reader. I will give you this space if you respond to me as an author.

There are many—far too many—books about education on the market. While some offer real contributions, many are written by either ideologues or salespeople. *Ideologues* seek to change the way you see education, the lens you use to look at the schools. Some ideologies want you to view teachers as lazy and unaccountable. Others will have you view schools as spiritually desolate places in desperate need of prayer or corporal punishment or as bastions of racial oppression. Others will have you look at schools as institutions that are desperately underfunded, or wastefully overfunded, or as places where there is not enough testing, or too much testing, or the wrong kind of testing.

For the most part, ideologies are not helpful in the realm of education. Ideologies offer neat theories and coherent causal narratives. But education is messy and complex territory with many different factors in play, and so it is not easily understood from a single perspective. Further, schools vary greatly within single districts and across states, making general statements very difficult. Pablo Picasso once said, "When art critics get together, they talk about Form and Structure and Meaning. When artists get together, they talk about where you can buy cheap turpentine." Using this analogy, teachers are the artists; educational researchers, political advocates, and administrators are the art critics. Rarely do teachers themselves advance any grand theory of education, have an ideology, or even a political position. Most teachers work together every day with very diverse colleagues and students to achieve concrete and practical tasks. They often have great ideas about how to do these tasks, along with hard-earned wisdom about how not to do these tasks. It is typically people outside of the classroom who advance theory or ideology, and they unfortunately have most of the power and influence.

The other type of education book is written by what I call *salespeople*. Sometimes these salespeople are researchers or scholars like me. They assemble a mass of persuasive data and statistics to show what is wrong with the schools. But the data are a pretext to sell you their own method to fix it. These fix-it strategies will be either educational or managerial. *Educational fix-it books* will offer some new curriculum or teaching technique designed to correct the problems the author has identified. Education is perhaps the most prone to this type of analysis and has succumbed to numerous fads and foolish policy changes over the decades based on all of this research. *Managerial fix-it books*, on the other hand, use research (or ideology) to argue that if only we make some type of policy changes—abolish teacher tenure, pay teachers more, formally address racial oppression or economic inequality, change the way we assess teachers, test students more, or less, or differently—our educational problems will be solved. My point is that these two kinds of education books are largely irrelevant to the actual process of teaching. These books are like the "Form, Structure, and Meaning" Picasso spoke of in the earlier quote. In this book, what I am really interested in is turpentine.

How the Book Is Organized

Each chapter of the book presents a different Thing about elementary education that might surprise you. I will talk about the positive aspects of each Thing and then explore the negatives. At the end of each chapter, I present a list of suggestions you might try as a parent or citizen to respond to or address this Thing. In Part I, I discuss the first four Things; in Part II, I discuss the last six. At the end of each part, I have a separate chapter where I pause and digest the various Things considered so far and brainstorm some possible solutions to them. The last part of the book presents a vision of an elementary school system where each of these ten Things has been changed or improved. It envisions a "New Day" for our elementary schools.

Let me lower your expectations a bit. I will not tell you everything that is wrong with education and then sell some one method to fix it. I will not offer some new theory or management technique based on my research which will transform education. I will not roll out some new educational fad promising to motivate students or improve test scores. If I do have a solution, it will be complex, multifaceted, and likely difficult to achieve in today's political climate. I should say too that I work hard not to blame teachers in this book, so if you are looking forward to some "teacher bashing," you will likely be disappointed. I will also not blame tests or testing for our woes.

If anyone is to blame for our schools' problems, *it is you*. That is right, you. That is a pretty bold and potentially reckless statement to make, particularly if you have not purchased the book yet! I insult the reader before getting out of the Introduction. I mean no offense. The premise of the book is that we the public, the educational non-experts, have relied far too much on politicians, administrators, and teachers to do the hard work of education for us. We expect more from teachers and schools than they can possibly achieve, and we leave ourselves off the hook when many of our kids fail. Perhaps we will rise to the challenge and take that first courageous step inside today's elementary schools. Are you ready?

CHAPTER 2

So Many Girls…So Few Princes

Back to the tour. You step through the front door and enter the school building. The first thing you notice is the smell of the school. It is almost the same as your own elementary school from years ago. You walk toward the front office and are greeted by the secretary, Mrs. Davis, a warm woman with big, welcoming eyes. She instructs you to sign in as a visitor. She then hands you a plastic tag to wear around your neck to identify you as a "cleared person." Mrs. Davis says you will spend the day in Room 315, a second-grade classroom up one flight of stairs and down the hall about ten doors to the right. She points out the room on a printed floor map and circles it with a yellow highlighter pen. Another teacher comes into the office to report that one of the busses is late. It is Miss Phillips, your daughter's Kindergarten teacher from three years ago. You briefly say hello as she gets her mail, exchange a friendly hug, and excuse yourself to start out for your classroom.

You make your way past the front office and wander through the hallways, admiring the student work on the walls. You notice some papier mache masks on the wall to the right and some graded essays hanging to the left. There are some athletic trophies in a case a little farther down, and a brightly colored bulletin board decorated with the names of this month's "Star AR Readers." You peek into the different classrooms as you walk by. In one room, Miss Abbie reads to a group of first graders in a circle on the carpet. In another, Mrs. Sanchez has her third-grade class practice addition with interlocking blocks.

In addition to the smell, the sights and sounds of the school are also familiar to you, taking you back to your own childhood. At this point, you may be flooded with memories from your own school days. Sometimes you will recall very specific images; other times you will recall powerful feelings. Some are bad, and some are good, but all are powerful. You see Room 315 approaching on the right. You timidly walk to the door to knock. The teacher steps out and you meet Miss Thomas, a bright-eyed and enthusiastic woman in her mid-40s. She invites you in, introduces you to the class, and points you to the back of the room where you will observe until dismissal at 2:45 p.m.

As you say hello to the now curious children and sit in your chair at an unoccupied desk, you think to yourself what nice and pleasant women all the teachers and staff have been thus far. Come to think of it, all the staff and teachers you have seen so far have been women. Other than the police officer directing traffic in front of the school, everyone you have seen working here is female. This is not just a fluke about your school, your district, your state, or your national region. It is true of almost all of schools in the country. In the United States, 87% of all elementary school teachers are female. About 97.7% of pre-K and Kindergarten teachers are female (UNESCO Institute for Statistics, 2019). There are similarly high numbers of female teachers in schools across the world, but the United States has the highest.

There are a variety of reasons for this gender imbalance, most having to do with *sexism* and *status*. In the past, discriminatory practices in education and labor directed women to work only in areas like teaching and nursing (Laughlin, 2000). These fields were viewed as suited for "women's work." The passage of the landmark *Title IX of the Education Amendments* of 1972 formally removed barriers that prevented women from entering previously prohibited fields of study and enabled women to enter career areas that were historically closed to them.

This is all to be greatly celebrated, but despite the great strides women have made into previously male-dominated areas, there has not been a corresponding flow of men into the female-dominated area of teaching. In fact, the percentage of women in elementary teaching grows *larger* with the passage of time. In 1981, for example, the percentage of male teachers in elementary school was 18%. Now it is 13%. Though many more career paths are now open to women compared to 30 years ago, the idea that certain fields are "women's work" still appears to be with us.

Why does this gender imbalance persist and grow in elementary schools? This is a complex issue with no single explanation. Some have suggested because women are the primary caregivers in their families, they are more interested in the teaching profession than men because they can work a similar schedule as their own school-aged children. Others argue that because of their nature or socialization, women are simply more attracted to "nurturing" work like teaching and healing than men are (Rich, 2014). For example, in my own college classes on the Psychology of Childhood or Developmental Psychology, it is typical in a class of 40 students for there to be only two or three male students registered. It seems for many men, working with or learning about children is not a very "macho" thing to do.

Cappuozzo (2011) notes that over the past few decades, girls have been invited to enter historically male-dominated fields like math and science, but boys have not been presented with similar incentives to enter female-dominated professions like education. Ingersoll, Merrill, and Stuckey (2018) surmise that since teaching is already dominated by women, many men come to associate teaching with work "not suitable for males." Others have spoken of a widespread cultural devaluation of work traditionally done by women. In this sense, men would not be attracted to elementary teaching because they do not value or respect what they see as "women's work" or "nose-wiping" as one of my male graduate school psychology professors derisively called it decades ago.

Tyre (2009) suggests that female teachers can also practice a subtle form of reverse discrimination when they interview male teacher candidates for a job. She cites an investigation conducted by Wilmette, Illinois, school principal Max McGee in which he asked his human resources director to conduct an experiment. The director asked the most successful male teachers to submit to the interview process again. Little did the interviewers know they were interviewing already successful male teachers. McGee found that the best male teachers responded to standard interview questions in a way that the largely female hiring committee found unacceptable and led them not to want to hire these male applicants. As an example, the committee asked in an interview how a prospective teacher would respond to a difference of opinion in a staff meeting. According to the committee, acceptable answers included words like "understanding" and "collaboration." But many male teachers answered this question in a way that suggested they were not interested in "coalition building." For example, a male interviewee said he "respected other people's right to disagree," which the committee judged to be too confrontational.

There is also a pernicious cultural stigma attached to males who teach in the preschool and elementary grades. Daitsman (2011), a former preschool teacher, notes that male preschool and elementary teachers are often assumed to be pedophiles, homosexuals, or just not "manly" enough for wanting to work with little children. I have seen and experienced this negative stereotype personally. It is quite real. Being seen as a potential pedophile is not a very attractive work climate to have to deal with, and so many men just stay away from it.

Additionally, men are also deterred from teaching because of how poorly educators are paid. Since many men feel a pressure to be the "breadwinner," a profession that averages $40,000 per year may not fit the bill in a young man's mind. Another factor taking men out of the elementary classroom is a phenomenon known as the "glass escalator" in which the men who do enter the teaching profession tend to be promoted more quickly to administrative positions than women (Williams, 1992). For example, while only 13% of elementary teachers are male, 50% of school principals are male.

All of this is to say there are some real obstacles to contend with on the path toward establishing a gender staffing balance in elementary education. What makes this issue even more difficult is the all-too-recent legacy of legally supported discrimination against women in employment. Given women's past victimization, there is a tendency to ignore the gender imbalance in schools or to treat it as if it were not a problem. After all, many reason, women have suffered enough with oppression and dealt with male-dominated fields for centuries. Maybe they deserve their own career area for a change. Besides, some others say, the gender imbalance in education does not matter anyway. All that matters is finding good teachers, regardless of gender.

Some readers may hear my words that there are "too many" women in elementary education and become angry. They may interpret my effort to establish a gender staffing balance as an attempt to take away the impressive and rightfully gained achievements women have made in education over the past 40 years, to "turn back the clock" as it were. Nothing could be farther from the truth. My point is not to take away any of the great progress women have made in so many areas over the past three decades or to claim that men are somehow oppressed. Gender balance is not a zero-sum game. Everyone wins when we have true equity in the workplace.

With very few exceptions, the women who do the work of elementary teaching do it incredibly well. They are dedicated, creative, organized, compassionate, patient, and practical. Elementary teachers work very hard for long hours. Public school teachers are five times more likely to have a part-time job than the average full-time worker in the United States

(U.S. Department of Labor, 2019). Most of them will do whatever it takes to reach their students. They get on the floor, sing, and dance. They wear ridiculous costumes to work. They spend an average of $479 per year of their own money getting materials in order to adequately teach their students (U.S. Department of Education, 2018). If you spend even a few hours watching these women at their craft, they will touch you to the point where you tear up and cry. All my mentors in elementary education have been women and I have tried to absorb as much of their wisdom and talents as I can.

The problem with the 87% figure is not with the women who are already part of education, *but with all the men who are not*. Any organization staffed by almost 90% of any one gender begins to develop certain problems as a result of the imbalance. What makes gender balance such a wonderful thing in almost all areas of life is that, with some exceptions of course, men and women tend to complement one another. That is, we each bring things to the table the other does not do as well, or as easily. We each have weaknesses that the other gender helps compensate, strengths the other gender does not possess in quite the same measure. In my experience, organizations without a gender balance become lopsided with a single gender energy that is not modulated by its complementary counterpart. As one of my supervising female elementary teachers said once in frustration when things started to get tense between her and a colleague on the six-member, all-female fourth-grade team, "there's just too much estrogen in this room for anyone's good!"

Let me pause and consider how discussions of gender and education typically go. Someone says something or presents scientific findings related to gender like, "women tend to be better at multi-tasking," "boys tend to be more active in the classroom," or "girls tend to be better writers." The critical reader or listener then rifles through his or her memory to find the single exception that will counter the claim. "Wait a minute," they say to themselves, "I am a woman and I am terrible at multi-tasking" or "I had a boy in my class last year who sat as still as the ocean" or "I have a girl in my class this year who is a terrible writer." With these exceptions in mind, we feel free to ignore the claim about "gender differences." On some level, this is a healthy strategy. We are bombarded by casual statements about gender all the time which are little more than harmful stereotypes. But if this critical attitude blinds us to gender differences which are supported by dispassionate scientific investigation, then our critical strategies run the risk of blinding us to the salient features of real children's lives. *Gender differences concern averages, not individuals.*

The nature of the claims I make about gender and education are modest and based on differences observed across great numbers of children. I am not talking about every single person, but tendencies across large numbers of people. The differences I discuss are aggregate differences which have some research to support them. They will surely not apply in every single individual case. Finding the single exception will not necessarily refute my claims of gender difference. So rather than say "boys" or "girls," "men" or "women," I will say "many boys" or "many women." I do this to reflect the reality that we are dealing with a continuum of traits and behaviors that are present in individuals in very different degrees. But it is important to remember that differences do not have to be individual to be real.

SOME NEGATIVE EFFECTS OF THE GENDER STAFFING IMBALANCE

Let us explore a few potentially negative effects of the elementary school gender staffing imbalance by returning to the scene of our tour. As you sit in the back of the classroom observing Miss Thomas hard at work, what may immediately catch your eye are several students sprinkled around the room who seem to be having a very hard time staying on task. They are out of their seats when they should be sitting and working quietly. Perhaps they are rolling on the floor when they should be at their desks. Perhaps they are using their pencil like a weapon instead of a writing implement or are poking the student next to them. You will probably feel some need to help the teacher deal with these students, to get the students to "behave." Some teachers try to ignore this kind of disruptive behavior as much as they can, reasoning the more attention they give to it just reinforces and makes it more likely to occur in the future.

Others deal with disruptive behaviors more directly. Perhaps the teacher will give the disruptive student a stern look, remind them of the rules, or move them to sit somewhere else. The teacher may threaten them with the loss of a privilege like recess or computer time. They may try to motivate them with the promise of some future reward. They may ask them to come up and "move their stick," by placing a clothesline clip from a happy face to a frowning face. They may ask them to "put themselves on yellow" on the traffic signal chart on the side wall. They may warn them that they may have to call mom, dad, or grandma to let them know how bad their behavior is. They may even take a picture or video of the misbehaving child and text it to the parent! They may need to move the student to a corner for a "time out" or even send them to another classroom or to the office. If you stay long enough, you are likely to see many of these "classroom management" strategies. Keep in mind, the teacher needs to do all this while also trying to teach a lesson to the other 25 or 30 students in the room.

Let me pause this scenario for a moment. You just imagined a disruptive group of students. When you pictured these kids in your mind, were they boys or girls? I bet you said boys. I did not use any gender-specific pronouns like "he" or "she" in my scenario. If you pictured boys as the disruptive parties, it does not mean you are prejudiced or biased. It simply means you are observant. Statistically speaking, most disruptive students *are* boys. Boys make up 90% of discipline referrals in school (Gurian & Stevens, 2004; Yang, Harmeyer, Chen, & Lofaso, 2018). About 5.28% of elementary students are suspended out of school in any given academic year (National Center for Education Statistics, 2017). The suspension rate in some districts can range as high as 13–24% of students. The rate of elementary male suspension is more than two times as high as the rate of female suspension. In a classroom of 30 students, these figures mean there can be as many as three students from a given classroom who will do something so bad at school, it will get them suspended from the school grounds for some time (usually for violence, drugs, having a gun or weapon, threats, or seriously disruptive behavior).

After about an hour in the school, you may be left with the sense that while the school works for most girls and many of the boys, there are a lot of disengaged, unhappy, unruly, and even violent young boys (and yes, sometimes some girls) which the elementary school has a lot of trouble reaching at all. These students also make it difficult for the teacher to teach and for the other children in the room to learn. These facts lead Tyre (2009) to speak of a "boy problem" in our schools. African American and other marginalized populations academically underperform whites and Asian Americans overall, but this difference masks the boy problem. When we compare males to females of similar races and backgrounds, the females *always significantly outperform the males* by factors of two, three, or four. What this means is that poor African American girls significantly outperform poor African American boys; affluent white girls significantly outperform affluent white boys.

Time spent disengaged or acting out is reflected in poorer grades and lower academic achievement for boys across all races, districts, and socioeconomic classes. Boys make up 70% of all the Ds and Fs given in schools (Gurian & Stevens, 2004). They make up 66% of disability diagnoses and are twice as likely to be held back in Kindergarten (Tyre, 2009, p. 5). If you need more data to convince you, take a look at the list of the Honor Roll at your own child's school, or the list of advanced readers, the awards ceremonies, standardized test scores, or enrollment in Advanced Placement classes if you have kids in high school. It is as though there are two schools in the same building: one for the people who can sit still and another school for the subset of boys (and a few girls) who cannot quite get with the program. This issue has been discussed very well and at length in books like *Raising Cain* (Kindlon, Thompson, & Barker, 2000), *Boys Adrift* (Sax, 2009), *The War Against Boys* (Sommers, 2000), and *The Trouble with Boys* (Tyre, 2009), so I will not belabor it further here. Suffice it to say the trends for many boys in school do not look good and get worse each year.

The plight of modern boys is surely a complicated issue with many biological, psychological, and social factors, but the gender imbalance boys experience at school (and sometimes at home too) is a big part of the problem. So, what is the precise correlation between gender staffing imbalance, academic disengagement, and disruptive behavior at school? Getting our heads around the effect of the gender staffing imbalance on boys involves looking at three separate components: gender identification, classroom structure, and containing high energy.

Gender identification. To begin, gender staffing imbalances are problematic because they deprive many boys of the simple identification with his own gender which female students can easily form with their teachers. Seeing oneself in one's teacher is a powerful bridge into the educational and social world. This issue of identification has been explored in the context of race (see Egalite, Kisida, & Winters, 2015) and has provided a persuasive argument for why members of marginalized groups need to see members of their own group in positions of power and authority. If you are black and all you see are white faces teaching you all day, it is harder to see yourself as a teacher or another important member of society. It can be an alienating experience. This same dynamic applies to gender.

What happens to many boys when they see themselves in their teachers? It is easier for you to imagine yourself doing what he is doing, being both smart and powerful, learning how he handles stress, solves conflict, balances his obligations, and organizes his time. When you talk with them, many male students say academic activities like reading and math are "girlie" and so shy away from them. Seeing that a man can do these things and still be a man is extremely important. Without such a gender identification, the young boy does not have the same kind of "hook" into school. School becomes "mommy stuff," and boys can become frustrated and alienated from the educational process. They start to behave exactly as they currently do: they fidget, daydream, act out, and fight.

From everything that I have seen, many elementary school boys are just plain hungry to have men in their lives. I recall several elementary teaching placements where young male children of all races and backgrounds would touch the hair on my arms or feel the whiskers on my face as if I were an unfamiliar zoo creature. They would constantly sit or stand next to me, wanting to spend all their time with "Mr. Dillon." Now, I am sure I am a nice person, but I am not naïve enough to believe that their attraction to me had all that much to do with me as an individual. I was a lone male in a sea of females. My maleness was by far the most relevant factor for these boys. The young males in the room were drawn to me like water in a desert.

These days we tend to think of gender as irrelevant, that male teachers (or parents) are more or less interchangeable with female teachers (or parents). This is true to an extent. Surely a woman can teach counting as well as a man can, and vice versa. Women can play powerful roles for boys, as men can for girls. But fathers and other male father figures have unique roles to play in a boy's life, which matter very much to the boys themselves (as do mothers and adult women for girls). The important question is not how we adults see and want to see gender, *but how children see it.* For most of them, gender is the most salient feature of the teacher (other than warmth and coldness). Kindergarten teacher and researcher Vivian Paley (1984) writes, "Kindergarten is a triumph of sexual stereotyping. No amount of adult subterfuge or propaganda deflects the five-year-olds' passion for segregation by sex" (p. ix).

Classroom structure. A second negative effect of the gender staffing imbalance concerns the whole way schools and classrooms are set up. Let us take a closer look at Miss Thomas' classroom. You notice right away the neat tables and chairs with crayons placed on them, stacks of large-lined writing paper, containers filled with pencils, piles of picture books. The placement of these materials right in the center of the room communicates to all who enter what is most important in this place: sitting, reading, and writing. It will look like heaven for those who like to sit, read, and write, but dreadful for those who do not. Off in the back of the room, tucked away in bins and shelves, you notice blocks, scales, action figures, balls, games, and other things that might absorb the more active student. This is not to mention the tantalizing view of the playground and basketball courts just out of reach through the window outside. Instead of being able to move and handle engaging objects in class, students are expected to sit in their chair or on the carpet on their little square, listen to stories about Thanksgiving dinner, and write their letters in coherent form. Maybe, it is promised, they can engage these interesting materials later as a reward. Some boys will accept this bargain, sit still, and stay on task. These will be the successful ones who derive a great benefit from school. But many others exclaim, "Why? Why do I have to wait until later? I will do something engaging right now." They will check out and may never return.

Part of the reason why the boys I cited earlier have a hard time staying on task in school is because the environment is not set up to bring out their natural strengths. It is structured this way in part because it is primarily staffed by women. As helpful as all my own pre-service and in-service education courses were, these classes almost always emphasized the calm, quiet, pensive, and collaborative learning styles of children. We teachers-in-training were taught to construct lessons and assignments that involved group planning, literacy, and numeracy concentration, all in a mostly quiet and noncompetitive setting. I rarely heard a lecture and was never trained to plan academic lessons that stressed individual achievement, competition, noise, and physical action. It is no accident that all but one of my teachers were women.

If you are a male and spend any time in a school, you notice this peculiar structure right away. With some exceptions, many young boys can experience women's preferred social and psychological processes as alien to their own. Please do not misunderstand. Boys identify with and benefit from women's psychological processes, but if that is all they get, it can gradually become alienating. Boys are constantly put in groups, given collective tasks on which they need to cooperate and share their thoughts and feelings openly with others through either speech, reading aloud, or writing. These are valuable skills for sure, but they do not play to many boys' natural strengths or preferences. In classrooms filled with both male and female children, it seems a far better idea to combine the cooperative learning strategies that now exist with more individualistic and competitive options, and then allow choice for participation from both genders. What would help is an option I will discuss in more detail in Chap. 14, where elementary classrooms would be taught by two certified teachers instead of one, ideally one male and the other female.

High energy. The third area where the gender staffing imbalance may negatively impact boys concerns some boys' maddeningly high level of energy. I recall when my own son was five years old. We were on vacation and had many activities planned. He was so engaged in each one, I kept waiting until he would tire and need a nap. By the end of the day, we had done about nine miles of hiking, spent several hours swimming, rowed in a canoe, set up a tent, and gone on a short nature walk. I thought to myself, "if he has this much energy on a single day over the weekend, what does he do with it while immobile at school all day?" Boys at school often look terribly out of place. They constantly wiggle in their seats, talk, get up, and move around.

Many women (and some men) do not understand and struggle to contain this high male energy in their students. They often look at these high-impact boys with an admixture of fear, fascination, and irritation. There is a great risk for them to misinterpret behaviors as violent or antisocial when they are not. Many boys are just being the active people they are. Schools can be terribly unwelcoming places for active people. Broward County schools in Florida, for example, recently banned running, even on the playground. Most schools also show zero tolerance for most forms of rough play or even fantasied aggression like running around the playground "pretending" to shoot each other with a finger made into a gun. When you ask a boy to write an essay or short story, it can be some violent or gory stuff. Sometimes this play is problematic, but often he is playing at being the best, most compassionate, most heroic kind of man imaginable. I have found that most male teachers understand this in boys, while many women struggle.

Schools tend to shut this behavior down to forestall problems, fearing the boys' energy will escalate into arguments or fights. They also work hard to help "civilize" boys, to make them calmer, more capable of focused concentration, more cooperative, and less impulse-driven. All of this is to the good, but what schools forget is that the civilizing process cannot squelch a boy's energy, aggression, and competitiveness, but only help channel it into more productive avenues. When we tell them not to be their active, aggressive selves, we do not teach them not to do it, we teach them to lie and hide it from us. If men and women worked in equal numbers in the schools, I believe there would be more flexibility of response to boys' often harrowing levels of energy.

The problem of boys' engagement in school will not be solved simply by having more male bodies in the building. But it will help. What boys really need are "boy-friendly" teachers. These are teachers who are sensitive to the unique needs and interests of boys (and other active students). Being a male yourself or having your own male child helps cultivate boy-friendliness, but it does not guarantee it. Women can be boy-friendly too. Boy-friendly women can have a similarly positive effect on boys as boy-friendly men, but you do not get the gender identification that comes with a male teacher. Schools need to move in a general direction of boy-friendliness, but also need to have many more male teachers than they currently do to serve the male students. In speaking of the "boy problem," one of my (female) professors from my teaching certification classes said there was an "epidemic shortage of males who go into elementary teaching." It is presenting, she said, "a crisis to society." I think she was really onto something.

> **What You Can Do**
> Here are some actions you can take as a citizen or parent in your own neck of the woods:
>
> 1. Talking about gender is politically explosive. Many principals and legislators are aware of the boy problem, but are scared to talk about it (back to the pothole concept). Do not allow this fear to prevent you from talking about what you see, tackling the boy problem, and dealing with the gender staffing imbalance in schools. Gender politics on the left and the conservative reaction on the right mask the inhospitable environment for learning we have created for many boys. Do not take your eye off that ball.
> 2. Know that the goal of elementary school has changed from when you were a child. School is much more rigorous and difficult than it used to be, and it is a lot less fun. Many Kindergarten and even preschool classrooms now start their days off with phonics or math worksheets. This might not bring out the best in your boy. Make sure you and your child are prepared.
> 3. Advocate for your child and trust yourself. Do not allow teachers to write your child off because he cannot sit still or diagnose him with an attention deficit or learning disability quite so quickly. It could just be that the school is not designed for your child's way of being. Talk with other parents. There is a saying that principals have, "One complaining parent is a fruitcake; three parents are a fruitcake with friends, seven parents are a force to be reckoned with." You are stronger than you think.
> 4. Do not worry so much about your child's future, whether he will get into Harvard and be a brain surgeon. Instead, think about who your child is deep down, what his or her gifts are, and what will make him or her happy in life.

(continued)

(continued)
 5. Pay teachers more. Show them real respect. Do what you can to raise their status and thus make the profession more attractive to males. The median teacher salary in 1970 was $40,000. It is the same today. Pay in other careers for women has gone up 25%. As a member of a democracy, you are in charge of the market pay rate for teachers. Support raising teacher pay in your district and candidates who do so. Earmark taxes specifically to teacher salaries if you are worried about taxes being raised and not used for teacher pay. Fight administrative bloat and the waste of money on non-teaching tasks.
 6. If you have a boy, push to get a competent male teacher. Just one could make all the difference to your son's elementary education. Pressure the principal and school board to hire more males (who don't want to be principals). If they cannot find a male, then be sure to advocate for a boy-friendly female. Bring this pressure for more male teachers to your school, your Parent-Teacher Association, and your principal.
 7. Consider starting boys in school one year later than girls. Boys are about a year behind most girls their age in most school subjects, so having them around girls who are "on their level" will make a world of difference to their self-esteem and later academic confidence.
 8. Consider single-sex classes or schools. These programs would have special active classes, outdoor learning activities, and different behavior and discipline policies than the typical school. If you have an active boy now, make sure the school understands that some "play violence" can be healthy and therapeutic (provided personal boundaries and class rules are respected and adhered to). Many boys are just trying to be heroes.
 9. Advocate for recess at your school. Ask your son what he likes about school, what his favorite class is. Nine out of ten will say recess or Physical Education. This preference matters a great deal.
 10. Be aware of your own bias and the negative stereotypes that you may bring to the idea of men wanting to be around little children all day long. Male teachers pick up on it easily and do not want to deal with your creepy prejudices. They would rather be somewhere they are welcome.

References

Cappuozzo, R. M. (2011). Calling my 'maleness' into question. In L. W. Watson & S. C. Woods (Eds.), *Go where you belong: Male teachers as cultural workers in the lives of children, families, and communities* (pp. 107–112). Boston, MA: Sense Publishers.

Daitsman, J. M. (2011). The teacher with the beard: A nurturing male helps children overcome bias. In L. W. Watson & S. C. Woods (Eds.), *Go where you belong: Male teachers as cultural workers in the lives of children, families, and communities* (pp. 47–54). Boston, MA: Sense Publishers.

Egalite, A. J., Kisida, B., & Winters, M. A. (2015). Representation in the classroom: The effect of own-race teachers on student achievement. *Economics of Education Review, 45*, 44–52. https://doi.org/10.1016/j.econedurev.2015.01.007

Gurian, M., & Stevens, K. (2004). With boys and girls in mind. *Educational Leadership, 62*(3), 21–26.

Ingersoll, R., Merrill, L., & Stuckey, D. (2018). An analysis of nearly 30 years of data on the teaching force sheds new light on the makeup of the occupation—And on staffing priorities. *Educational Leadership, 75*(8), 45–49.

Kindlon, D. J., Thompson, M., & Barker, T. (2000). *Raising Cain: Protecting the emotional life of boys.* New York, NY: Ballantine Books.

Laughlin, K. A. (2000). *Women's work and public policy: A history of the Women's Bureau, U.S. Department of Labor, 1945–1970.* Boston, MA: Northeastern University Press.

National Center for Education Statistics. (2017). Percentage of students suspended and expelled from public elementary and secondary schools, by sex, race/ethnicity, and state: 2013–14. Retrieved from National Center for Education Statistics Website: https://nces.ed.gov/programs/digest/d17/tables/dt17_233.40.asp

Paley, V. G. (1984). *Boys & girls: Superheroes in the doll corner.* Chicago, IL: University of Chicago Press.

Rich, M. (2014, September 6). Why don't more men go into teaching? *The New York Times.* Retrieved from https://www.nytimes.com/2014/09/07/sunday-review/why-dont-more-men-go-into-teaching.html

Sax, L. (2009). *Boys Adrift: The five factors driving the growing epidemic of unmotivated boys and underachieving young men.* New York, NY: Basic Books.

Sommers, C. H. (2000). *The War against boys: How misguided feminism is harming our young men.* New York, NY: Simon & Schuster.

Tyre, P. (2009). *The trouble with boys: A surprising report card on our sons, their problems at school, and what parents and educators must do.* New York, NY: Crown Publishers.

UNESCO Institute for Statistics. (2019). Primary education, teachers (% female). Retrieved from https://data.worldbank.org/indicator/SE.PRM.TCHR.FE.ZS

U.S. Department of Education. (2018). Public school spending on classroom supplies [PDF File]. Retrieved from National Center for Education Statistics Website: https://nces.ed.gov/pubs2018/2018097.pdf

U.S. Department of Labor. (2019). Labor force statistics from the current population survey. Retrieved from https://www.bls.gov/cps/cpsaat36.htm

Williams, C. L. (1992). The glass escalator: Hidden advantages for men in the "female" professions. *Social Problems, 39*(3), 253–267. https://doi.org/10.2307/3096961

Yang, M. Y., Harmeyer, E., Chen, Z., & Lofaso, B. M. (2018). Predictors of early elementary school suspension by gender: A longitudinal multilevel analysis. *Children and Youth Services Review, 93*, 331–338. https://doi.org/10.1016/j.childyouth.2018.08.008

CHAPTER 3

When Am I Ever Going to Use Any of This?

You have been observing as a visitor from the back of the classroom for about an hour now. Miss Thomas just finished her English/Language Arts lesson on the upcoming Thanksgiving holiday. How is it going so far? You would probably need a break, but lunch is not for another two hours. Depending on the teacher and the kids in the room, you may even need a strong drink! But believe it or not, as you watch your class get on with its day, you may eventually nod off to sleep. You would think it was that heavy breakfast you ate or maybe that you need another cup of coffee, but that is not what it is.

Once you pass the initial excitement of being in a room full of boisterous young children, you may just find the elementary classroom an extremely boring place to be. I do not mean the curriculum is boring or that teachers need to jazz up their lessons by making them more "hands on." Surely some teachers are engaging, and some are dull. Some school subjects are a drag, and some exciting. This will always be true. What I am talking about goes much deeper than the curriculum or even the teacher. It is a level of boredom and purposelessness experienced by many elementary students no matter how engaging the subject matter or talented the teacher is.

I am not proud to say this, but I sometimes leave the elementary school at the end of the day feeling sorry for what the students had to endure. I feel this way even when I am the one teaching them! It can be such a long and dreadful day for elementary schoolers. I shudder when

I hear politicians and administrators talking about making the school day even longer than it currently is. Who learns in six- or seven-hour-long increments anyway?

The problem of student boredom in the public elementary school has been examined by many researchers (e.g., Cai & Liem, 2017; Noel & Liub, 2017; Oliveira, 2015). Common solutions are well intentioned, but often off the mark. Some believe the problem would be solved if more teachers learned exciting teaching techniques to better engage their students (e.g., Chen, Wang, Lu, Lin, & Hong, 2016; Lee & Hannafin, 2016; Sabin, 2015). Others suggest if schools would integrate more technology into the classroom, today's "wired" students would be more tuned in (e.g., Light & Pierson, 2014; Moore, Gillett, & Steele, 2014; Niemi & Multisilta, 2016). However, the deep sense of boredom I speak of is not caused by the teacher, the curriculum, or the materials in the classroom. It has to do with the overall understanding children have of why they are at school in the first place, the story they tell themselves about why they have to get up in the morning and go to school at all. The reason why our elementary schools can be so tedious is that they do not have what children this age most need: *adventure* and *high purpose.*

Go into almost any elementary classroom across the country and you will immediately see what I mean. Lessons are simply offered to students with little or no explanation of what they are for. While it is true that teachers often cite the "standards" or objectives of a lesson, they do not often discuss how each lesson fits into an overall story. Transitions from one subject to another often lack coherence, "O.K. now put away your English books and take out your Math." It is hard for today's kids to see a connection between what they do in school and some larger thing in the world they care about. I think if adults could spend just one full day at school, from bus ride to dismissal, they would feel similarly exhausted and have much more sympathy for what their children have to endure. I completely understand why in some surveys over 30% of boys and 14% of girls say they dislike school "a lot." I dislike it "a lot" sometimes too.

Whenever I go to a school and have a spare moment with a child, I find a way to ask them why they go to school. Very young children are particularly interested in this question because they do not understand why they cannot be home with a loved one or do more interesting tasks than phonics or numbers. They will say, "I go to school because my Mom has to work," or "because I need to learn things." Older children are a bit more aware of legal and market forces. They will say something like, "I'll go to jail if I don't go to school," or "I go to school so that I can get a job," or "so I can go to college." But in all my decades of asking young children this question, *I have never heard one invoke anything having to do with adventure or high purpose.* I would probably fall on the floor if a kid said, "Where else would I want to be? It's the most exciting and adventurous thing I can imagine doing with my time" or even, "I go to school because it's fun." Let us take a closer look at high purpose, adventure, and why kids need these two things so much.

Adventure and High Purpose

High purpose is what most popular children's movie and literary heroes have in their lives. It is the sense that we are involved in something of immense, even world-saving importance. For the child, "most people" are preoccupied with living their mundane, day-to-day lives. They focus on "low" purposes like earning money, climbing the social, or corporate ladder. They do petty, banal, uninspired, unimaginative, and sometimes even bad things. Think here of how the Dursleys are portrayed in *Harry Potter and the Sorcerer's Stone* (Rowling, 1997). They work meaningless jobs and force their kids to attend mind-numbing schools which strip the magic out of life. Harry Potter does not attend The Hogwarts School of Witchcraft and Wizardry to merely learn his state-mandated Standards of Learning so he can get a decent paying job. He is there to learn vital skills which will help him save the world from the low-purpose power politics of Lord Voldemort and his ilk.

Adventure is the exciting and sometimes hazardous path one takes when trying to realize high purpose in life. Think here of young Percy Jackson who must leave the dreary school he attends to embark on a dangerous quest to figure out a way to save the world from nihilistic supernatural beings and the humans who serve them. The universe is being stripped of its cosmic meaning and Percy needs to stop it. Now *that* is an adventure! Compare Percy Jackson's day with the schedule of a modern elementary student. The contrast is striking. I turn to a closer look at the inner world of young children so we can appreciate why they need adventure and high purpose more than anything else at this crucial time in their lives.

The Romantic Child

Educational theorist Kieran Egan (1986) found that close to the age of six-and-a-half (first grade), many significant and turbulent psychological changes begin to take place. Other theorists have referred to these changes as the "five- to seven-year shift" (Piaget, 1985; Sameroff & Haith, 1996). During this time, the world emerges as a much more cold and autonomous entity than the more vibrant and enchanted world of toddlerhood (Egan, 1986, p. 29). Before elementary school, Egan (1986) suggests the world is experienced as a magical extension of the self, a place where trees sing and the sun smiles. Along with the new impersonal reality of the first grader comes a sense of autonomous time, space, logical necessity, and causality (Egan, 1986, p. 31). The world of the elementary schooler now runs according to its own inexorable laws, caring little for his or her plans.

Along with these changes in outer reality, the young child's inner sense of self also becomes more separate and distinct from the world around him or her. Previously the child enjoyed an intense connection with everything, but now what emerges is the painful realization that I am alone, alienated from the world around me (Piaget & Cook, 1954). What is worse, the child's trusted ways of making sense of things from early childhood do not work for him or her any longer. The child must learn to establish a new connection to a vastly different world.

The impersonality of the world and the alienation of the self combine to create a unique psychological dilemma which Egan refers to as "Romantic," harkening to the famous poets of the eighteenth century. Specifically, the child develops a great need to transcend a reality that is experienced as cold, mechanical, vast, and threatening, but also to somehow secure himself or herself in it. In response to the threat posed by this strange and alien new world, children tend to align themselves with those parts of the world which seem most powerful, brave, courageous, strong, and intelligent. Children at this stage will identify with heroes and heroines with extraordinary powers and become interested in such things as the *Guinness Book of World Records* with its chronicles of the smallest, the largest, the highest, the fastest, and the farthest (Egan, 1986, p. 31).

Families and schools who are sensitive to these psychological issues will first offer children a heroic and adventurous template which they can use to explore and make contact with their strange and scary new reality. But this is not what most schools and families do. Instead of helping children transcend reality, schools move in the opposite direction. They force children to attend to the smallest details of the world, such as minute aspects of history and civics, adding and subtracting small sums, learning about the geographical details of the North American continent, notes of the scales of music, the properties of ice, and so on. This is the *last* place young minds want or need to be.

Literature which is popular with elementary-aged children tends to be "Romantic" in nature. In these tales, a hero or heroine struggles against great odds to a glory and transcendence over threatening nature, persons, events, institutions, ideas, or nations. Children need school to be Romantic like the literature they love, not overly focused on the small and mundane details of the real world. This can be counterintuitive for many adult educators who want to teach young children all about the important facts of life. It is not that these facts are unimportant; it is that children need to approach them slowly and only from the narrative context of adventure and high purpose.

Lessons from Harry Potter

There are several popular Romances with which children between the ages of 6 and 12 become quite enchanted, even obsessed. Some of these include the *Harry Potter* series, *The Lord of the Rings* trilogy, the *Percy Jackson and the Olympians* series, the *Princess and the Goblin*, and many others. Given the strong resonance children have with these tales, these texts can help us understand the world of early childhood and how to better respond to it as educators. The first volume of the *Harry Potter* series is the prototypical Romance. It has enjoyed stunning popularity, selling more than five million copies and nearly $1 billion in worldwide film sales. I turn to *Harry Potter and the Sorcerer's Stone* to illustrate the major characteristics of the Romantic predicament and describe what children must do to resolve it.

To review, the six-year-old begins to experience reality as much more cold, mechanical, vast, and threatening than the infant and toddler years. Literature which is popular with children reflects this unwelcome psychological change. Harry Potter's world is represented as quite alien and hostile. The very first pages of the story begin with a disturbing description of Harry's surrogate family, Vernon, Petunia, and Dudley Dursley. They are presented as "Muggles," Harry-Potter-speak for people who do not see the magic and miracles going on all around them. They never ask questions about anything or think of acting in a way that is not acceptable or conventional. Further, the Dursleys are absolutely awful to Harry. He is forced to sleep in a dirty cupboard under the stairs crawling with spiders and other insects. His birthday is not celebrated, while the vile and rotund Dudley gets everything he wants. Harry must wear Dudley's old clothes. His round glasses are held together with tape due to the frequency with which Dudley has punched him in the nose.

A tall man named Albus Dumbledore shows up outside the Dursley's house late one night while Harry quietly sleeps. Albus describes a momentous event which everyone will soon be celebrating, everyone, that is, except the Muggles. Voldemort, the evil one, showed up at the Potter house 11 years ago that night and tried to kill baby Harry because of what he would someday become. Voldemort succeeded in killing both of Harry's parents, but he could not kill Harry. We learn that Dumbledore decided at that time to place the orphaned Harry with his only living relatives, the Dursleys, to protect him until he was old enough to begin his Wizard responsibilities. But the Dursleys have hidden Harry's noble origins from him his entire life. In fact, Vernon and Petunia have been determined to *stamp out* Harry's magical power and specialness because they want everybody to be ordinary. Far from the nuisance he is made out to be, the reader learns at the beginning of the novel that Harry is quite special and famous. We read, "…there will be books written about Harry—every child in our world will know his name!" (Rowling, 1997, p. 13). Harry is cosmically significant.

It is important to note when the story begins, Rowling tells us that Harry is getting ready to begin Middle School, a place where he will sit all day in rows doing uncreative and soul-numbing educational tasks. He dreads it. Harry is quite certain (and terrified) that he is becoming a full member of the ordinary, un-magical Muggle world. But Harry soon learns what the reader already knows: he is not just a regular 11-year-old who lives at #4 Privet Drive with mundane surrogate parents and a nuisance brother. He is a wizard!! Even more, he is the most powerful wizard in the entire universe who will soon be able to go to an exciting new school of magic that the Muggles cannot even see.

For the young reader, the beginning of this Romance symbolizes how the adult world actually looks and feels to them. Parents and teachers, the child believes, "just don't get it." For the child reader, the world outside is beginning to appear cruel, schedule-driven, and indifferent to his or her concerns. The magical and animistic ways of looking at the world which he or she relied on in early childhood are just not part of the adult world he or she is being ushered into. Harry shares the reader's struggles. It is why they love him so much. Deep down, children wonder, "What is happening to the invisible world of magic and spirit which adults are increasingly telling me doesn't matter?" "What special gifts do I have?" "What is unique about me?" The Romance gives children the great gift of hearing and experiencing a powerful message: "Yes, your parents and teachers treat you like you are just another number in a vast, mechanical world.

They ignore you, treat you unfairly, and favor your siblings. The world is vast, cruel, and impersonal. You are not sure where you fit in. But you are somebody. You have gifts they cannot see. You are not just some kid getting picked on by his brother; you are able to do magical things, figure out complicated spells, and you can walk through walls to enter an enchanted school which most other people don't even know exists!"

A Romance like *Harry Potter* addresses the young child's dire predicament by creating two worlds: a real one that most cannot see or appreciate and a false one that most (wrongly) accept as being the real one. The Romance helps the young reader by creating a safe and exciting fantasy world that he or she uses as a secure base from which to eventually establish a more viable way of living in the strange emerging Muggle/adult world. This reality-bridging is the primary function of the Romance. It is important to note that the goal of the Romance is not to invite the child into fantasy in order to stay there, but to enable the child from this place of fantasy to eventually make a connection to the "real world" on new and better terms. The span of this bridging process is the entire course of elementary school.

Good Romantic children's literature not only presents children with a true-to-life representation of their dire psychological situation; it bears hidden tools for resolving the Romantic dilemma of a cruel reality and an alienated self. Turning back to *Harry Potter*, we pick up the story where Harry discovers who he really is and prepares to enter the dazzling Hogwarts School of Witchcraft and Wizardry. Once inside the wizarding world, Harry discovers a curriculum that is music to the young child's ears. He has classes with titles such as, "Defense against the Dark Arts," "The History of Magic," "Charms," "Transfiguration," and "Potions." Compare these with the classes readers are likely taking—Social Studies, Reading, Math—and the contrast is apparent.

Shortly after arriving at Hogwarts, Harry and his friends learn that someone is trying to obtain the Sorcerer's Stone, an object whose power will enable them to have anything they desire. Given Hogwarts' many enemies, the Stone's falling into the wrong hands would be catastrophic. Harry and his two friends, Ron and Hermione, must therefore embark upon a quest to save the Stone and quite possibly the whole world. This odyssey takes them through trap doors, past a three-headed dog, countless human foes, through various magic spells and evil forces, a gruesome Troll, a dragon, and a unicorn. Each step along the way provides them with opportunities to use both their wits and the magical skills they have been learning in school. Toward the end of the story, we learn there is only enough invisibility potion for one of Harry's party to proceed past the guards, so Harry must take the last part of his journey alone. Here he confronts the final obstacle to acquiring the Sorcerer's Stone: one of his own teachers, Professor Quirrell.

We learn that Quirrell has long been doing Lord Voldemort's dirty work behind the scenes. Quirrell lets us in on his basic beliefs in a dialogue with Harry where he recounts how Voldemort disabused him of his childish ideas about good and evil. What Voldemort taught Quirrell is that there is no good and evil, "there is only power, and those too weak to seek it" (Rowling, 1997, p. 291). Quirrell pursues his life goals without regard to high purposes. Harry sees how grotesque this moral stance really is. This is the first tool the Romance offers the struggling reader to help resolve his or her predicament: while the human self is powerful, magical, strong, even godlike, it ultimately must be subordinated to something larger and even more powerful than itself. In this particular story, good and evil are forces larger and more powerful than the ego. Quirrell (and Voldemort) makes a fundamental mistake in not appreciating this truth.

The young reader, intoxicated with the idea of the ego's extreme powers and strength, must eventually learn this lesson in real life as well. It may take four or five years, but the question Harry and the young reader must ultimately decide is: what will my "larger something" be? The Romance helps the child appreciate that though they are strong, powerful, and special, they are not powerful in an ultimate sense. There are limits to the self's scope and power. This something-more becomes the "high purpose" to which the child devotes his or her life. This larger purpose helps bring childhood to a healthy and successful completion at the end of elementary school.

Returning to the story, after taking quite a beating, Harry eventually manages to get the Stone from the Mirror of Erised. We learn that Harry succeeds in getting the Stone because he did not desire to use it for himself, but for the service of others. When Harry regains consciousness after his battle, the reader confronts a scene that provides a second valuable tool for Romantic resolution. Dumbledore explains to Harry why Quirrell could not hurt him. The reason, he says, "is that your mother died to save you" (Rowling, 1997, p. 299). Love as powerful as the love Harry's mother had for him leaves a permanent mark and gives him protection forever. Love is the strongest force in the universe, stronger than evil, stronger than magic. Dumbledore tells Harry that this love is now a deep part of him and it alone is what makes him so powerful and famous.

Harry is ultimately successful on his adventure because he and his mother before him have chosen the most powerful force of all: self-sacrificial love. Contrary to the many religious protests of *Harry Potter*, witchcraft and magic do not save Harry or his mates. The real magic of *Harry Potter* is self-sacrificial love. And Harry obtained this power not from Hogwarts School of Witchcraft and Wizardry, but from his own mother's act of sacrificing her life to Lord Voldemort to save her son.

Love is the "something more" this Romance offers the reader as a "high purpose" toward which to live one's life. Love, the book suggests, is how you find a home in a cruel and often-indifferent adult world. This central insight about the power of love provides the abstract principle which can ultimately help a young reader negotiate his or her way out of the Romantic stage. Of course, different Romantic stories will provide different answers to the child. Some will suggest using your wits as a way forward, or forgiveness, or trust. The important point is that schools need to offer something similarly Romantic to elementary children. They need to provide conflict, alienation, drama, extreme characters, adventure, and climatic resolution to frame the entire school experience and each lesson in it. Once students have this sense of adventure and high purpose, they are willing to learn almost anything they see as helping them toward these important ends.

I once viewed a documentary many years ago called *Childhood* (Akuginow & Haines-Stiles, 1991). Part of the series examined children in a traditional African society. There was a scene with a group of school-aged boys sitting in a circle outside around a village elder. This elder was the "teacher" and the boys were at "school." The children were quietly listening to this man give a boring, technical talk for quite some time. There were no behavior problems, no time-outs. But this was no ordinary school. The boys were there because they were selected to become drum players for their group, a role in society with a great deal of status and deep religious significance. The boys were sitting through a lesson on how to make a drum to prepare for their future role in society.

What is different about this African scenario from a modern classroom is that the children in the traditional culture have a clear sense of why they are sitting in the circle listening to a technical lesson in the first place. They feel their boring work in class serves a higher purpose. They know they have embarked on an adventurous course to an exciting future adult position. How do children feel in our more formal educational settings? What story do they tell themselves about why they are in class? What exciting adult roles do they see themselves preparing for? Elementary children desperately want to learn to become skilled adults, but they first need the frame of high purpose and adventure. This frame helps them understand why they are learning all these important things in the first place.

Several researchers have developed and tested lessons that incorporate adventure into the curriculum. Mortlock (1984) introduced what he calls "Adventure Education," which joins outdoor education and high adventure like climbing or paddling. Following in this tradition, Fernández-Río and Suarez (2016) used the exciting and popular physical activity of "parkour" as an adventurous frame to organize physical education lessons. Doering, Scharber, Riedel, and Miller (2010) developed what they call an "Adventure Learning" curriculum for online instruction. In the *PolarHusky* program, for example, students can go on a virtual 3000-mile sled dog journey in which they must plan, learn about various locations, and collaborate with experts and other students. The umbrella of the sled adventure integrates the different subjects students learn, for example, History, Math, and English. Other researchers have developed computer adventure games to improve performance in such areas as Geography (Wiebe & Martin, 1994) and Reading (Grabe & Dosmann, 1988). While these attempts have creatively integrated adventure into the school, what is missing is the sense of high purpose that transforms an adventure from a mere physically thrilling experience to a developmentally and morally significant event.

Industry Versus Inferiority

The psychologist Erik Erikson (1964) found that the elementary-aged child is deeply preoccupied with questions which involve what he calls *industry*. Industry is the feeling that I can do things which are important and valued by the adults around me. Genuine industry only begins when I can clearly see an inspiring vision of what it means to be a productive adult in society. As in the example of the children in Africa, once I am captivated by a heroic sense of the future, I will then apply myself to the educational tasks that I see as leading me toward this vision. Industry takes many years to develop and is typically fostered in the school and the home between the ages of 6 and 11, the elementary years.

By 11 or 12, the child should feel that he or she is making real progress toward some inspiring vision of him or herself in the adult world. If industry has developed by the end of elementary school, the child can do remarkable things. He or she can hold down a part-time job, responsibly and independently complete household chores, constructively participate in extracurricular clubs and sports, earn grades in school that reflect his or her ability and intelligence, and make realistic and successful plans of daily and weekly activities. How many of today's kids can do these things by the end of elementary school? Many of my college students still cannot do a lot of these things in their 20s.

For Erikson (1964), the failure to achieve industry by the end of elementary school will leave the middle schooler and young adult with a deep sense of "inferiority." Inferiority is the sense that I do not have much that is valuable to offer the adult world emerging in my future, that I am less than others whom I believe have greater gifts. When I do not have industry, research shows I have lower standards and expectations of myself for success (Ward, Mergendoller, & Tikunoff, 1982). I perceive that teachers and bosses expect less of me. I have a hard time holding down a job, I am irresponsible around the home, my grades are poor, and I struggle to manage my time to complete daily or weekly goals (Juhasz, 1982). And when I do have successes, without industry I tend to interpret them as "just getting lucky" rather than a reflection of my inherent strengths and abilities. I have a deep sense of despair about my future and I am more likely to suffer from depression and mental health issues in my teen and adult years (Ward et al., 1982). I believe the rising number of diagnosed mental disorders, delinquency, and violence in teens is in part connected to the failure to achieve industry by the beginning of middle school.

If Erikson is correct, we should judge the success of the elementary school years not by how well students perform on state-mandated tests, but on whether children leave this period with the necessary sense of industry that will take them into the turbulent adolescent years. By 11 or 12, do children see themselves on an exciting path toward full participation in the adult group around them? Do they derive a sense of esteem and value from being able to competently do things that adults value? When schools simply line up the standards for a grade level in a decontextualized list, what is missing is an engaging story of adventure and high purpose which makes the standards intelligible and attractive. Without adventure and high purpose, standards are just subjects we "cover" over the year without much rhyme or reason.

Today's elementary schools teach children valuable knowledge and skills. The problem is that children are not retaining much of it and are often bored to tears. Political debate focuses on the fact that children are not learning enough of the important things they need to know. How many times have we heard the alarming figures that 57% of children cannot locate the Atlantic Ocean on a map or do not know who George Washington was? Embarrassed administrators then turn up the heat on schools to achieve more learning outcomes. But this kind of worried "standards-based" talk misses the larger context of high purpose, adventure, and industry that preoccupies elementary-aged children. It is not that this standards-based knowledge is not worth knowing, it is that *this knowledge is not what children need to know at this time in their lives.* They have more pressing preoccupations that must first be addressed before moving on to itemized facts and information. Ironically, when we first tend to what children most need, it makes it easier to teach them discrete skills.

The Zombie Apocalypse

If we pay close attention, the fictional stories children love to read and hear show us what they want school to be like. From everything I can see, children want school to serve a higher purpose and take them on an adventurous course into adulthood. Children are more than willing to learn practical skills and competencies so long as they believe these lessons will help them realize their dreams of the future. The problem is that there is little drama to school, no picture of a dire world situation that needs to be rectified and transcended, no exciting vision of the future toward which to work. If they *can* conjure a vision of what their school helps them work toward, it does not inspire much excitement. Looking at how we are portrayed in the stories children like, our adult world looks like a place full of Muggles to them, or worse, a zombie apocalypse where the adults only appear to be alive but are really dead. Who wants to be a part of that?

Without inspiring images of adventure and high purpose, school is simply drudgery, something like a painful trip to the dentist that your parents say is "good for you." Kids respond to the drudgery of school in one of three ways. Some deal with the drudgery by outwardly complying but inwardly detaching from the process, looking forward to more exciting things after school, at lunch, or recess. Teachers tend to regard these students as the "easy ones." But this outward compliance is different from inner passion. These children are simply going through the motions of education and will cease such motions when there is no longer external reinforcement. A second group of kids is not as disciplined and able to compartmentalize as the first. They will "act out" and misbehave in protest of the drudgery. Teachers tend to regard these students as the "difficult ones." Every class has several of these. The third group deals with the absence of adventure and high purpose by making school largely a social enterprise, a dramatic "High School Musical" where the only preoccupation is the ups and downs of our various loves and hates. These students manufacture their own sense of adventure and high purpose, and graft it onto the boring school day. They attend school for their friends rather than for what they are learning.

Adventure and high purpose can be integrated from the level of the individual lesson all the way to the entire school or district. What is important is that a dramatic moral or spiritual conflict is initially staged. For example, perhaps the earth stands in mortal danger from pollution and climate change. What is required are "Eco-Leaders" who will save the planet from its ailments and enemies. Who is ready to help? School lessons then adventurously serve this higher purpose. Or perhaps all the beauty is fading in the universe and what is required are "Aesthete Athletes" who will prepare for a life of identifying and protecting beautiful things (e.g., paintings, books, ideas, places). Perhaps disease and ignorance menace the globe. What is required are "Enlightenment Elders" who will prepare to cure disease and spread knowledge. Perhaps the threat of tyranny is afoot. What is needed are "Citizenship Soldiers" who will prepare for a life of democratic engagement and rational discussion. Potential dramatic conflicts are nearly endless. As important as they are, these frames are often absent from public educational settings because they get us into values, religion, politics, and spirituality. Since these are such difficult subjects for adults to discuss and agree upon, we remove them completely and make education about decontextualized competences and skills. This is a huge mistake.

Let me conclude by returning to the second-grade classroom you have been visiting today. What are the actual stories and images in the students' minds about what their 9:00–10:15 Math lesson was for? Why do they think they are sitting there doing their work today? When I ask them, most have no clue why they are learning any of this and cannot see any connection between what they are learning in class and their future lives.

Many students will try to make a connection on their own if one is not explicitly provided for them. Let us imagine a student; I will call him Jeffrey. After a lesson on adding two-digit numbers, Jeffrey pipes up and asks Miss Thomas, "When am I ever going to use this?" This is a common refrain heard in classrooms across the land. Teachers can get a little defensive in the face of questions like this. They may not know what to say. They also have limited time, and so giving an answer may take them far afield from the content of their lesson. Miss Thomas may ignore the question, thinking Jeffrey is just being fresh. If she answers the question at all, she may say something like, "Well, don't you think someday you'll need to balance your checkbook or follow a simple recipe to make a cake? How will you be able to do any of that without being able to add two-digit numbers?" This is the only kind of answer I have ever heard from teachers in response to the "Why-do-I-need-to-know-this?" question.

While correct on some level, Miss Thomas' answer misses the deeper hope and desire expressed in Jeffrey's question. Though he does not say it explicitly, Jeffrey is really asking, "How is this lesson connected to the heroic image I have of my own adult future? How will it help me deal with menacing reality? What higher principle of living will it help me serve?"

While they are not often explicitly discussed, schools *do* provide children with implicit narratives of why they must go to school. They are just not that engaging to children. If we look closely at Miss Thomas' "checkbook" answer, it indirectly conjures an image for Jeffrey of him someday sitting at his desk calmly balancing his checkbook or combining flour and other ingredients in his kitchen to make a cake. Do we really expect this image to inspire a child or meet his or her developmental needs? It sounds like a Muggle future to me! Most children will not have the courage to challenge these boring visions we proffer them and so they either drop their questioning and comply, act out in protest, or dream of recess later. This is because teachers and students never really sit down and discuss what school is all about.

When I step back from the public elementary school curriculum and try to discern the embedded images of the future adult world toward which all the lessons and subjects are leading, it looks something like this: "Jeffrey, someday you will be a mid-level insurance adjuster. You will need to sit still at a desk and behave yourself quietly for long periods of time. You will need to enter large numerical sums into a computer and analyze them to provide the most realistic risk assessment you can for your employer. If you cannot add and write properly, you will never be able to do any of this. If you cannot sit still, you will never make it. If you cannot follow instructions, you will be lost. That's what this is all about. That is why you are going to school day in and day out." Now, this image would surely help Jeffrey see a connection between what he is doing in his classes and his future, but would it excite him? Would it inspire him? Would it lead him to the sense of high purpose and spiritual adventure he sees and wants when Harry Potter goes to school at Hogwarts or when Percy Jackson goes to school at Camp Half-Blood? Should we be surprised if he rejects it?

Though slightly humorous, this image of the insurance adjuster is not far from the actual image of the future for which many modern schools prepare students. It is not often explicitly articulated, but it is what kids see when they piece together all the lessons, school subjects, and standards. In Chap. 6, I discuss how schools might be reformed to better address children's deep need for high purpose, adventure, and industry. And I look at some schools that are already doing this. In the next chapter, I turn to another challenge that contributes to classroom boredom: the astounding number of supervisors, managers, administrators, and principals who do not teach for a living but have a surprising amount of control over those who do. For now, I leave you with some things you can think about and try in your own situation.

> **What You Can Do**
>
> 1. Why do you send your children to school? What is the story you tell them when they ask? Is it a gripping story? Write your answer down. Share it with your children.
> 2. Judge your child's teachers and school not only by how well the students perform on state tests, but upon whether it is helping your child develop an inspiring vision of himself in the adult world.
> 3. Does your child's school provide drama, adventure, fascinating characters, to frame the school day or year? Do the people who work there seem excited and inspired by what they do? Would you be excited to go there?
> 4. Do you believe that even very young children are deep thinkers and feelers who are gripped by life's mysteries and existential dilemmas? If not, why? Were you that way when you were young? What do you recall wishing your parents would know and understand about you when you were in school?
> 5. What stories enchant your child? What are they about? What vision of life are they presenting? Watch, listen, and learn from your child what she really likes, what she dreams about, and what she really wants to do with her time.
> 6. What is your mission, vision, and high purpose in life? Do you wake up with a sense of your day as an adventure? How attractive would adulthood look to your child if you were the only model of it? If you do not have these things, what can you do to get them? They may be the biggest gifts you can give your children. How comfortable are you discussing the different high purposes of life with other adults? If you have great resistance, the public schools will continue to be places that teach only decontextualized lists of intellectual skills.

REFERENCES

Akuginow, E. (Producer), & Haines-Stiles, G. (Director). (1991). *Childhood* [Documentary]. London: Ambrose Video Publishing.

Cai, E. L., & Liem, G. D. (2017). 'Why do I study and what do I want to achieve by studying?' Understanding the reasons and the aims of student engagement. *School Psychology International, 38*(2), 131–148.

Chen, H., Wang, H., Lu, Y., Lin, H., & Hong, Z. (2016). Using a modified argument-driven inquiry to promote elementary school students' engagement in learning science and argumentation. *International Journal of Science Education, 38*(2), 170–191.

Doering, A., Scharber, C., Riedel, E., & Miller, C. (2010). 'Timber for president': Adventure learning and motivation. *Journal of Interactive Learning Research, 21*(4), 483–513.

Egan, K. (1986). *Individual development and the curriculum*. London: Hutchinson.

Erikson, E. (1964). *Childhood and society* (2nd ed.). Oxford, UK: W. W. Norton.

Fernández-Río, J., & Suarez, C. (2016). Feasibility and students' preliminary views on parkour in a group of primary school children. *Physical Education and Sport Pedagogy, 21*(3), 281–294. https://doi.org/10.1080/17408989.2014.946008

Grabe, M., & Dosmann, M. (1988). The potential of adventure games for the development of reading and study skills. *Journal of Computer-Based Instruction, 15*(2), 72–77.

Juhasz, A. M. (1982). Early adolescents and society: Implications of Eriksonian theory. *Journal of Early Adolescence, 2*(1), 15–24.

Lee, E., & Hannafin, M. J. (2016). A design framework for enhancing engagement in student-centered learning: Own it, learn it, and share it. *Educational Technology Research and Development, 64*(4), 707–734.

Light, D., & Pierson, E. (2014). Increasing student engagement in Math: The use of Khan Academy in Chilean classrooms. *International Journal of Education and Development Using Information and Communication Technology, 10*(2), 103–119.

Moore, A. J., Gillett, M. R., & Steele, M. D. (2014). Fostering student engagement with the flip. *Mathematics Teacher, 107*(6), 420–425.

Mortlock, C. (1984). *The adventure alternative*. Milnthorpe, UK: Cicerone Press.

Niemi, H., & Multisilta, J. (2016). Digital storytelling promoting twenty-first century skills and student engagement. *Technology, Pedagogy and Education, 25*(4), 451–468.

Noel, L., & Liub, T. L. (2017). Using design thinking to create a new education paradigm for elementary level children for higher student engagement and success. *Design and Technology Education, 22*(1), 1–12.

Oliveira, A. W. (2015). Reading engagement in science: Elementary students' read-aloud experiences. *International Journal of Environmental and Science Education, 10*(3), 429–451.

Piaget, J. (1985). *The equilibration of cognitive structures: The central problem of intellectual development.* Chicago, IL: University of Chicago Press.

Piaget, J., & Cook, M. (1954). *The construction of reality in the child.* New York, NY: Basic Books.

Rowling, J. K. (1997). *Harry Potter and the sorcerer's stone.* New York, NY: Scholastic Press.

Sabin, J. T. (2015). Teacher morale, student engagement, and student achievement growth in reading: A correlational study. *Journal of Organizational and Educational Leadership, 1*(1), 1–24.

Sameroff, A. J., & Haith, M. M. (1996). *The five to seven year shift: The age of reason and responsibility.* Chicago, IL: University of Chicago Press.

Ward, B. A., Mergendoller, J. R., & Tikunoff, W. J. (1982). Introduction to the junior high school transition study. *Journal of Early Adolescence, 2*(4), 311–317.

Wiebe, J. H., & Martin, N. J. (1994). The impact of a computer-based adventure game on achievement and attitudes in geography. *Journal of Computing in Childhood Education, 5*(1), 61–71.

CHAPTER 4

"And Then God Made School Boards"

Miss Thomas' English/Language Arts lesson is over. She stands up and tells the students to close their workbooks and take out their Math books. They sing a song to mark the transition, "*It's time, it's time to do, it's time to do, something new.*" As Miss Thomas gathers her materials, you notice a man in a suit quietly enters the room. He nods to the teacher as she begins her lesson and sits at a desk in the back of the room next to you. You notice he has a checklist with item boxes containing statements such as "Teacher presents content in a coherent fashion, building on previously mastered content and connecting material to content to be learned in the future," and "Teacher uses questions appropriate to the material, and structures activities requiring students to use higher order thinking." He is already scribbling notes on his form.

Miss Thomas continues with her lesson, but you notice she has now become a little nervous. She acts like she is onstage. The man observes her with his clipboard in hand for another 20 minutes, adding more notes to his boxes, gets up, and leaves as silently as he entered. Miss Thomas continues with her lesson for another half hour or so, visibly more relaxed now that the man is gone. She gets the class ready for lunch by having the children fetch their lunchboxes. The students line up at the door and you walk together down the hall to the cafeteria.

The two of you start to chat as you walk. You ask her who the man was who came into class. "Oh, that was the principal. We're being evaluated this month. They pop in unannounced to see if I am using the proper

© The Author(s) 2019
J. J. Dillon, *Inside Today's Elementary Schools*,
https://doi.org/10.1007/978-3-030-23347-1_4

lesson plan format and that I am following my daily schedule." Though she is a 23-year teaching veteran, she lightly complains that for the past 7 or 8 years she has had to comply with more and more regulations, paperwork, student assessments, and red tape from principals, assistant principals, counselors, district supervisors, and assistant superintendents. For example, last year the school instituted a policy where teachers must fill out a lesson plan into a proscribed template for the six subjects they teach and submit a whole week's lesson plans to the principal every Monday morning. It takes her almost all Sunday to get this work ready each week. She is given hardly any planning time during the week to get this done. As another example, she says this year the district adopted a "conscious discipline" classroom management program which all teachers must now use. It has had mixed results. She says it works for some students, but not nearly all. She is given little flexibility to adopt a different approach with those other students. Miss Thomas seems frustrated, even slightly burned out from having to jump through so many administrative hoops. She tells you of a boy in her class whom she feels needs some extra help with his reading. In order to get this help, she must gather data each day on his performance and record it in a chart for the next six weeks. This is on top of the other paperwork she must complete for several of her other students. She complains about having very little freedom to do what she sees fit in her classroom and wonders out loud whether she should return to the advertising career she left before she got into teaching. "At least I was taken seriously there," she says sadly.

I mentioned earlier that I recently finished my initial elementary school certification classes and my state exams. I am now ready to take the step into the elementary teaching world. But as I contemplate what this might look like for me, I am filled with some real trepidation. I have long felt called to teach young children. My own educational experiences as a child were extremely positive and I want to help other children benefit from all that early education can offer them. But when I tell people I plan to enter elementary teaching from a career in the college classroom, they look at me like I am crazy. Surprisingly, the people who try to talk me out of elementary teaching the most are elementary school teachers themselves! Sadly, many of them tell me they would not go into the field if they had it to do over again. They warn me to stay where I am on my comfy university campus. With comments like these—and there are many—it is clear something is happening in our schools that is wearing our teachers down, leaving them bitter and sometimes resentful. You do not meet many good ambassadors for the elementary teaching profession from the elementary teaching profession. You do see some former teachers extolling the joys of the classroom on the lecture circuit, but they left their classrooms behind years ago.

Miss Thomas' experience in this scenario matches research on teacher retention and job satisfaction. Ingersoll (2002) finds a whopping 46% of all new teachers in the United States leave the profession within their first five years. These numbers are similar to the divorce rate, which is often spoken of as a "crisis." Other researchers disagree with Ingersoll, citing five-year attrition numbers that are closer to 20% or 30% (Fensterwald, 2015; U.S. Department of Education, 2015). Most of the dispute depends on how you count "leaving the profession." Ingersoll counts a teacher who goes into Administration as leaving. I cannot get into the details here, but I find Ingersoll's (2002) numbers to be more valid than his critics'. I agree with him that if a teacher leaves the classroom, but stays in the school Administration, it is effectively "leaving teaching."

The annual turnover rate in teaching professions is 43% higher than that in non-teaching professions (Ingersoll, 2002). For the teachers who stay in their teaching jobs past the first five years, the situation does not look much better than the ones who leave. Half of all public school teachers say they feel "great stress" in their job several days a week. In 2013, only 39% of teachers reported feeling "very satisfied" with their job. This is down from 2008 when 62% of teachers had said in the same poll they were "very satisfied" with their job (Markow, Macia, & Lee, 2013).

Why are so many public school teachers so distressed? What makes some schools such unpleasant places to work? And why have satisfaction ratings gone *down* so precipitously over the past seven to ten years? People outside of education may think it is the low pay or lack of respect for the teaching profession. But that is not what it is. When teachers are asked, they cite the lack of planning time, workload, having to tolerate inappropriate behavior from students, and lack of influence over school policy as the primary reasons for their decision to get out of teaching. They also note that recent school reform initiatives, with their emphasis on firing "bad" teachers, assessing teachers by student standardized test scores, and rewriting tenure and collective bargaining laws, unfairly make them into the enemy in the education debate (American Federation of Teachers, 2017). Looking closely at these reasons for leaving, you might notice they have nothing to do with pay or teaching. *They are all about management.* As one teacher on my third-grade teaching team tearfully put it when she resigned at the end of the semester after four years of teaching, "I love the kids, I just hate the bureaucracy."

Who created this toxic environment for teachers? Consider again the common teacher complaints: lack of planning time, unreasonable workload, lack of influence over school policy, attacking teachers' unions, and tying job security to test scores. Who implemented these things? It was a band of people I ominously refer to as "the Administration." The Administration is a vast and twisted chain of managers, supervisors, and their support staff. It is a hierarchically organized structure in the form of a chain-of-command pyramid composed of various offices, each with its own role and domain of responsibility. Understanding the structure of the Administration will enable us to understand why it so frustrates teachers and impedes student learning.

The Administration

The Administration begins at the Federal level with the President of the United States, who can set educational priorities affecting all public schools in the nation. We have seen examples of the enormous influence of this level over the past decade with the "No Child Left Behind" initiative of the George W. Bush administration or the "Race to the Top" initiative of the Obama administration. The Federal level also includes the U.S. Supreme Court, which decides whether schools comply with the Constitution, and the U.S. Congress, which enacts the President's policy recommendations into law and provides the states with additional funding (provided they comply with federal directives).

The Administration at the Federal level also consists of the Secretary of Education and the U.S. Department of Education, which governs educational budgets, rules, and regulations. There is an additional role for the Department of Health and Human Services, which funds the Head Start program, and the Department of Agriculture, which funds the Federal School Lunch program. This Federal part of the Administration is housed primarily in the U.S. Department of Education in Washington, DC, though there are offices in other Federal agencies. The Federal level of the Administration employs about 3912 people and has a $68 billion annual budget which is drawn primarily from Federal taxes. The Federal level of the Administration provides about 8% of the total funding for local school budgets.

As we go down the administrative chain to the State level, we come to the Governor, the State Legislature, and the State Supreme Court, who have roles corresponding to those at the Federal level. They establish educational standards and priorities, provide funding, and adjudicate potential violations of the state constitution on matters pertaining to education. From here, we move to the State School Board, which typically consists of elected officials who oversee the entire state educational system and ensure that the state complies with state and federal mandates. Then there is the state education leader, sometimes called the Superintendent of Schools or the Chief Education Officer, who executes the day-to-day details of the school board's vision on spending, staff, facilities, and curricular programs. From there, we move to the State Education Administration, sometimes called the Office of the Superintendent, which implements the Superintendent's policies and directives. State education offices are typically housed in state capitals and in field offices throughout the state. The State level of the Administration provides 47.1% of education funding, which is drawn primarily from state income, sales taxes, and state lottery money (if the state permits one).

As we move farther down the administrative chain, we come to the District School Board. They establish the school budget in their district, set rules and district policies for schools (e.g., field trips), and set specific curriculum learning standards in conjunction with state and federal directives. Then there is the District Superintendent, who is the leader of the District School Board, along with District Administrators, who administer programs, funds, rules, and regulations given to them by the district and state boards. In some states, District Administrations are the counties; in others they are larger regions of the state. This part of the Administration is housed in district offices in counties or regions. The District level of the Administration provides 44.9% of education funding, which is primarily drawn from local property taxes.

As we move down the chain even more, we finally get to the local school. There is even more Administration within the school itself. The Administration at the local level starts with the school Principal. He or she is responsible for the day-to-day operation of the school, hires teachers and staff, publicly represents the school to the community, and mediates conflicts among students, staff, parents, and members of the community. He or she also interacts with and answers to the various District, State, and Federal authorities described above. Some schools also have Assistant Principals who help with behavior management, budgeting, training, staff supervision, and curriculum. There are also a growing number of "resource teachers" and "team leaders" within schools such as curriculum specialists and teaching team supervisors, along with counselors, and other staff officials in the school who do not teach their own classroom, but supervise and "help" other teachers who do. After all those layers of Administration, you finally get to Miss Thomas!

There are four surprising things to point out about the Administration. First, nobody in the Administration teaches children. What is more, the farther you go up the chain of the Administration, the farther away you get from teaching real students. Many in the uppermost layers of the Administration do not have a degree in education, have never taught a child in a real class for a single day of their lives, or have left the classroom for good decades ago. For example, Betsy DeVos, the current U.S. Secretary of Education, has a degree in business economics and no formal training in education. Her mother was a school teacher, but the only real experience DeVos has with schools was serving as a volunteer mentor for 15 years in Grand Rapids. She is now the head of the entire Federal Department of Education. This problem is not just limited to DeVos. While many states require their Superintendents and other administrators to have a degree and even a license in education, that is recently starting to change to make room for military and business leaders, so-called turnaround specialists. At least ten states have passed legislation over the past decade which makes it easier for people with no education experience to become principals or superintendents. This opens various alternative pathways to certification besides a degree in education.

An Administrator's job involves staffing and managing resources related to education, but not the life of learning that takes place in the classroom. As a random example, consider the daily schedule of Jon Felske, the former Superintendent of the Wyoming and Godwin Heights school districts in the state of Michigan. He gets to the Wyoming Public Schools office at 6:30 a.m. and reads about 51 e-mails. His schedule proceeds from there.

7 a.m.: Meets with Finance Director and other administrators, discusses staffing assignments, federal grant compliance and a bill to cut school employee pay. 8:11 a.m.: Adjourns meeting, leaves for Rogers High's senior class awards breakfast. The day continues in this fashion.

For the sake of space, I leave several of Felske's other meetings off my description and pick up the Superintendent's day after lunch.

1:12 p.m.: Return to the Wyoming office for meeting with an attorney about an employee grievance. 1:55 p.m.: Reads e-mail from the director

of Wyoming's online Frontiers program about possible funding cut, and calls the office of the state Superintendent. 2 p.m.: Returns call to disgruntled parent, leaving a message. 2:12 p.m.: Pulls into Newhall Middle School parking lot in hopes of watching part of Field Day.
This all continues until about 8:00 p.m. with the Superintendent's attendance at a High School graduation ceremony (The Grand Rapids Press, 2010).

While Administrators like Felske generally work extremely hard and for long hours, their schedules rarely take them into the classroom (other than for a brief visit) or even into contact with a regular teacher.

Second, the Administration has a great deal of power. This is the most important feature of the Administration in the United States. We have set our educational system up so that the farther up the chain and away from the classroom you go, the more power and influence you have over the day-to-day lives of teachers and students. It is exactly the opposite of how it should be. Members of the Administration do not teach for a living, but they oversee those who do. They manage not just salaries, hiring, benefits, and physical plants, but also the content of the curriculum, pedagogy, and classroom discipline.

Teachers have surprisingly little to say about what is taught in their classrooms, how to teach, with what materials, or even how long to teach each subject. One Georgia teacher I interviewed spoke of going outside to teach her science lesson about photosynthesis. Her principal told her she was only to use the field during recess time because it would be distracting to the other students in the building who would see her class through the windows. As we saw in the example at the beginning of the chapter, many teachers feel they basically jump through a series of hoops all day and are not given much autonomy or respect for the knowledge and skills they have. As we will see in the next chapter, this kind of job structure will attract candidates who are prone to "do what they are told" and not rock the boat.

Consider another example of the scope of administrative power and micromanagement. Some school districts have devised what they call "teacher proof" lesson plans (see Taylor, 2013). They are called "teacher proof" because the lessons are so detailed and directive, they are "safe" from being changed and adapted by teachers. Imagine you are a trained professional with a degree in your field and your supervisor (who may lack a degree in the field or much recent teaching experience) does not trust you enough to create or adapt your own lessons. They feel they must protect the children from you! Ironically, while they are given little control over what or how they teach, it is the *teachers*, not the administrators, who are held accountable for the performance of the students come assessment time. As Pamela, a first-grade teacher I interviewed in Pennsylvania told me, "If you are going to fire me for how kids do, then let me teach them."

Third, administrators are paid *vastly* more money than teachers. For example, the average annual salary of superintendents in Georgia, where I live, is $148,371. Teacher salaries in Georgia start at $39,190 and average $54,890. The highest elementary teacher salary paid in the entire state is $76,320, one half of what the average superintendent makes. This inequity is not only morally obscene, it erodes morale, provokes resentment, and causes many teachers from the very beginning of their careers to scratch and claw their way out of the classroom into the Administration where they can make a halfway decent living to support their family. The lure of power and money in the Administration takes many talented teachers out of the classroom.

Fourth, given their lack of intimacy with and knowledge of real classrooms, many of the Administration's ideas and initiatives are often time-consuming for the teacher and ineffective for the students. Teachers say many administrative directives are designed more to placate their own bosses or angry parents with window dressing than to really help students learn and grow. Real learning is hard and time-consuming; management quick-fixes and policy changes are easy. They say many of the Administration's ideas, like the use of technology in the classroom and online teaching platforms, are designed more to save the Administration money than to promote student learning. Often, administrative initiatives are imposed on teachers without a true calculation of the cost to teachers' already-limited time and energy. Special Education teacher Sam Burton notes, "There is an implicit (and offensive, frankly) assumption that I am not already working to capacity—that when a new format for reports is introduced which will require an extra 15 hours of work over a two-week period, that I have 15 more hours spare" (Burton, 2014).

Further, the assumption behind many Administrative initiatives is that the teacher is the only influence in the student's life. Their proposals put the teacher completely on the hook for student performance and leave out the contribution from the child's family and community, which have been shown to have more of an effect on student performance than any other factor. It is like planting seeds in dry ground in the middle of winter and being told to make them grow. When you ask if you can get some water or heat, you are told to do your job. It is a mixture custom-made to produce burnout.

The "And Then God Made School Boards" subtitle for this chapter comes from the nineteenth-century writer and satirist, Mark Twain. The original passage is longer than this. Twain did not have God making school boards *first*. His full statement is, "In the first place, God made idiots. That was for practice. Then he made school boards." From Twain's point of view, the Administration is a perfect idiot. I will take a close look at this curious creature by examining four concrete ways the Administration stifles teachers and impedes student learning: (1) creating what I call a "total management mentality" which sees all problems in education as having a management solution, (2) establishing an unnecessarily adversarial relationship with teachers, (3) filling administrative positions with individuals with limited managerial skills, all of which lead to, (4) the spawning of a toxic work climate created by managerial fear, insecurity, and an excessive need to control.

TOTAL MANAGEMENT MENTALITY

As I have shown, the school system as a whole is structured in a way that gives power and influence to people who are the most remote from the classroom. It is *designed* to have administrators be aloof, detached, and empowered to enact sweeping changes to every aspect of the educational enterprise. They get paid their comfortable salaries not to teach, but to go to meetings, read reports, attend conferences, and design new policies which they "roll out" and impose on those below them. And they have cleverly set it all up where *they* are not the ones held accountable if their ideas fail; *teachers are*. This way of structuring the education system leads to the formation of what I call a "total management mentality" in which every problem in education becomes a problem with a management solution.

Since all problems must be solved with more Administration, the total management mentality inevitably leads to the endless replication of supervisory positions and the wasting of vast sums of money on non-academic, administrative expenses. For example, between 1950 and 2009, the number of U.S. public school students increased by 96%. The number of teachers increased in the same period by 252%, but the rate of increase of Administration and support staff increased at a whopping 702% (New England Center for Investigative Reporting, 2014; Perry, 2013; Scafidi, 2013). When you sketch out the various layers of management and oversight as I have above, it is a bit shocking to see how many overlapping and often redundant parties are involved in what is basically a local, community-based enterprise.

What needs exist in the public schools to justify such a vast disparity in resource allocation? Why were so many more administrative positions required during this time? Simply put, there are none. Educational administrators are a self-protecting, self-perpetuating group whose main purpose is to expand their administrative domains, not enhance student learning or faculty development. They respond to needs of their own creation. Ginsberg (2011) argues that most teachers are at least driven by the school's main purpose: education and student development. Today's full-time administrators, on the other hand, view management as an end-in-itself.

Of the $639.5 billion in budget spending by U.S. public schools for the 2015 fiscal year, $344.3 billion was spent on instruction. At the same time, $118.7 billion was spent on administrative costs, about 19% of total education spending. It is important to note I am not including in this $118.7 billion figure any money spent on pupil transportation or upkeep of buildings, only costs associated with administrators and their services. Our priorities in educational spending are out of whack. This is no surprise, of course, since it is administrators who establish the spending priorities! Much more of our existing educational resources should go to teachers and teaching.

Administrators are quick to defend their staffing increases. They maintain that given the expanding size and importance of their responsibilities, they need more resources to get the job done. School administrators, they say, lead and manage organizations with operating budgets projected at close to $400 million. Most superintendents direct an average yearly budget of $22 million, with 375 staff, and over 3500 students. This is comparable to what a CEO of an industrial corporation must manage. A few school districts have operating budgets on the scale of Fortune 500 companies, with revenues of $3 billion or more. All of this is surely true. My point is, why did we set things up where management positions like this are even necessary? How has the system become so centralized and vast that you need a highly skilled CEO to run an academic enterprise?

The problem of the total management mentality is not only about endlessly replicating positions and wasted money, but about an overall mindset. This mindset sees all problems in education as management problems with a technical solution. This mindset shirks responsibility and places the onus for learning in "someone else" above or below me. And perhaps most sadly of all, this mindset is not just part of the Administration, but comes to be adopted by rank-and-file teachers and employees.

"It's management's responsibility," they come to say. "Don't blame me, I'm just doing what I'm told." In addition, with the total management mentality, teachers and families do not see themselves as the major stakeholders in the education of students. Teachers become passive employees, following policy, just doing what they are told. Parents and families become passive consumers, just employing a government service and expecting a magical result.

Adversarial Posture

The vast administrative chain I sketched above is only about 75 years old, a fairly recent development in the United States. As Rousmaniere (2013) points out in her exhaustive study of the history of the educational administration, prior to 1945, schools in the United States were loosely organized with highly local forms of administration. She writes, "school leaders worked under limited organizational structures, with minimal guidelines and expectations of their work. This thin administrative framework left them largely reliant on their own administrative leadership skills and directly dependent on community approval" (p. 7). Why did this change to the rigidly organized hierarchical pyramid we have now? The expansion of the Administration in education mirrors the overall expansion of administrative domains taking place in other areas of American society in the twentieth century (e.g., food production, labor rules, and environmental laws). As it expanded, it did so in a way that mimicked the corporate structure believed to be effective in solving complex problems. As such, the educational system was transformed into a business model with conflicting interests between management and labor. The education system became not only more bureaucratic and centralized, but more adversarial as well. In this model, members of the Administration are the "managers" and teachers are "labor." Students and parents are the "consumers."

A day at the school can feel like a tense drama between bosses and employees, with demands, counterdemands, grievances, unions, union reps, lawsuits, and strikes. While this can lead to teacher-blaming and teacher burnout (Brandt, Burgess, & Watts, 1999), the ones ultimately harmed are the children. When teachers and their bosses are pit in an adversarial relationship to one another, who advocates for the students? A far better idea would be to construct a system where teachers and administrators were on the same team working for the students.

Who Becomes an Administrator?

Not only is there a total management mentality in the Administration, but many of the people promoted into management are not very good managers (of course, some are very good). In this section, I take a close look at who gets promoted in education and why. While there are many inspiring and talented leaders in education, the current system of staffing the Administration has three problematic aspects: (1) it tends to reward managerial incompetence, (2) promotes teachers to administrative positions who are simply burnt out from their years in the classroom, and (3) attracts individuals who desire control over others rather than the professional development of teachers and the intellectual development of students.

First, many managers are incompetent and are not held accountable for their failures. The teachers I interviewed told me that almost half of the administrators they have worked for were incompetent in varying degrees. A 30-year veteran teacher in Georgia tells me, "The biggest thing the public would be surprised to know about the schools is just how bad administrators are. Parents think the people in charge have it under control, but they really don't know what they are doing." Stories like this abound in the teachers' lounge. Almost every teacher I talked with told me that school administrators are often not the most qualified person for the job, but rather the most senior person who has played politics skillfully. I have heard countless stories of how the promotion system in education rewards the total management mentality and punishes a teacher-centered approach. From a teacher's point of view, the dregs and not the cream often rises to the top.

Part of the reason for this problem is that the incentives for promotion in education are often perverse. There are some studies which show that promotion in education is related to teaching effectiveness (Chingos & West, 2011), but effectiveness as a teacher is nearly always defined as having students with high standardized test scores. There are many reasons for having students earn high scores, and teaching effectiveness is not always one of them. Often, the better teachers are given the more difficult students and so these teachers' test score averages suffer. Shana Frazin, who was an elementary teacher before working for Teachers College, says, "Lots and lots of schools reward incompetence so that the least effective teachers get the easiest class…whereas if you're good, you get more piled on your plate" (Hechinger Report, 2011).

Second, the promotion structure in education attracts teachers who are often desperate to get out of the classroom. Faced with the daily grind of grading papers, dealing with recalcitrant students and ungrateful parents, the prospect of a lifetime career out of the classroom in a position with significantly higher pay, greater social esteem, and the capacity to exert real influence is almost too attractive to pass up. Teaching is among the most stressful professions (Hakanen, Bakker, & Schaufeli, 2006). As a result, many teachers can experience professional burnout in just their first year (Mearns & Cain, 2003). Instead of having professional development programs in place to help teachers work through the inevitable burnout issues they all face, teachers are forced to hide their stress and look for an exit. Many find this exit in the form of a promotion to the administration. Teachers I talked to say many people in education are attracted to becoming part of the Administration not because they are good at management or because of their track record with great policy initiatives that help students, but because they are burned out from teaching in the classroom. There are not many fields where being burned out from the job will land you a promotion, but education is one of them.

Third, in teachers' descriptions of bad administrators, nearly all of them could be described as "control freaks" or some other personality disorder. A first-grade teacher from California spoke of a time when she was short about nine chairs in her room. With their permission, she gathered extra chairs from other teachers' rooms on her team since there were no children using them. When the principal entered the room, he saw the new chairs and confronted the teacher in front of the students. He was upset she did not check with him first. He made the children put the chairs back in the other rooms and then made her ask him permission to move them. She then had to move the nine chairs back in the room as before. I could go on and on with stories like this, but hopefully the gist is clear. Kets de Vries (1990) goes even farther than this and suggests that the many "turnaround specialists" brought in to help ailing schools are not only control freaks, but psychiatrically disturbed narcissists and sociopaths.

Toxic Culture

Workplace toxicity is almost guaranteed when the Administration is as massive, hierarchical, adversarial, management-oriented, and filled with as much managerial incompetence as it is today. All of these elements combine to produce a toxic culture that scares new teachers off in their first five years and dispirits the ones who stay. This toxic culture mirrors the common teacher complaints about their job: high workload and lack of planning time, teacher-blaming, lack of influence over curriculum and educational policy, having to tolerate intolerable student behavior, administrative and public obsession with high-stakes tests, and poor administrator people skills.

Heavy workload and lack of planning time. The Administration's total management mentality and lack of familiarity with the daily rhythms of the classroom lead them to try and squeeze as much "labor" out of teachers as possible. Because of this, most teachers are given precious little time during the day for planning, their classes are often too big, and their workload too heavy. They are often forced to do an immense amount of work in the evenings and over the weekend. On top of this, they must comply with often onerous levels of tedious paperwork and other administrative decrees. Their lives adopt an unsustainably frenetic pace with the added stress and worry that comes with juggling unachievable external demands. It is a recipe for burnout.

Little influence over policy decisions and teacher-blaming. As I mentioned above, the adversarial structure of the Administration gives them almost all the power and responsibility for academic policy, curriculum, pedagogy, and assessment. Teachers are the "labor" hired and expected to execute the decisions made by management. Teachers' expertise and training are often ignored, leaving them to carry out initiatives they do not fully endorse or believe in. At the same time, the risks of failure are not evenly spread throughout the system. Teachers are mostly held responsible when students fail. There is not a collective sense of ownership for student success shared by the Administration, teachers, students, parents, and the surrounding community. My position is that if teachers are held responsible for student failure, they should be given the ability to shape educational policy. If they are not given real academic power, they will continue to burn out or leave the profession.

Outrageous student behavior. If you spend a few hours in many elementary schools, you will see that teachers are often forced to tolerate behavior from students that is inappropriate, disrespectful, vulgar, disruptive, aggressive, and even violent. I will discuss this issue in more detail in Chap. 13. Many teachers report that administrative procedures to deal with these increasingly outrageous student behaviors are often ineffective, overly political, and result in days and months of dealing with behavior no other adult would tolerate in any other context. I have seen students bite teachers and then be asked by their principal what they may have done to encourage it.

The administrative failure to create a culture of respectful behavior is one of the most common complaints teachers make about their job. They do not all make this complaint since some schools deal with discipline very effectively, but if the Administration does not deal with discipline well, as is often the case, it will make the teacher's life a nightmare. In a recent survey of parents who removed their children from public school and sent them to a private school, 85% of parents said that they chose a private school because it provides a "better learning environment" free of distracting behavior problems (Council for American Private Education, 2013). The children who cannot afford private school are thus forced to deal with an environment that is not always conducive to learning.

Obsession with high-stakes tests. The total management mentality of the Administration leads to a narrow focus on assessing the "productivity" of their employees: the high-stakes test. I believe these tests provide us with valuable information about what students know and do not know. However, they are not the only index of student learning and there are many more factors to explain low student performance than a poor (or good) teacher. Many teachers fight desperately to get transferred out of schools where students consistently earn low test scores (or engage in high numbers of inappropriate behaviors). This creates a crisis in many districts where teachers must be hired without a certificate to teach the most at-risk students. Experienced teachers know even they cannot turn around underperforming students in a single year. Evaluating teachers this narrow and unfair way is a recipe to drive them out of areas where they are most needed, or out the field entirely.

Pathology and poor social skills. If you talk to any teacher who has been in the schools more than a few years, they will fill your ear with the various hurtful, vindictive, sadistic, even illegal things their principals and other administrators said or did to them, their students, or their colleagues. This is because many administrators have risen in the ranks not for their people skills, but because of their promise to "get things done," sometimes regardless of the human cost to those around them. Tom Rademacher (2017), who was named Minnesota Teacher of the Year in 2014, recounts in his book a principal talking about a student whose father was in prison by saying, "It's no wonder they're violent, it's in their blood." He reports many teachers being yelled at by principals in front of parents or students, or being told to "shut up" during meetings. Some principals will disappear for long periods of time or close the door in their office for the entire day. Another teacher recalls being attacked by a student and dragged down the stairs by her hair. She took two days off to process the incident and was reprimanded upon her return for not taking her job seriously.

I could go on and on with this. The important point is not just the quality of the candidates who often fill these administrative posts, but the fact that so often nothing happens to correct their behavior when they do something inappropriate. Socially and professionally inept administrators are often not held accountable for their boorish behavior but are simply transferred to another school or continue in their current position with no serious consequences. Administrators are often protected by what Rademacher (2017) calls a bubble of false professionalism in which everyone around them works to protect their career, status, and feelings. They are also often very good politicians who are owed favors by their own bosses which they call in to squelch complaints or grievances. This corrodes teacher morale in an immense way. Bosses are supposed to protect us and the environment we teach in, not contribute to its poisoning.

The Good Ones

I have painted a picture of how the Administration is grinding at teachers, creating layers of bad policy and procedure, forcing them into burnout and early retirement. So as not to leave this chapter on a bad note, I want to look at the many instances where teachers like, or even love, their principal or superintendent and see if this might point to how an Administration might be fashioned in a way that facilitates thriving in teachers and learning in students. I will explore this issue in much greater detail in Chap. 6. For now, let me say that this supportive type of Administration needs to become much more the norm than it is now.

The first point and most important point to make in this context is that having good administrators is extremely important to teachers. When elementary teachers are given the choice on surveys between a school where administrators give "strong backing and support to teachers" versus a school that "paid a significantly higher salary," 81% of them say they prefer a more supportive Administration to a higher salary (National Comprehensive Commission for Teacher Quality, 2007). What are the specific things teachers say make for a good administrator?

1. Good administrators are a "teacher's teacher." They are reluctant to assume an administrative post and plan to return to the classroom after a fixed period. They do not desire a lifetime career in Administration. They have long and deep experience in the classroom and a desire to return to it.
2. Good administrators have excellent people skills and a positive leadership style. They demonstrate respectful and professional relations with teachers. They model the kind of behavior they expect from their teachers. They have an ability to resolve conflict and can fairly and decisively discipline inappropriate teacher behavior. They also have a feedback mechanism in place where teachers can discuss things that are not working and have their concerns addressed in the form of policy or office procedure changes.
3. Good administrators seek to create a total learning environment, not a total management mentality. They do whatever is necessary to create the kind of school climate that is conducive to student learning and to protect teachers from whatever will undermine their teaching. That includes working to get teachers the basics they need to do their job, fighting for enough planning time for them to produce effective lessons, "having their back" when parents criticize or undermine them, and establishing a school climate that is as free of student disrespect, aggression, and inappropriate behavior.
4. Good administrators allow teachers an expanded role in the process of curriculum formation, execution, and assessment.
5. Good administrators work with teachers, parents, and the surrounding community to set an inspiring vision of the future for its students (see Chap. 3). He or she works to establish clear and achievable goals for realizing this vision. Perhaps most importantly, he or she works to create an overall school culture with standards, rituals, symbols, ceremonies, and stories that make up the "vibe" of a school and make it an enchanting place to be.

What You Can Do
If you are a parent or citizen, it is important to realize that the Administration works for you. They should be helping you to realize your educational aspirations for your children. Here are some things you can do to help create a more efficient and humane administrative structure in the public schools.

1. Recognize the total management mentality is pervasive in many segments of society. It dominates the educational Administration, as well as the minds of many teachers. You should not fall for it. Most problems in education are hard, time-consuming, and expensive. These issues cannot be solved with fancy curricula, technology, teaching methods, and teachers alone. Most problems in education are not problems of management. Do what you can to focus on teaching and learning and not management.
2. Follow the money. Educate yourself on how much money in your district and school is going to teaching versus how much is spent on Administration and other non-educational expenses including new staff positions, expensive new office software, or highly paid consultants. As a stakeholder, you can pressure decision-makers to route as much of the existing budget to educational expenses rather than supervisory positions.
3. Advocate for a leaner and meaner educational system. Vote for candidates who focus on local problems and solutions rather than national or state problems and solutions. When national or state politicians start to talk about education and all the things they are going to do about it, be skeptical, very skeptical.
4. Do whatever you can to ensure that actual teachers and people with educational training are promoted to administrative positions. Be skeptical of lifelong administrators and supervisors who have never taught or have been out of the classroom too long. Be wary of the promises of former military officers or business tycoons who say they will "turn around" the ailing schools with all their leadership acumen. They cannot do it. The skills they have which were effective on the field of battle

(*continued*)

(continued)

or in the boardroom will not work in the classroom. It is a completely different enterprise and the skill sets do not transfer.
5. Focus on your child's passions, gifts, talents, and vocation. What does he or she love to do? What is he or she really good at? Worry less about their future job prospects, college admission, and test scores. That pressure skews the educational system away from real teaching and learning toward quick-fixes and gimmicks to boost test scores.
6. Help your teacher teach. She works very hard amidst nearly impossible conditions. Praise her. Encourage her. Support her. If you have an issue, bring it up after saying at least one positive thing about what she is doing. Go to her first with a problem rather than "going over her head" to her principal. If she says your child had a bad day, believe her. It is likely it was far worse than she is letting on. Do what you can at home to help the learning projects that are going on at school. Make sure homework gets done, books are read, and screens turned off. You are as big a part of your child's education as the teacher and the school are.

References

American Federation of Teachers. (2017). 2017 educator quality of work life survey [PDF File]. Retrieved from https://www.aft.org/sites/default/files/2017_eqwl_survey_web.pdf

Brandt, S., Burgess, D., & Watts, D. (1999). Is the level of teacher burnout more significant among elementary education teachers or elementary general education teachers? *The Corinthian, 1*, 40–54. Retrieved from https://kb.gcsu.edu/cgi/viewcontent.cgi?article=1118&context=thecorinthian

Burton, S. (2014, August 30). A teacher speaks out: 'I'm effectively being forced out of a career that I wanted to love'. *The Independent*. Retrieved from https://www.independent.co.uk/

Chingos, M. M., & West, M. R. (2011). Promotion and reassignment in public school districts: How do schools respond to differences in teacher effectiveness? *Economics of Education Review, 30*(3), 419–433. https://doi.org/10.1016/j.econedurev.2010.12.011

Council for American Private Education. (2013). Survey identifies why parents choose private schools [PDF File]. Retrieved from https://www.capenet.org/pdf/Outlook390.pdf

Fensterwald, J. (2015, July 16). Half of new teachers quit profession in 5 years? Not true, new study says. Retrieved from https://edsource.org/2015/half-of-new-teachers-quit-profession-in-5-years-not-true-new-study-says/83054

Ginsberg, B. (2011). *The fall of the faculty: The rise of the all-administration university and why it matters*. New York, NY: Oxford University Press.

Hakanen, J., Bakker, A. B., & Schaufeli, W. B. (2006). Burnout and work engagement among teachers. *The Journal of School Psychology, 43*(6), 495–513. https://doi.org/10.1016/j.jsp.2005.11.001

Hechinger Report. (2011, March 3). What teachers want (in a principal). *The Hechinger Report*. Retrieved from https://hechingerreport.org/what-teachers-want-in-a-principal/

Ingersoll, R. M. (2002). The teacher shortage: A case of wrong diagnosis and wrong prescription. *NASSP Bulletin, 86*(631), 16–31.

Kets de Vries, M. F. (1990). Leaders on the couch. *Journal of Applied Behavioral Science, 26*(4), 423–431. https://doi.org/10.1177/0021886390264003

Markow, D., Macia, L., & Lee, H. (2013). The MetLife survey of the American teacher: Challenges for school leadership [PDF File]. Retrieved from https://www.metlife.com/content/dam/microsites/about/corporate-profile/MetLife-Teacher-Survey-2012.pdf

Mearns, J., & Cain, J. E. (2003). Relationships between teachers' occupational stress and their burnout and distress: Roles of coping and negative mood regulation expectancies. *Anxiety, Stress, & Coping, 16*(1), 71–82. https://doi.org/10.1080/1061580021000057040

National Comprehensive Commission for Teacher Quality, & Public Agenda. (2007). *Lessons learned: New teachers talk about their jobs, challenges, and long-range plans* (Issue 1) [PDF File]. Retrieved from Public Agenda Website: https://www.publicagenda.org/files/lessons_learned_1.pdf

New England Center for Investigative Reporting. (2014, February 6). New analysis shows problematic boom in higher ed administrators. *HuffPost*. Retrieved from https://www.huffingtonpost.com/

Perry, M. J. (2013). Chart of the day: Administrative bloat in US public schools. *AEI*. Retrieved from http://www.aei.org/publication/chart-of-the-day-administrative-bloat-in-us-public-schools

Rademacher, T. (2017). *It won't be easy: An exceedingly honest (and slightly unprofessional) love letter to teaching*. Minneapolis, MN: University of Minnesota.

Rousmaniere, K. (2013). *The principal's office: A social history of the American school principal*. Albany, NY: State University of New York Press.

Scafidi, B. (2013). The school staffing surge: Decades of employment growth in America's public schools part II [PDF File]. Retrieved from the Friedman

Foundation for Educational Choice Website: https://files.eric.ed.gov/fulltext/ED543118.pdf

Taylor, M. W. (2013). Replacing the 'teacher-proof' curriculum with the 'curriculum-proof' teacher: Toward more effective interactions with mathematics textbooks. *Journal of Curriculum Studies, 45*(3), 295–321. https://doi.org/10.1080/00220272.2012.710253

The Grand Rapids Press. (2010, August 17). A very long day in the life of Superintendent Jon Felske. Retrieved from https://www.mlive.com/news/grand-rapids/2010/08/a_very_long_day_in_the_life_of.html

U.S. Department of Education. (2015). *Public school teacher attrition and mobility in the first five years: Results from the first through fifth waves of the 2007–08 beginning teacher longitudinal study* [PDF File]. Retrieved from National Center for Education Statistics Website: https://nces.ed.gov/pubs2015/2015337.pdf

CHAPTER 5

The Bottom of the Barrel?

We return to the scene of the school visit. You have been chatting with Miss Thomas in the hallway as you lead a line of children to lunch. You drop the class off at the cafeteria and go with her a little way down the corridor to the teachers' lounge where you can get a few minutes respite from the raucous second graders. Several other teachers are already in there eating their lunch. The room is filled with animated discussion and homemade food. The two of you sit down across from one another and begin to eat. You pick up where you left off in the hall. You ask Miss Thomas about her past work in advertising. The conversation moves to where she went to college and what she likes to do in her spare time. You love to read and so you ask her what she has been reading lately. She notes that she really has no time to read. "Come to think of it," she adds, "I've never been much of a reader, or a writer for that matter." She speaks of her own history in school and matter-of-factly notes that she has always been just an average student, which she says helps her identify with many of the kids in the classroom who struggle with schoolwork as well. As you get to talking with your teacher, it becomes clear she does not enjoy or do many of the things she teaches her students all day.

In this chapter I look at the elementary teacher's own personality, schooling, and intellectual habits. This is the only place in the book where I will be remotely critical of teachers. Teachers are blamed for far too many problems in education, but they surely have a role to play. It pains me to say this, but some of our weakest college students go into teaching. As with Miss Thomas described above, teachers are often not actual practitioners of the arts they teach. They are not mathematicians, great readers, writers, or scientists. Some are, of course, but many are not. In this chapter, I review several studies about the kinds of college students who go into education and their intellectual habits once they become teachers. Put simply, there are no numbers I have seen about the intellectual abilities and scholarly habits of either elementary education majors or current elementary teachers that look in any way encouraging to me. Secretary of Education Arne Duncan recently said in a speech, "In the United States, a significant proportion of new teachers come from the bottom third of their college class, and most new teachers say their training didn't prepare them for the realities of the classroom" (U.S. Department of Education, 2014). What would lead him to this dire assessment of his own teaching force? In this chapter I explore some of the reasons why. I focus first on what kinds of students are attracted to a career the public schools.

In my first year preparing to become an elementary teacher, all the candidates had to write an essay about why they wanted to become an educator. I found this exercise fascinating. I asked the other students in my class for their reasons for going into teaching and they willingly shared their essays. I then asked students who had other sections of this same class for their answers. Before long, I assembled more than a hundred essays from aspiring teachers on, "Why I want to go into teaching." I found what people found attractive about teaching clustered into four distinct categories that I call the Mother, the Sergeant, the Sheep, and the Underachiever.

Women's Work: The Mother

I said in Chap. 2 that teaching in general, and elementary teaching in particular, has historically been cast as a "low-status" occupation in the United States, a "gut major," "women's work," or "nose-wiping." Many teachers will tell you stories of the first time they told their parents of their decision to go into education. Parents can say the most denigrating and hurtful things. A first-grade teacher I worked with recalls her father lamenting, "You'll never make any money!" Another first-grade teacher's father exclaimed, "But you're smart enough to be a doctor!" A third-grade teacher remembers his mother reacting to the news he would major in education by saying, "We raised you to do something important with your life." This same mother then said she wanted her son to pay back all the money they "wasted" on his college tuition! I recall my uncle's old chestnut he would share over holiday dinners when I was first thinking of a career in teaching, "Those who can, do; those who can't, teach." Over my long career as a college professor, I have had several calls from worried parents begging me to talk their child out of going into education. "Please, Dr. Dillon, she respects you. Tell her how she's blowing her chance at a good career." Obviously, these parents forgot they were talking to another teacher!

None of this discounts the many positive things people say about teaching, for example, "If you can read this, thank a teacher," or "I touch the future; I teach." Despite these comments, there is a decidedly negative perception of the teaching field in the minds of millions of American citizens. In a 2018 poll of attitudes toward public schools, 54% of Americans said they did not want their child to become a public school teacher. This was the first time since this question was first asked back in 1969 that a majority of Americans said no to this question (PDK Poll, 2018). In a recent study of the attitudes toward different occupations held by the top third of college graduates, only 66% of students polled said they agreed with the statement, "I would be proud to tell people I was a teacher." Only 37% agreed that "people who have this job [teaching] are considered successful" (McKinsey & Company, 2010). This negative view of teaching in the United States is not shared by other countries in the world. In Finland, for example, teaching is rated as one of the most admired professions, ahead of lawyers, architects, and medical doctors (Sahlberg, 2015, p. 101).

This low view of the teaching profession in the United States is not just an inner attitude. These negative views receive concrete expression in the form of the low salaries we pay teachers compared with other professions. A recent study by the Economic Policy Institute finds that teachers earn 19% less than similarly skilled and educated professionals in other fields. Further, this "teaching penalty" has increased significantly, from 2% in 1994 to 19% in 2017 (Allegretto & Mishel, 2018). The negative cultural attitude toward teaching is also expressed in the way we treat teachers as employees who need to "do what they are told" by their bosses. The administrative structure outlined in Chap. 4 reflects the belief that we do not completely trust our teachers' intellects, initiative, and professional autonomy. The allegedly smarter and more competent administrator needs to tell them how to do their work.

Given the low status, one wonders what motivates young candidates to go into elementary education in the first place? Obviously, there are many noble souls who are drawn to the profession out of a love of learning and a desire to help the next generation develop into all they can be. These candidates can see past the cultural denigration of teaching to a deeper truth about the field. At the same time, there are others who are, perhaps unconsciously, attracted to the teaching profession precisely *because* it is perceived as less rigorous or challenging than other professions. Some do not expect very much of themselves intellectually. Others, like Miss Thomas, have struggled themselves in school and are not the best students.

Still others are attracted to the profession *because* it is seen as "women's work." I call this group of teachers, the *Mother*. Mothers tell you they got into teaching because they simply love little children. They always have. They want to spend their days with them, caring for them, and nurturing them. They speak of the students with the care and affection of a mother. One third-grade teacher I worked with referred to the students as her "babies." She would frequently hug them, tell them she loved them, and even ask them if they loved her. For the Mother, the children's intellectual development is more of an afterthought and takes a backseat to the powerful affection she has for them and her deep desire they feel loved and valued. In my work interviewing candidates to hire to teach college, I frequently ask them why they want to teach. I would say a full third will give a variation of the Mother response, stating they want students to know they are cared for, valued, that they are smart, important, or loved.

Care and affection are extremely important qualities to have in an elementary (or any) teacher, but in the Mother this emotional investment can sometimes mask the teacher's own intellectual deficits and divert vital time and energy away from rigorous instruction and holding students to high standards even if it upsets them. The Mother's reasoning looks like this: "It doesn't matter how much I know or how good I am at teaching, how much time I spend on instruction, how hard I grade, or even how much my students learn. The most important thing is how much I care…and I care a lot." This strong affection can interfere with the discipline and rigor necessary to facilitate intellectual development and skill mastery in students. So long as the elementary teaching profession is seen as "women's work," it will continue to attract candidates who see teaching in just this way.

Drill and Kill: The Sergeant

I mentioned in Chap. 3 that many elementary schools lack a sense of vision and high purpose. Without these guiding forces, teaching is simply the presentation of isolated skills and learning objectives without a framing narrative. Without adventure and high purpose, standards are just subjects we "cover" without rhyme or reason. This kind of teaching is often very concrete, technical, and uninspiring. You simply "do your lesson" without connecting the skill or knowledge to any larger picture, to other skills, or to a deeper purpose. Your work as a teacher does not involve creatively applying a general principle to a concrete case, for example, how can two-digit addition help us be heroes? You just "do" two-digit addition and move onto the next subject. Teachers call this kind of instruction "drill and kill." This phrase was originally coined as a negative description of a teaching style that stifled children's curiosity and questioning through the repetitive practice of isolated skills. However, the *Sergeant* proudly describes his or her teaching approach as just this. They delight in the prospect of practicing important skills to mastery and hope to turn their classes into well-oiled machines.

Aspiring teachers understand many currently employed teachers "drill and kill" all day long. It is impossible to go into the schools at your teaching placements and not see this setup. Candidates who go into teaching know they will need to be able to tolerate long periods of extremely tedious instruction, often delivered without creativity, inspiration, or vision. This is especially true during the second half of the academic year as schools prepare for their high-stakes tests. Some candidates are horrified by this prospect and decide to enter another career entirely. Others secretly hope to transform it. But many others are fascinated and attracted to elementary teaching for this very reason. They like the laundry list of skills that are laid out in the "curriculum map" for their grade at the beginning of the year. It has a certain focus, direction, and discipline to it. It seems like "real work." They like the concrete focus and immediate feedback they get about how they and the students are doing. They love the results, the test scores, and they genuinely believe they are helping.

Of course, rigor and discipline are important qualities in any teacher. The problem with the Sergeant is that their focus on the mastery of isolated skills runs the risk of killing the spirit of three-quarters of the classroom. For those who do not like the drill, school becomes a humiliating place to be, filled with drudgery and personal failure. Further, these teachers fail at the most vital task of all during the elementary years: to awaken in each child an exciting vision of the future and an awareness of the gifts he or she brings to the adult world. If students dread coming to school over time, it causes a serious long-term problem which strikes at the heart of the child's self-confidence and overall relationship to learning. Students may finish the school year and eventually graduate someday, but it is at a great psychological and emotional cost.

Just Tell Me What to Do: The Sheep

In Chap. 4, I discussed how the school system is over-supervised and prone to the total management mentality, where every problem is seen to have a management solution. In this hyper-administrative context, the teacher's role is to deliver a curriculum that has been pre-fabricated for her. After years of learning about this administrative arrangement in college and experiencing it in their internships, candidates who go into teaching are fully aware it is set up this way. Many hate this arrangement and change their major to something besides education for this reason. Others who dislike this setup go into teaching with the hope they will eventually enter the ranks of the Administration where they can finally be "in charge" and exercise some degree of professional autonomy. Still others believe they can do their good work with children despite the administrative hoops, disempowering oversight, and red tape. They plan to ignore the Administration or otherwise deal with it. There is another cluster of teachers, however, who are attracted to the teaching profession *because* of the high levels of management and low levels of professional autonomy it affords them. They are what I call the "Sheep." They are docile, agreeable, selfless, loyal, obedient, often uncreative, and seemingly content in their disempowerment. They like being part of a team and do not ever want to "rock the boat."

In my work as a psychologist, I often have occasion to use the Myers-Briggs Type Indicator (MBTI). The MBTI is a personality measure based on the theory of Carl Jung who proposed that people experience the world using four principal psychological functions. The mother-daughter team of Katherine Myers and Isabel Briggs operationalized Jung's theory, arguing that these functions can be understood in terms of four major dimensions: where we gather energy (Introversion or Extroversion), how we gather information (Sensing or Intuition), how we make decisions (Thinking or Feeling), and how we act upon decisions once we make them (Judging or Perceiving). The assumption behind the MBTI is that people have specific "preferences" in the way they deal with these four dimensions of human experience. Some suggest these preferences are innate; others suggest they are deep-seated learned habits which are very difficult to change. The MBTI gives the test-taker a four-letter score based on the assessment of his or her particular preferences across these four dimensions.

When you look at the MBTI scores of elementary teachers, their rate of each personality type mirrors those in the general population, except for one area: the Introverted Sensing Feeling Judging (ISFJ) type, also known as the *Protector*. Elementary teachers have more than *two times* the number of ISFJ types compared with the national population. The national average for the ISFJ is 13.8%; for elementary teachers it is 29.9% (Rushton, Morgan, & Richard, 2007). The Keirsey Group describes Protectors as deriving "a great deal of satisfaction from caring for others...as devoted and loyal to their superiors." They "value tradition, whether it be cultural, institutional, or familial. They believe in the safety of a traditional social hierarchy, and do everything they can to uphold custom and convention." For Protectors, "regulations are tried and true, and they rarely question the effectiveness of going by the book. They expect everyone to conform to the established rules, feeling a personal responsibility to ensure that standards are not only adhered to but honored" (Portrait of the guardian protector ISFJ, n.d.).

Notice the major adjectives used to describe the Protector: give loyalty to superiors, value tradition, uphold convention, respect social hierarchy, rarely question going by the book, and expect others to conform to the established rules. The Protector's predominant value is not seeking knowledge, creativity, or freedom, but loyalty to tradition. The reason why nearly one-third of elementary teachers have this personality type is because the profession is set up to reward them. Make no mistake about it, these individuals are a Principal's dream! They are punctual, tireless workers, never miss a day of work, respectful of authority and the rules, and they don't make waves. These are all good qualities, of course. Groups cannot function without a healthy amount of cooperation and compromise. But the downside is that these teachers do not raise questions when questions should be raised. They do not exercise autonomy where autonomy is most needed.

The Easiest Major: The Underachiever

For a variety of reasons, a career in teaching in the United States does not always attract the top academic talent. Students in college who go into education have some of the lowest IQ, SAT, and Graduate Record Exam (GRE) scores of any major in college (Ackerman & Heggestad, 1997; Olson, 2014; Wai, Lubinski, & Benbow, 2009). Half of all students who go into education are in the bottom half of their high school graduating class (McKinsey & Company, 2010). Only 23% of college students who get jobs in teaching come from the top third of their class in college, and only 14% of that small group ever go on to work with the most at-risk students, where there is such a great need for their intellect and teaching skills. The world's top-scoring education systems, like South Korea, Finland, and Singapore, all draw 100% of their teachers come from the top third of the college graduates (McKinsey & Company, 2010).

Parents with kids in public schools are aware of this dirty little secret. In a recent *Public Agenda* poll, a majority of parents with children in school (53%) believe that people who choose to go into teaching tend to be "just average," compared with other college graduates (Public Agenda, 2003). These parents see the talent pool up close every day and render a less-than-stellar judgment. But these parents are not quite correct; teachers are actually even intellectually *lower* than average compared to other college graduates.

Despite the fact that education draws some of the weakest students in college, education majors have the highest GPA of any major (O'Shaughnessy, 2010). This leads many to the conclusion that education classes and teacher training are not as intellectually challenging as other majors in college (Sawchuk, 2014). From my own recent experience going through the education major, I am sorry to say this view is accurate. As helpful as my own education classes were, they were among the easiest classes to get an A in that I have ever taken. I would often get a four- to five-page paper back from my professors with nothing but a "check plus" at the top as a grade. We quickly learned that our professors merely checked to see that we adhered to the page count and did not assess the quality of our writing at all. I had assignments that were deliberately constructed to have students go to Wikipedia to obtain information. We would spend hours of class time doing meaningless busy group-work projects rather than learning techniques to teach. My GPA was 4.0, and that was while I was working full time and raising a family. There was very little reading, writing, discussion, and thinking involved with the process.

It was only when I got to the state certification test that I realized how incomplete my training was. I purchased and took several full-length practice tests for the state exam. These yielded horrible scores and revealed huge gaps in vital content areas such as reading and math instruction, child development, and classroom management. Given the gaps, I had to study nonstop for months to make up the deficits. At many points I grumbled to myself, "Why didn't we learn these reading instruction theories and methods in the class I just took called, '*Reading Instruction*?'" Though I had a 4.0 GPA in my classes, I initially scored in the 40s on my practice certification exams. For the most part, undergraduate education classes lack the academic rigor present in other majors and run the risk of attracting candidates to education *because* they are less challenging. It is a major designed to attract the *Underachiever*. One Physical Education (PE) teacher I got to know well in one of the schools I was placed in told me he went into PE because "it was the only major where you could get a workout in class and didn't have to study much."

Lest we think this academic underachievement is confined to education majors while they are in college and that once they get into the intellectually dynamic elementary school setting, they suddenly become more academically oriented, it is not so. Currently employed teachers do not generally like to read and write themselves. McKool and Gespass (2009) found less than half of elementary teachers report reading for pleasure daily. Twenty-six percent of elementary teachers report spending *no time at all* on reading, ever. This is consistent with other research showing that preservice and currently employed teachers do not read regularly and report little pleasure in reading (e.g., Applegate & Applegate, 2004; Smith, 1989).

This is a huge problem. As I will show in Chap. 7, the modern elementary school curriculum is centered on massive literacy and numeracy skills. It is designed to prepare young people for college and a professional career. If many of the people administering this curriculum are not practitioners or masters of these skills themselves, it creates a problem on two levels, one that is *technical* and the other that goes to *credibility*.

Technically speaking, if you do not practice the skills you teach yourself, you really cannot teach them very well. Your knowledge is a mile wide and an inch deep. Once the teaching process moves from the mere presentation of information to the phase where students begin to ask probing questions, make puzzling errors, and where the teacher must apply what she knows to new domains and real-world contexts, the teacher's lack of practiced knowledge and ability becomes quickly evident. For example, one of my own professional interests is abstraction, how readers can draw out deeper meaning from texts. My lessons in elementary school that deal with abstraction are much more effective than my lessons on Georgia history, where my knowledge is scant. I recall very well a lesson on Georgia geography, where I knew next to nothing. My lesson was much less confident and creative. It relied on simply presenting information rather than having students actively engage with it. I could not answer many of the students' probing questions. Because of my lack of mastery, I wanted to shut students' questions down rather than confidently field them.

The second aspect of teacher academic underachievement goes to the question of morale and credibility. Imagine you went into a health club where all the personal fitness trainers employed there were morbidly obese. Would you have a lot of confidence in their leadership? Their health tips? The metaphor is crude and unfair to our schools in some ways, but many of our public elementary teachers are analogous to these overweight fitness trainers. They do not practice what they preach, and it becomes evident to the public over time. A teacher needs to be living the life of the mind to be effective. At the same time, living a life of the mind helps students trust you, respect you, and generally listen to what you say. The question is, how do we begin to attract the kinds of student candidates we want to staff this largely academic venture? The answer is reformed teacher training.

Teacher Training, Where It All Begins

As much as we focus on teacher quality and getting rid of "bad teachers" in this country, the topic of teacher training is oddly not a big part of the political discussion. Where did all these allegedly "bad teachers" come from? And how did they manage to pass a state exam certifying they were competent to teach young children when many allegedly turn out to be incompetent? The answer lies in low-quality teacher training programs and poor certification exams. When you take a close look at the quality of teacher training in the United States, the situation does not look good. A recent study by the National Council on Teacher Quality (Greenberg, McKee, & Walsh, 2013) concludes that teacher training programs "have become an industry of mediocrity, churning out first-year teachers with classroom management skills and content knowledge inadequate to thrive in classrooms with ever-increasing ethnic and socioeconomic student diversity" (p. 3). I will discuss the problems in teacher training in terms of three major areas: unity, quality, and academic rigor.

Unity. While we have a national *Common Core* curriculum for the major subjects taught to children in elementary school, we do not have a similarly unified national curriculum for college students in teacher training programs. Ours is a wildly piecemeal approach based on widely different views of what teachers need to know, what kinds of classes they need to take, and what kinds of internship experiences they need to have in order to become a "good teacher." In addition, there is no common set of standards to assess the quality of teacher preparation across the country to decide which programs are doing a good job preparing today's teachers and which are not. The National Council on Teacher Quality (NCTQ, 2016) offers a list of 19 standards for elementary teacher training programs, but these (or any other) set of standards have not been adopted nationally.

What is more, many schools of education are unwilling even to provide information on what they do in their education classes. There is therefore no way for national bodies or external researchers to determine the quality of different schools of education across the country. In forming its national report, the NCTQ notes it had to hire attorneys in nine states to deal with education programs who argued their syllabi are their "intellectual property" and therefore do not have to be shared. How can we assess the quality of teacher education when there are no national standards, no national accrediting body, and no mandate that schools even provide information about what they are teaching in their preparation programs?

To top it all off, each of the 50 states is responsible for assessing the quality of its own schools. This is rather like asking students to grade their own papers. U.S. Secretary of Education Arne Duncan recently noted that for the past 12 years, more than 50% of the states had not rated a single teacher training program as inferior. Duncan and the Obama administration tried to make the assessment of teacher training programs more rigorous by providing funding and incentives to close inferior programs and make state licensing exams more challenging, but this work stalled.

Quality. Teacher training in the United States is not only piecemeal in terms of academic standards, but the quality of training programs is also uneven between and within states. What this means is that a degree from the University of Ohio is not necessarily as good as a degree from the University of Minnesota. Teachers with these two degrees could have potentially wide differences in training, knowledge, and skills. At the same time, teaching degrees within states are not reciprocal either, making a degree from the University of Georgia and the University of West Georgia potentially quite different degrees. For example, the NCTQ ranks my own training program at the University of West Georgia in the 76th percentile of all training programs, while Albany State University, just 170 miles down the interstate, ranks only in the lower 4th percentile. A degree from either university would enable me to teach in Georgia elementary schools. At the same time, our country has embraced several dubious "alternative pathways" to certification such as Teach for America and other waivers for teacher training that do not involve a degree from a standard academic program. This compromises the quality of the teacher preparation process even further.

It is odd that the United States has what I regard as an oversized state and federal role in the elementary school curriculum, but not a similar national role for teacher training and preparation. When it comes to teacher training, individual schools and states are given wide latitude to determine what is taught in their programs. What is called for is just the opposite: *more* national control over academic standards and curriculum for teacher training programs and *less* national control over academic standards and curriculum of the elementary schools themselves. We need a national teaching preparation curriculum that equips teachers to perform in today's schools and prepares them to exercise their professional judgment as autonomous agents once they enter the workplace. If we properly train teachers to be competent professionals to begin with, we will not need so many layers of supervision and oversight to make sure they are doing the right thing once they are hired. I will develop this idea in more detail in the next chapter.

Rigor. As I mentioned earlier, classes in teacher preparation programs are often not academically rigorous or intellectually challenging. This leads not only to poor teacher preparation but to the potential of attracting teacher candidates who are academically underachieving. The recent NCTQ report on teacher training programs concludes that getting into a teacher training program is much too easy. Only one-quarter of teacher training programs deny admissions to students in the lower half of their class, while the highest achieving countries, like Finland and Singapore, limit all entries to the top third (Greenberg, McKee, & Walsh, 2013, p. 4). I will share just a few more examples. Three out of four elementary teacher preparation programs do not teach best practices in reading instruction. Fewer than one in nine elementary programs prepare candidates in content at the level necessary to teach the new *Common Core* state standards currently being implemented in classrooms in over 40 states. Just 7% of programs ensure that their student teachers will have uniformly strong experiences by being placed with effective teachers rather than just willing volunteers (Greenberg, McKee, & Walsh, 2013, p. 4).

Why *Should* We Teach Anyway?

What kinds of candidates do we want to attract to teach in our schools? We need to figure this question out before we start talking about how to train teachers, what classes they should take, and what scores they need to get on their certification exams. The central questions of this section are the following: What does it mean to be a "good" or "prepared" teacher? And why *should* people go into teaching in the first place?

Compassion, rigor, and teamwork are all ingredients of a good teacher, but in isolation these qualities become caricatures leading to the Mother, the Sergeant, or the Sheep. These qualities all need to be present in a candidate alongside a larger vision which holds that intellectual activity is the very purpose of life and the only basis for a satisfying existence. From this point of view, the primary function of the schools not to help kids get good jobs when they grow up, to get them into good colleges, or prepare them to do well on their state-mandated tests. Rather, schools help students learn skills that enable them to grow as people and embark on the adventurous odyssey of life in pursuit of high purpose. Academic *overachievers*, not underachievers, are required to do this work.

The main reason why we sometimes do not produce good public school teachers is because the public is not united on what education is for. And many in the public do not value education very much. Imagine if our surgeons and medical doctors were all drawn from the bottom third of the college student pool. Would we tolerate it? Probably not. It would likely be declared a national emergency. The fact that we allow this problem to persist in education reflects the fact that we do not think elementary education is all that important, or that the costs of mediocre teachers are not that high. But they are.

Attracting and training good teachers is not only a management problem where we need to change laws or policy, but it is a problem of vision. The issue does not need a get-tough politician, a business manager, turnaround specialist, or military commander to fix things. It requires an overall philosophical shift, a collective reorganization of priorities in the culture at large. Such a shift would lead to a change in the administrative structure of elementary schools that currently gives teachers low levels of professional autonomy over matters of curriculum and instruction. To attract the kinds of teacher candidates we want and need, it will not be enough to have high-quality teacher education, good pay, as well as safe and stimulating working conditions. Teachers need to know they will enter into a work environment where they will be valued and treated like the professionals they are so they can fulfill the inspiring vision that got them into teaching in the first place: helping children learn and grow, equipping kids with skills for high purpose, and building a better society and world.

Please do not misunderstand the message of this chapter. We should not romanticize teachers. Solving the teacher training problem is no magic bullet. Attracting and training the most intellectually qualified and talented teachers in the world will make a very small impact on students so long as the current administrative structure of schools and the familial/ community context of most students remains unchanged. Teachers are just one part of an overall learning context. I will show in later chapters that society and family context are even *more* important factors to student success than teacher quality. Contrary to the political narrative we often hear about education, teachers can only facilitate a limited amount of learning in students when working by themselves on the task of education. But good teachers are an important part of the total educational context.

What You Can Do
Attracting the highest caliber teachers is a multifaceted problem. No one party is responsible for the whole thing. How can you do your part to begin to turn this issue around?

1. Fight the cultural devaluation of teaching. The shift in cultural mindset discussed in this chapter begins with you. You are the biggest part of the culture. This shift demands you muster the courage to be countercultural. The culture says education is women's work, unimportant, something only to help people get good jobs. You must stand apart and proclaim that the most important part of school is to help children discover who they are, what they are called to do, and to inspire them to embrace the mission of high purpose in life. It is among the noblest of life callings. Think deeply about what is in your heart when you think about teachers. I have discovered from my research that many of us carry around painful memories from our own experiences in schools that negatively cloud what we now think and feel about education. A lot of our feelings and beliefs about education reflect what we believe about our own intellects, our own academic skills, and our own often fraught relationship with school and teachers. So, take a good look at all that. Be honest. Share your thoughts and feelings with others. Do not let the "experts" make all the decisions on these important matters because you think you are not smart enough.
2. Encourage your own children to go into teaching, or at least do not discourage them when they tell you they may be interested in doing it. They may be called to it. If they ever come to you with ideas of teaching, it likely means they have been inspired by their own teachers and see this life choice as an exciting one filled with adventure and high purpose. The children of the future need your children to teach. Please do not discourage them.

(continued)

(continued)

3. Educate yourself on what is involved in teacher training in your own state. Be aware of what the teachers who work in your schools know and what they do not know. Educate yourself on your teacher's salary, benefits, and workload. Many careless statements are made about education and teachers that are just not true, and many consequential political decisions are made from ignorance. Work hard not to traffic in educational misinformation and lies.
4. Be aware of the different motivations to teach and the different types of teacher, especially the Mother, Sergeant, Sheep, and the Underachiever. Ask yourself, "what *should* draw a teacher to a life in the classroom?" "What kinds of teachers do I want my own children to have?"
5. Demand as much teacher and teaching-team empowerment from your Principal and Administration as possible. Insist that teachers be given the widest possible latitude in curriculum, pedagogy, and assessment. This will help to attract the kinds of intelligent, professional, and competent teachers to the classroom that nearly everyone wants.
6. Work to pay teachers in a way that reflects their training, their value to you, and the salaries of comparable professions. This is not necessarily about raising taxes. Funds can come from radical cuts in administrative positions and costs. If taxes are involved, I would suggest creating specific ballot measures where voters approve targeted salary increases for teachers. It must be clearly stipulated that additional revenues *cannot* be used for administration, upkeep of buildings, retirement accounts, or the government's general operating fund to build roads or pay down government debt. Ballot measures to pay teachers more have widespread appeal when voters are given concrete assurances that all the additional funding will go to teacher salary increases. Higher salaries will not only help many teachers make ends meet who are currently struggling, it will also help to attract the kinds of competent professionals we want and need in our classrooms. People will not consider a career a "profession" if they cannot support a family on the salary it pays.

References

Ackerman, P. L., & Heggestad, E. D. (1997). Intelligence, personality, and interests: Evidence for overlapping traits. *Psychological Bulletin, 121*(2), 219–245.

Allegretto, S., & Mishel, L. (2018). *The teacher pay penalty has hit a new high: Trends in the teacher wage and compensation gaps through 2017.* Retrieved from Economic Policy Institute Website: https://www.epi.org/publication/teacher-pay-gap-2018

Applegate, A. J., & Applegate, M. D. (2004). The Peter effect: Reading habits and attitudes of preservice teachers. *Reading Teacher, 57*(6), 554–563.

Greenberg, J., McKee, A., & Walsh, K. (2013). *Executive summary teacher prep review: A review of the nation's teacher preparation programs.* Retrieved from the National Council on Teacher Quality Website: https://www.nctq.org/dmsView/Teacher_Prep_Review_executive_summary

McKinsey & Company. (2010). Attracting and retaining top talent in US teaching. Retrieved from https://www.mckinsey.com/industries/social-sector/our-insights/attracting-and-retaining-top-talent-in-us-teaching

McKool, S. S., & Gespass, S. (2009). Does Johnny's reading teacher love to read? How teachers' personal reading habits affect instructional practices. *Literacy Research & Instruction, 48*(3), 264–276.

National Council on Teacher Quality. (2016). *NCTQ teacher prep review standards and indicators: Traditional teacher preparation program standards.* Retrieved from https://www.nctq.org/dmsView/NCTQ_-_Standards_and_Indicators_-_Traditional_Programs

Olson, R. (2014). Average IQ of students by college major and gender ratio. Retrieved from http://www.randalolson.com/2014/06/25/average-iq-of-students-by-college-major-and-gender-ratio

O'Shaughnessy, L. (2010, April 5). 5 hardest and easiest college majors by GPA's: Why aren't more college students earning degrees in engineering and the sciences? *CBSNews.* Retrieved from http://www.cbsnews.com/news/5-hardest-and-easiest-college-majors-by-gpas/

PDK Poll. (2018). Teaching: Respect but dwindling appeal. Retrieved from http://pdkpoll.org/results

Portrait of the guardian protector ISFJ. (n.d.). Retrieved from https://keirsey.com/temperament/guardian-protector/

Public Agenda. (2003). *An assessment of survey data on attitudes about teaching including the views of parents, administrators, teachers, and the general public* [PDF File]. Retrieved from Public Agenda Website https://www.publicagenda.org/files/attitudes_about_teaching.pdf

Rushton, S., Morgan, J., & Richard, M. (2007). Teacher's Myers-Briggs personality profiles: Identifying effective teacher personality traits [PDF file]. *Teaching and Teaching Education, 23,* 432–441. Retrieved from http://www2.sfasu.edu/cte/Michelle_Files/HMS_300_Web_Content/Teacher_MBPTI.pdf

Sahlberg, P. (2015). *Finnish lessons, 2.0.* New York, NY: Teachers College Press.

Sawchuk, S. (2014, November 12). Is teacher-preparation rigorous enough? *Education Week.* Retrieved from http://blogs.edweek.org/edweek/teacherbeat/2014/11/is_teacher-preparation_coursew.html?qs=grade+inflation

Smith, M. C. (1989). Reading attitudes of pre-service education majors. *Reading Horizons, 29*(4), 230–234. Retrieved from https://scholarworks.wmich.edu/reading_horizons/vol29/iss4/2/

U.S. Department of Education. (2014). Parent voices for world-class education: Remarks of U.S. secretary of education Arne Duncan to the national assessment governing board education summit for parent leaders [Transcribed Speech]. Retrieved from https://www.ed.gov/news/speeches/remarks-us-secretary-education-arne-duncan-national-assessment-governing-board-educati

Wai, J., Lubinski, D., & Benbow, C. (2009). Spatial ability for STEM domains: Aligning over 50 years of cumulative psychological knowledge solidifies its importance. *Journal of Educational Psychology, 101*(4), 817–835.

CHAPTER 6

What to Do About These Four Things

So far, I have presented four surprising "Things" about today's elementary schools: the large gender staffing imbalance, a lack of adventure and high purpose, the many layers of bureaucracy, and the fact that we often do not draw from the top of the academic pool in selecting and training teachers. I was careful to mention in the Introduction that mine is not a "fix-it" book where I lay out all the terrible things about education and then present a single solution to correct everything. Education has far too many moving parts for something like that to be possible. While I do not propose a single solution or even a set of solutions, I do have some ideas to contribute to the society-wide effort to improve the educational situation. In this chapter, I try to digest these four items and brainstorm some solutions.

At bottom, the first four Things I outline are all about *vision* and *personnel*, about the future toward which we educate children and the people we hire to do it. I focus in this chapter on how personnel might be recruited, trained, utilized, and promoted differently than they currently are. And I consider our collective visions of the ideal teacher, the ideal school, and who should have the power to formulate these visions. Currently, education's visions come from "the experts." For us to begin to improve our schools, more avenues must open for parents, the larger community, and the children themselves to have a hand in this important envisioning process.

Our Vision of Teachers and Schools

I start with some basic questions. What are elementary schools for? What does an ideal school look like? An ideal teacher? What do elementary school children really need to learn? How much of their day do they need to learn it? Whose visions should get to determine the shape of the schools? I invite you to envision with me some answers to these fundamental questions. As I will discuss further in Chap. 12, a big part of the problem with our public schools is that the public has not contributed a great deal to the discussion. Most of us have not thought through, nor have we been asked to share, why we send our kids to school in the first place, what we want them to learn, and the qualities of the people we want to teach them. I hope our society can begin a more inclusive and transparent process where we all openly share the images we have about the ideal school, the ideal curriculum, and the ideal teacher that will inspire us and our children.

Before we start the envisioning, I note the ideas which often come immediately to mind when we talk about education are often not our own but reflect larger cultural assumptions which we often take for granted. Finding the best images of schools and teachers therefore requires that we adopt a critical stance toward our highly commercial culture and tune into our deepest, highest selves. It is particularly important to be aware of how much "educational capitalism" reigns in our thinking about schools (see Hill-Jackson & Lewis, 2010, p. xvi). With educational capitalism, we think of the school's primary function as teaching our children the knowledge and skills that will enable them to get a good job and be financially successful in today's economy. Recall the scenario of the insurance adjuster I considered in the context of young Jeffrey's question about what all his math lessons were for. This commercial understanding of the role of the teacher and the school is perhaps the most dominant of all the public's images of what education is all about.

While preparing for work in a capitalist economy is surely an important goal, schools should play a deeper and more liberating role in our children's lives. Schools should free children's intellects to be able to distinguish fact from fiction, enable them to articulate and express their ideas and feelings, develop habits and practices that will enable them to participate in the democratic process, help children discover the truth about themselves and the universe, just who they are and what they are here to do. While the economic viability of children is surely a consideration, it is among the last items on my list of what elementary schools should do.

Many parents, politicians, and businesses, however, put college admission and student earning potential at the very top of their list. They buy into educational capitalism hook, line, and sinker. Unfortunately, this view prevents schools from being able to realize their central humanistic mission of developing people. More importantly, it produces a restless panic that leads parents to push their children toward the best colleges starting in preschool and Kindergarten. It causes schools to lay out a rigorous, college prep curriculum-for-all which they then endlessly assess. We can do better than that.

Schools tell a story. Parents, administrators, and politicians often collude with the capitalist system and turn education into a handmaid of the economy. The price we pay is the health, happiness, and true development of our children. So before listening to the "public" at large, *I suggest we listen to the children.* What do children want and need from school? What are their hopes and dreams for the future? I have spent years investigating the things that really grab kids' attention. If you have ever taught children yourself, you know it is difficult to get them to focus on anything in school, so when they are truly engaged by something, it is well worth our time to see what has taken such a hold of them. So, what grips children, stops them in their tracks, and fills them with enchantment? From what I can see, elementary-aged children are *transfixed by the story form.* They cast their lives in terms of story and they process most of the information they learn into narratives. Thus, to meet children's real needs, their educational journey needs to be encased in a meaningful story.

Some schools already do this. Jacy Douglas and the teachers she works with at Parkside School in Baileyton, Alabama, spent two summers changing their drab school building into the "Wizarding World of Harry Potter" with classrooms designed to resemble Slytherin, Ravenclaw, and Gryffindor (Frisbie, 2018). Rooms and hallways are complete with gothic columns, ancient portraits, shelves with potions and spell books, suits of armor standing guard, vivid murals, insects, snakes, wands, a fireplace, sofas, and dining tables. Schools in my own hometown of Atlanta and other cities have also recently become Hogwarts (CBS News, 2015; Edgeworth, 2018). The story does not need to be Harry Potter, of course. This is just an example of how the educational journey of the entire school could be framed within a single gripping narrative.

While encasing the entire school into one narrative may be difficult for many to achieve, doing it at the level of the individual classroom is easier. Many teachers across the country base their individual classrooms on story "themes." I have seen teachers organize their classrooms and their school year around the story theme of *Star Wars, Magic School Bus, The Wild Wild West, Pirates of the Caribbean, 20,000 Leagues Under the Sea, Olivia Saves the Circus, A Trip to the Safari*, and many more. They use this theme to integrate all the lessons and traditional subject areas of the curriculum. Costumes, characters, activities, and decorations all support this central narrative. These teachers appreciate how most elementary children need the framing device of story to inspire them and to add relevance and coherence to an otherwise disconnected set of subjects.

Schools invite adventure. We know children's minds are narratively structured, but what kinds of stories do elementary-aged children need? As discussed in Chap. 3, elementary-aged children need *romantic* stories, odysseys in which a hero or heroine struggles against great odds against threatening circumstances to a glorious transcendence. In addition, their stories need binary opposition, antagonists, heroes, and a lot of emotion. Such stories mirror their precarious developmental condition, enable them to make strides toward psychological growth, and help them perform what would otherwise be tedious academic tasks.

Consider the popular PBS children's program *Cyberchase*. The central drama of the show is that the Motherboard, the ruler of Cyberspace, has been infected with a virus hatched by the evil villain Hacker (dire initial situation). The virus severely weakens the Motherboard and prevents her from being able to protect Cyberspace. Three regular kids are enlisted to engage a heroic effort to protect the world from the Hacker and his dark assistants, Buzz and Delete. They team up with the helpful bird Digit to form the Cybersquad. In each episode, the children must learn an important math or problem-solving skill—fractions, balancing, division, tessellations, and so on—which enables them to save Cyberspace from Hacker's total domination (transcendence over threatening conditions). This is a perfect romantic frame within which to present elementary schoolers an otherwise dry set of lessons.

Most schools and teachers implicitly understand children's deep need for story and adventure. They are constantly on the move to devise exciting games, competitions, mascots, and other scenarios to promote reading, math skills, test taking, and other things the school seeks to impart. The problem is that these devices are often not believable for children, are not dire or romantic enough, or are presented in a piecemeal fashion that just looks "corny" to them. For example, I recall being ushered from the third-grade class I was teaching into a large auditorium for an assembly on the upcoming state tests. On the stage was a giant Hawk who ran up and down the aisles squawking about how we would "Screech into Success" on the tests! While some children were engaged and mildly entertained, this character had no real meaning for them and was not part of an overall narrative of which they were a part. Also, for story and adventure to be effective, we need to do it for longer than 15 minutes at an assembly.

One can find several exciting examples of an integrated approach to romantic drama and adventure in the elementary schools. Consider Peter Lourie. He travels the world and offers adventure-writing workshops to elementary and middle schools. He shows up to the school, in costume (like Indiana Jones) and discusses his excursions on the Mississippi River, the Rio Grande, the Amazon jungle, and the trail of Lewis and Clark. Lourie has written over 16 children's books on these different places. When he comes to a school, Lourie focuses on one part of the world he has visited. He shows them slides, videos, audio tapes, notebooks, pictures, and other artifacts. After this, he shares how he moves from an initial idea all the way to a finished book.

With Lourie's approach, students use the concept of an adventure on the Lewis and Clark trail or the Amazon jungle to learn about history, math, geography, science, social studies, English/Language Arts, and writing in a way that is relevant and exciting to them. The romantic adventure to this exotic place will frame all the subject areas to be taught. Before Lourie arrives, teachers prepare the students by reading his books; they draft papers on the geography of the journey, make photo essays, conduct science experiments, write newspaper articles, and formulate research questions. They cover months of standard academic lessons using the adventure frame.

When Lourie arrives for his visit, he shares his own process of writing and learning during his adventures. The students share their work in a workshop format, read each other's work, and give each other feedback. Lourie and the teachers then work with the students to improve each other's writing and thinking (Livingston, 2009). There are more examples of an integrated approach to romance and adventure, but it requires some real planning and forethought. The teachers who have tried it report the effort is difficult, but far better than the dry educational format we use now.

Making schools more adventurous places would also partly be addressed by the establishment of a gender staffing balance. This is not a guarantee of adventure, of course, but a more equal balance of male and female teachers would make it more likely that schools would be sufficiently focused on both adventure and learning. To this day, my own son's favorite year in elementary school was the only year in his school career when he had a male teacher. They studied Native Americans, built tepees outside in an authentic village, made dioramas, tools, and weapons, wrote and acted out historical scripts, wore costumes, and told stories.

Whether they are achieved through a gender staffing balance or not, schools-of-adventure have many of the following features: (1) story themes which organize as much of the material to be learned as possible, (2) fixed and engaging rituals to mark the beginning and end of the day, as well as the transitions in between lessons, (3) plenty of time for free and active play between lessons, (4) at least one recess period where physical contact and vigorous activity are permitted (perhaps in a special area), (5) desk work which allows for play with things like blocks, cars, and Silly Putty, and (6) lessons which incorporate movement, active discovery, and outdoor activities like stargazing, canoeing, cycling, disc golf, fishing, parkour, and ultimate Frisbee. Schools-of-adventure also have alternative discipline policies which do not penalize students who simply have a hard time sitting still.

Ideally, schools-of-adventure are places where different styles of learning are represented within a given lesson or at different points throughout the day. In this sense, there would be room for quiet, pensive learning as well as more active and physical learning. This differentiation would be present in each lesson and throughout each grade of the elementary years. To the extent that the need for adventure correlates with student gender, schools-of-adventure could encourage experimentation with different gender arrangements in the form of single-sex schools, single-sex classrooms, or single-sex lesson periods (Sax, 2005). The past 10–15 years have seen the growth of the single-sex public school academy. Over 200 public schools to date are also reorganizing their schedules so that kids are taught core subjects in either all-boys or all-girls classrooms for part of the day (Tyre, 2009, p. 214). These initiatives make the most educational impact in at-risk African American and Hispanic students of both sexes (Tyre, 2009, p. 217).

An all-boys school, an all-boys classroom, or an all-boys class period has other benefits as well. The major benefit is that many students who typically disengage from school because it is not friendly to their more active way of being will find the format more inviting. Such arrangements also tend to attract teachers to the school who either are males themselves or at least have a desire to shape their teaching in a way that engages boys.

Such an environment helps allow a place for boys to try academic things in an environment where they are less prone to be judged or to feel inferior to girls who frequently outperform them. Girls receive similar benefits from being around their own gender counterparts. These gender initiatives are all to be encouraged, but it is also important to keep in mind that a single-sex school or classroom is not itself a pedagogy or a magic bullet. A boring class without adventure taught by a man is no better than a similar class taught by a woman. While it does not necessarily lead to higher test scores or college graduation rates, it does lead students to pursue subjects not traditionally associated with their gender, to follow their own talents rather than their gender.

Schools lift to high purpose. Children do not just want adventure for adventure's sake but want their lives to serve a higher purpose. As with the heroic Jackie, Matt, and Inez from *Cyberchase*, children want to learn skills to save the world from what ails it, to make it a better place. Many schools use the concept of a "theme" to organize their school year. They are often called "Theme Schools" (Meier, Knoester, & D'Andrea, 2015). Some of these schools are good examples of what I mean by schools-of-purpose. Not all chosen themes lift to high purpose, but many do. For example, some schools focus on climate change, pollution, scientific discovery, animal health, political power, social action, the ties that bind (community health), or solving community problems through invention.

There are many worthy and pedagogically effective high purposes to choose from. But we should choose one for each school rather than have nothing at all, as most do now. As with the story form I discussed earlier, the school theme should not just be an afterthought, but be used to integrate and provide coherence to the entire curriculum and the different academic subjects in it. High purpose gives children a clear and inspiring vision of where all their learning is leading. They can see what the skills taught in school can be used for. It gives them a firmer sense of what they are doing in school in the first place.

What is the high purpose to which we can agree to have our schools aspire? What ails the world right now? Could we not together specify and agree upon some things? Disease? Climate change? Ignorance? Oppression? Greed? Nihilism? Consumerism? Any one of these would suffice as a high purpose and would seriously engage most children's minds. High purpose can be a touchy topic for adults to discuss, of course, but it is far too important to children for us to ignore. An engaged, democratic community can make it happen if the process of deliberation is structured properly.

Schools promote exciting and meaningful work. Children want to see how they can contribute to adult society. They may act like they do not care sometimes, but they do. Learning skills valuable to adults is one of their central developmental preoccupations during the elementary school years. They are willing to do almost anything in school if it is connected to what they see as an exciting role in the grown-up world. In the main, children are not lazy or apathetic when it comes to schoolwork, so long as they can see a connection between what they are doing and an exciting view of the future. The characters in the stories children love like *Cyberchase*, *Harry Potter*, and *Percy Jackson* work tirelessly at their crafts. Young students will do the same. They desperately want to develop what Erikson (1964) calls *industry* by the end of elementary school rather than a sense of *inferiority*. Children will tune out from school, become disengaged, or even antisocial when they have concluded they have no useful role to play in the society of the future. There are a variety of reasons why children come to feel this way. Most have to do with home life and social messages, but school can contribute to cultivating inferiority as well. Children with a sense of inferiority do not believe that their tomorrow will be better than today, that they can succeed if they work hard, and that the give-and-take of school is worth it. And so, they slouch in their seats, check out, or worse, get themselves into a whole lot of trouble at school and the neighborhood.

Many schools recognize the lack of a real connection to the world of work is a major problem and are trying to do something about it. In response to a report released by the Council of Chief State School Officers Task Force on Career-Readiness, my own state of Georgia, along with many other states, developed learning outcomes and teaching materials to begin the process of "career-readiness" in elementary school. This program explores 17 different career clusters, such as Information Technology; Architecture and Construction; Finance; and Law, Public Safety, Corrections, and Security, to help children learn about the different jobs in the adult world, develop a positive attitude about their future, and appreciate the connection between academic success and career-readiness. I have seen and put together my own lessons for this program. My children went through this program as well. This is surely a good start, but I am struck with the sense that this program is largely an instance of "educational capitalism." The school's role is to simply present to children the jobs that exist in the world and then try to figure out where the child "fits." What is often left out is what I refer to as the "career vision" component of the career counseling process in which the child forms his or her own exciting vision of the future and then uses that to search for existing jobs in the world which match it. Surely, as the child matures, this vision will need to be tempered by "reality," but when we simply present adult "jobs" to young children, it often leaves them uninspired. These lessons on career-readiness have been among the most boring and uninspiring teaching I have seen in my teaching career. I would suggest we wait for this all-too-realistic presentation until at least middle school.

Further, many of the careers we present to children when we do these career modules in class are disconnected from the notion of high purpose. We simply talk about careers in Agriculture or Information Technology, what kind of training is involved, what the person does all day, and how much money he or she makes. As with Harry Potter and the Cybersquad, meaningful and exciting work is connected to both high purpose and a vital part of our being that is deeper than money and job tasks. Work, especially for a child, is not simply about "making a living" or earning a good salary. On a very important level, the children have an admirably heroic approach to work that many of us adults do not. "Career clusters" proffered to children in the absence of vision and high purpose will always fall flat.

Schools have inspiring teachers. I have argued in this chapter for an elementary education system that fosters schools-of-vision, schools-of-adventure-and-high-purpose, and schools that promote exciting and meaningful work. In this section, I examine the kinds of people we want to teach in these schools. What are our visions of a "good teacher?" Who are the kinds of people best able to prepare children for a life of adventure, high purpose, and meaningful work? The short answer is that inspiring teachers are those who have embarked upon the adventurous course of learning and discovery in their own lives. They enjoy reading, investigation, discussion, and research. They have also embraced some form of high purpose in their own life and career. They are dedicated to larger values besides just the technical mastery of teaching and classroom management. They view education as the moral enterprise it is.

The reasons to teach are varied and complex, but the principal motivation of an inspiring teacher is the desire to work in collaborative teams with other teachers to facilitate the learning and personal development of children. One may wish to love them, care for them, have them listen to us, or do well on state-mandated tests. One may even love to follow the rules and traditions of the school. But the principal motivation to teach should be to creatively exercise one's talent and professional autonomy to teach children the skills and knowledge they need to live meaningful and exciting lives of high purpose.

Of course, teaching is not only about vision, but concerns skill and proficiency as well. Inspiring elementary teachers must also know specific things and have quite specialized technical training. They know how to work collaboratively in teaching teams. They know how to work with children and families from the diversity of backgrounds represented in this country. They know a variety of effective ways to teach different learners to read, write, to do different levels of mathematics, to do experiments, and problem-solve. They know a variety of successful classroom management strategies based on different learners. And they know how to gather information about how well students are learning what they teach and to make appropriate adjustments based on this feedback.

Muggle schools and zombie teachers. Why are so many of today's public schools *not* about adventure, high purpose, exciting and meaningful work? Partly it is because we have designed schools to meet *adult* needs, fears, and visions, not children's. Schools are not necessarily built for children, nor have we involved children much in their formation. Partly this is because the envisioning process has been co-opted by a fierce educational capitalism which sees schools as job training grounds and teachers as the trainers. Another major reason is that the envisioning process I have been outlining is extremely thorny and controversial. Try to imagine gathering with your neighborhood or community to discuss a central narrative or a guiding theme for your school. Try to imagine a discussion about the high purpose which your schools will serve. Depending on the community, there may be a great diversity of opinion. There will probably be conflicting views. Many may wish that schools not get into this territory at all and decide instead stay on the safer ground of learning and standards disconnected from story, adventure, high purpose, and meaningful work. To some, this terrain feels very close to religion and philosophy, which they prefer to avoid in polite conversation out of fear of endless debate and intractable squabbles. Despite these fears and hesitations, I believe it is possible for public discussion of these matters to be productive and democratic. But it will surely take some work and courage on all our parts.

The alternative to the public envisioning process I propose is to settle for the narrow and often uninspiring vision of the schools we have now. This is unacceptable. From everything I have seen listening to children, their stories, movies, and literature, our schools look like "Muggle schools" to them. Muggle schools are blind to invisible spiritual reality and higher purposes. They are often soul-numbingly dull, based on isolated facts disconnected from an exciting view of the future which are repetitively presented by rote and then obsessively tested. And they are staffed by zombies, adults who are walking around as if they were alive but are really dead (and survive on "eating the brains" of real, living people). We can do better.

Personnel Reform

I begin this section with some basic questions about school personnel. What are the qualities of a good principal? Who should be hired to be an administrator and why? What administrative positions are necessary in today's school system and which could be eliminated? How can we attract the highest caliber, most qualified applicants to teach our children? How do we train teaching candidates to be able to do this work well? And why are so many men not going into elementary teaching?

Toward a gender staffing balance. We have broken down many barriers to racial and gender equality, not just by changing laws, but by taking affirmative action to undo past discrimination or structural barriers. In education, we currently have thousands of scholarships to support women going into the so-called Science, Technology, Engineering and Mathematics (STEM) disciplines. In addition, there are millions of public and private dollars supporting internships, research, and outreach to attract females to consider a major or career in a STEM field. The lack of women in the STEM disciplines is seen as a "crisis." In many ways it is, but the worst figure I have seen is about a 75% to 25% mismatch between males and females in the Computer and Mathematics fields. Recall, the imbalance at the elementary school level is **90%** female to **10%** male, a much sharper one than that in STEM. Males have not suffered the same amount of past discrimination in education, but the fact that the imbalance is so high should at least raise a similar level of public alarm.

What I propose is a national program like those designed to attract females to STEM disciplines. Public and private dollars would be spent on public outreach programs to young boys designed to attract them to a career in education. These would include TV commercials, posters for schools, and speakers to visit primary and secondary schools to talk about what an exciting career the teaching field can be. In addition, there should be public and private funds to support scholarships for young men who declare education as their college major. There are several initiatives already underway such as "Call Me Mister," "NYC Men Teach," "The Academy of Men in Education," and "Real Men are Teachers" which provide tuition assistance for male students pursuing teacher education in college. These programs also provide these men with academic support, a cohort system, and/or assistance with job placement. There are also a few scholarships targeted to supporting men who go into teaching, like the Charles Richard Drew Memorial Scholarship or the Hubertus W.V. Willems Scholarship. The problem is that these programs are piecemeal, inadequately funded, and not integrated into a national strategy that has enough sense of urgency. In addition to a national funding program to recruit and support males to teach, I suggest a national high school service program where boys are encouraged and supported to intern as part of a service-learning class at a local elementary classroom for a semester (see Tyre, 2009, p. 29).

The gender imbalance in elementary schools is yet another politically sensitive issue. I understand why talking about this as a problem has been avoided for so long. When I have tried, my interlocutors often interpret initiatives to recruit males as somehow undoing the progress of females. It is therefore vital that efforts to recruit more males into the profession are not mistakenly seen as a zero-sum game, that is, promoting male access to education means somehow erasing the impressive and long overdue gains women have made and still need to make in many career areas.

It is important to realize that affirmative action for males in education is already going on. As I was training to teach elementary school, everyone told me I would have no trouble getting a job when I graduated. They said this not because I was so smart or talented, but because I was a man. Principals are simply desperate to hire male teachers. The affirmative action model we have now is very blunt: to take any reasonably qualified male with a teaching certificate. The problem with this model is that we want to attract the right kind of male to the teaching field, not just any male. We therefore need to be much more organized and proactive about our male recruitment efforts.

A teaching-centered administration. It will not suffice to simply rail against the Administration as I have so far. Some Administration is surely needed, and schools would be lost without them. The question is, what are the necessary levels of Administration to have? In providing an answer, I make a distinction between what I call an *academic administrator* and a *true administrator*. A true administrator manages the necessary non-academic functions the school performs such as maintaining the physical plant, organizing and disbursing employee benefits, arranging student transportation, dealing with grievances, labor disputes, legal issues, as well as complying with civil rights, and other relevant federal and state laws pertaining to the schools. An academic administrator, on the other hand, deals with the development, implementation, and assessment of the curriculum, best pedagogical practices, teaching workload, length of class periods, providing learning support, "coaching" other teachers, special education, and testing. In today's administrative climate, these two types of administrator blend into each other and are often performed by the same people. Administrators who plan the budget and manage retirement accounts somehow get themselves involved with the curriculum. True administration and academics should remain separate. Simply put, the true administrator should have no power over the academic aspect of the school. Academics is the provenance of teachers.

The only necessary academic administrators are the academic officers in the state board of education, the local school board, the school principal, and possibly an academic dean. These positions should be chosen and staffed by certified teachers, not by elections or appointments by politicians or true administrators. Unless explicitly reserved to the state by its constitution, I do not see any basis why teachers should not be involved with the hiring of academic administrators. If there are provisions in a state preventing this, they should be changed. My vision will avoid and ultimately eliminate the adversarial climate in schools where we see teachers as "resources" that need to be employed and told what to do by managers. In my approach, the academic administrator is a teacher's teacher with a track record of teaching excellence, vision, organizational, and people skills.

The academic administrator who should be given the greatest amount of power and latitude over curriculum, instruction, and school discipline is the school principal, along with the teaching team of the individual school. Within broad state goals and curriculum maps, these individuals should be given nearly complete control over the curriculum, the hiring and firing of teachers, assessment, testing, workload, length of class periods, and the school discipline policy. In addition, any academic administrators like principals, assistant principals, counselors, and team leaders must not only be trained teachers themselves, they must teach during a good part of each school day as part of their job. In my vision, there would no longer be any full-time academic administrators. Further, academic administrators would hold their positions for a period of no longer than five years. The notion of a "permanent" academic administrator or a career in Administration should be forever abolished. One should enter the academic administration with the full expectation of eventually returning to teaching. Some may argue that administrators develop keen skill sets over time and that rotating them back into the classroom would cause a "brain drain." This is surely a risk, but it is also true that administrators do not necessarily continue to learn and grow the more time they remain in their jobs. I suggest that incoming academic administrators would shadow current academic administrators for a period of their school day a year before their new job begins in earnest. It is far better to have reluctant administrators than administrators who scratch and claw their way out of the classroom to get their higher-paying job which requires no teaching.

This new arrangement will have multiple benefits. The first is the reduction or perhaps the elimination of the total management mentality in the schools. Recall, with this mentality, we see all school problems as problems of management, requiring a management solution. Most academic problems are not management problems at all and find their best solutions when teachers and principals put their heads together to solve them. With more power and professional control, more highly qualified teachers will enter the field. With the dignity to shape one's one academic destiny, teachers would have a high degree of "buy in" to their job and would be much more likely to stick with it over time. Further, their days will no longer be spent implementing and assessing a curriculum that is not their own. This management arrangement would also enable teachers and teaching teams to implement their own behavioral discipline policies to create the kind of communities that will support learning. They would also likely structure the day with more planning time and time for collaboration.

The Tenth Amendment declares all powers not specifically enumerated by the Constitution to the Federal government are reserved to the *states*. The U.S. Constitution does not mention *any* powers to provide education to the Federal government. Therefore, public education is primarily a state responsibility. The current Federal involvement in education does not appear to be productive and is likely disempowering to states, districts, and individual teachers. I suggest we take a large chunk of their 4300 employees and $60 billion budget and use it for instruction to cut class sizes and hire more teachers. The remainder of their budget would be left to perform the true administrative functions I enumerated above, particularly to provide funding to support equal educational access which may be limited by students living in impoverished conditions or with various disabilities. It should also support educational research and development about the quality of the educational system, as well as to encourage states and localities to continually improve themselves (Harris, Ladd, Smith, & West, 2016). If we move in the direction I propose, the Federal government would be much less involved with curriculum and instruction and more involved with the establishment of educational standards and assessment for the training and recruitment of teachers across the nation.

States should therefore be directly involved in the development and supervision of the curriculum, teaching methods, and textbooks in their schools. Several state constitutions explicitly give the states the power to form the curriculum. Some state constitutions even endow the state with the power to select textbooks and other educational materials. States can also authorize other educational officials or bodies to establish, select, and regulate the curriculum. Many states delegate a great deal of their autonomy to localities, allowing them to develop their own curricula based on broad state goals and model curriculum frameworks. Local school districts are also free to develop the curriculum standards beyond what is explicitly required by the state. They often do not do this. I advocate a movement toward the maximization of local control in the area of curriculum and instruction. As states delegate more and more academic power to the localities, the state role in education would largely recede to focus on true administrative tasks such as school funding, construction, transportation, managing employee benefits, and so on.

Teacher recruitment. How we recruit, train, and select good candidates to teach in our schools is tied to the previous discussion of the overall vision we have of the schools and teachers. The vision of the ideal school attracts the teacher; the vision of the ideal teacher is used to train him or her to do the work. In this section, I discuss some concrete ways to transform our schools and teacher training programs to ensure we have a vast pool of teachers-of-vision from which to hire.

Building upon points I made in previous sections, schools will gradually become places of vision, adventure, and high purpose. As schools allow teachers to fulfill inspiring visions, new teachers will be drawn to, and stay in our schools. In addition, as the Federal and state roles in the academic component of schools are curtailed and the teaching team's role is enhanced, teaching will have more of the dignity and autonomy that exist in other professions. This will attract more talented professionals to a career in teaching. Sahlberg (2015) notes when teachers in Finland, who have among the highest job satisfaction (and standardized test scores) in the world, consider losing their professional autonomy in schools, having an outside inspector judge the quality of their work, having a merit-based compensation policy, or a high-stakes accountability system, their entire career choice would be called into question.

What I am talking about here is moving toward a permanent end to the adversarial management-labor culture of mistrust and the creation of a collaborative culture of cooperation between teachers and administration. Teachers must be involved with policymakers and principals in all aspects of planning, implementing, and assessing the curriculum. When teachers have professional autonomy like this, they are more inspired to teach than when they are forced to deliver preset programs and then submit to external assessments to judge how well they have performed.

As the emphasis shifts from a management focus on getting as much "labor output" from the teacher as possible, the working conditions of teachers will change to become much more hospitable and sustainable than they are now. The total learning mentality will replace the total management mentality. Teachers will not spend all their time teaching and assessing a curriculum that is not theirs. They will have more time for research into best practices, collaboration with colleagues, and opportunities for planning, grading, and professional development. The amount of time spent teaching in U.S. elementary schools is nearly two times as many hours per week as in Finnish schools, and yet Finnish students seem to learn more, and teacher job satisfaction is higher (Sahlberg, 2015, p. 124).

As we change the vision of the principal and other academic administrators from "boss" or "supervisor" to a part of the educational team, teachers will rely more on their principals' guidance and leadership. Teachers will benefit from principals who work at the same task alongside them. They would all be part of the same union and bargain with state officials together on contracts and working conditions. As the "merit-based" competitive environment changes, teacher will begin to trust and rely on each other more than they currently do.

Teacher training reform. I mentioned in the previous chapter how more national control over academic standards and curriculum is needed for teacher training programs, while *less* national control is needed over academic standards and curriculum in the elementary schools. I call for a national teaching preparation curriculum which equips all elementary teachers to perform in today's schools and prepares them to exercise their professional judgment as autonomous agents once they enter the workplace. Modeled upon the *Common Core* curriculum, I suggest the Department of Education, in cooperation with the states, should outline a set of learning outcomes that will be used to assess the quality of teacher preparation across the country.

Broadly speaking, these standards would involve training teacher candidates how to work effectively in teaching teams, how to work with children and families from diverse backgrounds, how to teach students with both active and more traditional classroom learning styles, learning best practices in reading and math instruction, along with other major content areas of the elementary curriculum. There should also be clear standards that outline what quality teacher mentors and internship placements should involve. Teacher candidates should learn best practices in classroom management, differentiated instruction, and be trained to read educational research, to gather and share data on how well their own students are learning. Teaching candidates should learn not only to teach but to conduct their own scholarship and research (Sahlberg, 2015, pp. 126–127). Eventually, standards to teach in U.S. elementary schools should be increased to require a master's degree in education.

Teacher preparation programs should also be mandated to share with national authorities what they are teaching in their classes and to assess these national learning outcomes at the end of teacher training each academic year. Programs should then be given a grade on a national report card. States should no longer be responsible for assessing the quality of their own schools. An independent national entity should be responsible for this. In addition, states should eliminate the increasingly popular use of "alternative" pathways to certification such as Teach for America and other waivers for teacher training that often water down the teacher preparation process even more than it is now.

Classes in teacher preparation programs should become much more academically rigorous and intellectually challenging. This could be achieved if teacher preparation programs were required to draw teaching candidates from the top half of the college student class rather than the bottom. And if more candidates could be recruited in middle and high school to enter a career in education, teacher training programs could become much more selective and academically rigorous.

We can continue what we are doing now and get poor results: low-quality teacher training, academically underachieving teaching candidates, and large numbers of new teachers who leave the field in their first years of teaching. Or we can try something new: attract high caliber teachers by improving teacher training, keeping administrative oversight of teachers and student testing to a minimum, increasing the professional autonomy of teachers, and handing over school and district level leadership to experienced educational professionals and teaching teams. This might go a long way toward developing a world-class elementary teaching corps who are equipped to present our current, academically challenging curriculum to all elementary students. I turn to that curriculum now.

References

CBS News. (2015, March 13). Hogwarts-inspired middle school in the heart of Atlanta. Retrieved from https://www.cbsnews.com/news/ron-clark-academy-atlanta-sets-success-confidence-future/

Edgeworth, C. (2018, August 3). Hogwarts themes classrooms and hallways inspiring students at Cullman County school. Retrieved from https://www.cbs42.com/news/local/hogwarts-themed-classrooms-and-hallway-inspiring-students-at-cullman-county-school/1345761220

Erikson, E. (1964). *Childhood and society* (2nd ed.). Oxford, UK: W. W. Norton.

Frisbie, C. (2018, August 9). Magical teachers transformed their school into a real-life Hogwarts for their students. *WGAL*. Retrieved from https://www.wgal.com/article/harry-potter-school-hogwarts-makeover/22654468

Harris, D. N., Ladd, H. F., Smith, M. S., & West, M. R. (2016). *A principled federal role in PreK-12 education* [PDF File]. Retrieved from Brown Center for Education Policy at Brookings Website: https://www.brookings.edu/wpcontent/uploads/2016/12/gs_20161206_principled_federal_role_browncenter1.pdf

Hill-Jackson, V., & Lewis, C. W. (2010). *Transforming teacher education: What went wrong with teacher training, and how we can fix it.* Sterling, VA: Stylus.

Livingston, K. E. (2009, December 23). Students explore storytelling with a real-life adventurer. Retrieved from Edutopia Website: https://www.edutopia.org/storytelling-adventure-peter-lourie

Meier, D., Knoester, M., & D'Andrea, K. C. (Eds.). (2015). *Teaching in themes: An approach to schoolwide learning, creating community, and differentiating instruction.* New York, NY: Teachers College Press.

Sahlberg, P. (2015). *Finnish lessons, 2.0.* New York, NY: Teachers College Press.

Sax, L. (2005). *Why gender matters: What parents and teachers need to know about the emerging science of sex differences.* New York, NY: Doubleday.

Tyre, P. (2009). *The trouble with boys: A surprising report card on our sons, their problems at school, and what parents and educators must do.* New York, NY: Harmony.

PART II

The Wall of Separation, Administrative Bloat, and Boundless Accommodation

CHAPTER 7

Platonic Curriculum; Epicurean Society

Back to the tour. You have finished your lunch in the teachers' lounge, fetched the children from the cafeteria, and walked with Miss Thomas back to your classroom. You are a little tired now. At this point, you have seen an English/Language Arts (ELA) lesson, a Social Studies lesson, and a Math lesson. You think about the "standards" listed on the board which comprised the meat of those lessons. For Social Studies it was, "Define the concept of government and the need for rules and laws." For ELA it was, "Identify the main topic of a multi-paragraph text as well as the focus of specific paragraphs within the text." For Math it was, "Draw a picture graph and a bar graph (with single-unit scale) to represent a data set with up to four categories. Solve simple put-together, take-apart, and compare problems using information presented in a bar graph." You think to yourself, "Wow! This is challenging stuff for second graders." Several of the students asked you for help at various points and you struggled with some of the answers.

My own children's school has a yearly event called "Curriculum Night." It is at the very beginning of the academic year. Most parents who attend Curriculum Night view it as an opportunity to meet their child's teacher and learn a little about what they will do all year. When you get there, books and materials are laid out on the desk, and the teacher gives a brief presentation about her policies, procedures, and what will be covered in "the curriculum." The *curriculum* is a broad term for the subjects that comprise a course of study in school, for example, English/Language

Arts, Math, and Science. The curriculum also consists of the goals and learning outcomes that teachers expect children to achieve over the school year. These goals and outcomes are commonly called *standards*. There are different kinds of standards. Some are about what a child is expected to know, for example, "Describe the life and contribution of James Oglethorpe to Georgia history." Others are about what a child should be able to do, for example, "Students will be able to count without using fingers to 10." Still others refer to how the child should be disposed to act in the future, for example, "Students will demonstrate persistence in the face of difficult reading passages," or "Students will resolve conflicts cooperatively." The curriculum also includes the various instructional methods and materials the teacher uses to achieve these standards and the batteries which will be used to assess whether students have learned the standards they were supposed to.

The most important part of the curriculum is the standards. The standards determine what teachers will do each day in class and what students will learn, as well as what will be assessed at the end of the unit or academic year. When teachers are trained, they are given a lesson plan template they must use to prepare all the lessons they will use throughout the day. A lesson plan is basically a chart that organizes a 30–115-minute period of teaching time. At the top of each lesson plan, the teacher is expected to insert the standard or standards which will be taught in that lesson. Teachers are also expected to make clear to the students what the standard of each lesson is before they teach it. I have seen many teachers have their students copy the text of the standard verbatim in their notebooks before beginning a lesson. I have also seen principals visit to evaluate teachers who ask the students in the middle of a lesson if they know what standard they are focusing on. Teachers may get a negative evaluation if the students do not know this vital information.

If you survey the elementary curriculum for each state, you will find over 100 standards for each grade. The number of standards increases as the child gets older, with the number growing to nearly 400 by the last year of high school. There are standards for Math, English/Language Arts, Social Studies, and Science. Even the "specials" like Music, Art, and Physical Education (PE) have their own standards. Given their central importance to education, I take closer look at these standards and focus on several questions: Just who formulates the elementary standards? What are these standards designed to do? And what is their general nature?

Who Formulates the Standards?

The "standards movement," as it is often called, began in earnest in the United States in the early 1990s, though it had been underway for 75 years before that (see Miyamoto, 2008). As mentioned in the previous chapter, the power to write academic standards belongs to state boards of education, with a handful of states, like Minnesota and New Hampshire, that require the state legislature to formally approve all academic standards. In formulating its standards, a state board typically delegates the task to "educational committees" and "workgroups" which consist of researchers, educational professionals, principals, and members of state and national teaching organizations. These committees also solicit input from selected teachers and parents during the development and comment periods of the process.

Individual school districts have some small input in the formulation of standards, though their power resides mostly in being able to devise the benchmark assessments used to test whether students have learned the standards for a grade rather than to write the standards themselves. Schools and teachers within a district have some limited flexibility with instruction, that is, how subjects are taught and learned, but not with the curriculum itself, that is, *what* is taught and learned. Teachers, schools, and districts are "given" the curriculum they are to teach by the state.

By the late 1990s, the standards movement had so taken hold that each state had its own formal set of curriculum standards specifying what all its K-12 children needed to learn in school by the end of each grade level. Each state also had its own definition of "proficiency," that is, the knowledge and achievement students needed to demonstrate in order to advance to the next grade. While this was surely an advance over no state standards at all, there was now a patchwork quilt of 50 different state curricula of widely differing quality. Further, research showed that the academic performance of students generally reflected the socioeconomic status of the districts and schools in which they were located. Specifically, wealthier communities tended to expect and achieve more from their students than their more economically disadvantaged counterparts (see Caldas & Bankston, 1999; Kozol, 1991; Roscigno, 2000). Poor standardized test scores and negative feedback from colleges and employers also indicated that students graduating from U.S. public high schools often did not have the basic knowledge to perform their jobs adequately or the higher-level skills to enter and succeed in college (see U.S. Department of Labor,

1999). This lack of standardization, inequality, and poor learning outcomes were the major reasons why states decided to formulate and adopt a set of national academic standards that would apply to all students and all schools across the nation. This, they hoped, would finally close performance gaps, help states all sing from the same song sheet, and raise the standards for everyone, regardless of their circumstances.

Beginning in 1989, the governors of all 50 states, their chief state education officers, the U.S. Department of Education, and the President of the United States formulated six educational goals for the entire United States to achieve by the year 2000. This came to be known as *Goals 2000*. These goals included having children leave the 4th, 8th, and 12th grades with demonstrated proficiency in English, mathematics, foreign languages, civics, geography, economics, the arts, and history. These national goals were codified by Congress in the year 2000 and the federal government began to provide funding for states who agreed to implement these higher academic standards and assessments. This was followed by the *No Child Left Behind Act* of 2002, which built on *Goals 2000* and incentivized the national effort at standardization, equality, and higher academic standards even more. While power to write academic standards belongs to the states, the federal level of the Administration has effectively inserted itself into the formulation of academic standards over the past 30 years by using funding to incentivize states to "voluntarily" adopt various national curriculum standards. Cash-strapped schools are hard-pressed to forgo this funding and so often comply with national directives they might otherwise resist or ignore.

The national push for standardization of the curriculum culminated with the states developing the *Common Core State Standards Initiative* in 2009. The *Common Core*, as I will refer to it for short, sought to build upon the best existing state standards and coordinate them into a single national set. However, it did not limit itself to six general aspirations as in *Goals 2000*, but now got into the nitty-gritty details of the entire English and Math curriculum. Plans are currently in the works for a similar national *Common Core* curriculum for Science and Social Studies. This *Common Core* effort was coordinated by the U.S. Department of Education together with the National Governors Association and the Council of Chief State School Officers. Workgroups and feedback groups consisted of researchers, educational professionals, teachers, academic administrators, and members of national organizations such as the National Education Association, the National Council of Teachers of Mathematics, the

National Council of Teachers of English, the American Federation of Teachers, and other national bodies. At this point, 42 states along with the District of Columbia have adopted the *Common Core* curriculum for Math and ELA, which now exists alongside state elementary standards in subjects not covered by the *Common Core*. In states without the *Common Core*, educational standards are completely state-based, though they often borrow liberally from *Common Core* standards.

What Are Standards Designed to Do?

In formulating the standards of the current *Common Core*, or any current set of state curriculum standards, the educational committees and workgroups established by state boards of education gather at conferences to discuss what all children at each grade level need to know, know how to do, or be disposed to act. In addition to relying on best practices, research, and practical wisdom, any gathering to formulate or reformulate educational standards is undertaken to correct or improve upon some perceived area of concern. The formulation of educational standards always has an aspirational and future-oriented aspect. Recall in the context of the national standards movement described above, recent gatherings were initiated by the shared sense that the existence of different educational standards across districts and states was leading to unacceptable achievement gaps between students of different races and socioeconomic backgrounds. But there was also concern that employers and colleges were complaining of an increasing lack of preparedness of students graduating from America's public schools. In addition, there was a common understanding that the lagging performance of American students on standardized tests when compared to international competitors was leading to an erosion of the United States' position as the world's leading creative and economic superpower. All of this contributed to a push not only to standardize the curriculum between states, *but also to raise overall academic standards,* to make the curriculum more challenging and intellectually demanding. And this is exactly what they did.

During the development process of *Goals 2000* and *Common Core*, workgroups articulated clear "college and career-readiness" goals which all students were expected to reach by the time they graduated high school. They wanted all future students to be educated so that they could graduate high school ready to succeed in entry-level college courses or in training for high-skilled careers. For example, the planning document that guided workgroups in setting the *Common Core* curriculum standards states that "the standards created will not lower the bar but raise it for all students" (Common Core State Standards Initiative, 2019). The *Common Core* standards "seek to ensure *all students* are prepared for all entry-level, credit-bearing, academic college courses in English, mathematics, the sciences, the social sciences, and the humanities" (Common Core State Standards Initiative, 2019). While planners were well aware that not all students would attend college, the career-readiness goals of workgroups operated on the assumption that the American economy of the future would be based on knowledge and information more than manufacturing and unskilled manual labor. They assumed that success in the "growing and sustainable" industries of the twenty-first-century economy would require *the same set of high-level cognitive skills needed for success in entry-level college courses,* that is, "reasoning, justification, synthesis, analysis, and problem-solving" (Common Core State Standards Initiative, 2019). This is the reason why I call the *Common Core* curriculum (and most state curricula, for that matter) a *college prep curriculum.*

In the case of *Common Core,* for example, the broad college and career-readiness goals articulated by workgroups defined what students should know by the end of the K-12 educational journey. What the workgroups did then was "backward plan" by formulating the specific steps at each grade level which would guide students toward the eventual goal of college admission and career-readiness. These specific steps came to comprise the standards we have now for each grade level from Kindergarten to 12th grade. In the current educational climate, the elementary standards form the beginning of a process of college and career-readiness which are then built upon by middle and high school.

This is a huge change from any other curriculum of the past, the implications of which we have unfortunately not fully appreciated. No more would Kindergarten, for example, be the place where children would "play in the garden" to build skills and confidence for school. Rather, Kindergarten begins a process of college preparation with rigorous goals for Math and English. Many students are overwhelmed right off the bat and quickly fall behind. Tyre (2009) has pointed to the proliferation of preschool "academies" which sprang up around the same time which helped to begin this furious college prep process with Math and Phonics worksheets given to students as young as two or three.

Furthermore, the focus on college preparation also came to almost completely eclipse other educational goals. No more would school focus on citizenship, character, virtues, or preparation for a trade. No more would elementary school be a fun and inviting place to explore the world and learn about yourself, what you like, what you are good at. Schools quickly became all about college and high-skilled labor, and the pressure is often intense. Questions revolved not around whether this was a sound idea for all students, but who would and would not be "left behind" in the march toward college and career-readiness. Rather than multiple avenues of success, schools became dominated by just one road.

What Is the Nature of the Standards?

Today's college prep elementary standards are highly literate, numerate, and abstract. At times they do reference mere information or meaningless facts, but overall, they stress higher-order process over information and content. Note the keywords used in formulating the standards: *reasoning, justification, synthesis, analysis,* and *problem-solving*. These cognitive processes are among the highest levels of Bloom's famous taxonomy of educational objectives (Bloom, Krathwohl, & Masia, 1956) and are a central part of each *Common Core* standard. Every one of the *Common Core* standards was designed to "include high-level cognitive demands by asking students to demonstrate deep conceptual understanding through the application of content knowledge and skills to new situations" (Common Core State Standards Initiative, 2019).

Consider this example from the current *Common Core* standards for English/Language Arts for Kindergarten: "With prompting and support, students will identify the main topic and retell key details of a text." Five-year-olds are here encouraged not only to listen to and recount the details of a text, which is hard enough, but then to abstract the main topic from the content, something many college students struggle to do. Consider another ELA *Common Core* standard from Kindergarten: "With prompting and support, students will describe the connection between two individuals, events, ideas, or pieces of information in a text." Again, students are prompted here to go beyond the data and make an abstract, intellectual connection between concrete elements. They need to be able to say, for example, that the event at point A in a text is like, or shares a common structure with, a separate event at point B.

These abstract, higher-order standards do not just pertain to reading and literature, but to all academic subjects. Here is a Kindergarten standard from Mathematics, "Students will classify objects into given categories; count the numbers of objects in each category and sort the categories by count." Take a close look at this standard. Students are prompted not simply to name or count objects, which alone may be a challenge for many five-year-olds, but to organize concrete material under a single abstract concept, for example, "That group has six in it and is like that other group which also has six. These are all groups of six; those are groups of four." While some state standards in elementary school deal with very concrete facts or rote skills, particularly Social Studies and Science, the standards that take up most of the actual teaching time (English and Math) are all about manipulating symbols in one's mind, abstracting patterns, comparing, contrasting, and classifying.

Public school teachers in grades 1–4 schedule approximately 68% of their school time for the "core curriculum" subjects of Math, Reading, Writing, Science, and Social Studies (Perie, Baker, & Bobbitt, 1997, p. ix). Of this time they spend on the core curriculum, public school teachers devote 50% to English/Reading/Language Arts (more than 2 hours per day), 24% to Mathematics (1 hour per day), and 13% (35 minutes per day) each to social studies and science (Perie et al., 1997, p. 8). These abstract operations are the major part of the elementary educational experience.

When I first started my training to become an elementary teacher in 2010, the *Common Core* was just hitting the ground in schools for the first time. Many teachers met the standards with a great deal of frustration, anxiety, and resistance (see Burks et al., 2015; Cherry-McDaniel, 2014; Glaus, 2014). Schools did not always do a good job preparing teachers for this new curriculum and given the "high-stakes" assessment environment where teachers are judged and let go based on student test performance, teachers feared this new and very difficult material they had to learn to teach from scratch was going to end up hurting them when all the dust settled.

Given my background in cognitive development and child psychology, I had a very different reaction. My own Ph.D. dissertation was about the effect of teaching techniques which place demands for higher-order thinking upon elementary students. When I did my dissertation over 20 years ago, many of these ideas were new to the elementary setting. But with the *Common Core*, high-level cognitive tasks dominate the entire school day. As an elementary teacher in training, I was enchanted with the possibilities and thought it was brilliantly organized.

At the same time, I worried about this new curriculum, but for different reasons than many of the teachers. The quasi-Darwinian high-stakes testing environment which surrounded these new standards seemed extremely unhelpful and was causing teachers to do whatever they could to have children perform adequately on the assessments rather than to really learn and grow. In addition, my research showed that the success of the high-level cognitive demands we place upon students is not dependent upon limited exposure, but total immersion. It is one thing to ask teachers to place high-level cognitive demands upon students when they teach; it is another to then expect and even demand a high level of learning for all students regardless of social inputs, family background, aptitude, inner attitude, and disposition. Engaging in higher-order thinking for just a few hours each day at school cannot work without large-scale family and social reinforcement of these processes. This national approach put all the responsibility for academic achievement on the teacher and did not ask much of anything from the other stakeholders: the parents, family, neighborhood, culture, and even the child him or herself.

I have come to think of our modern elementary school curriculum as "Platonic," after the philosopher Plato who outlined the skills and abilities students should learn in his ideal school in his masterwork, *The Republic* (1987/380 BCE). Plato's essential skills are largely about discerning patterns, categories, and forms (as well as developing skills and virtues for democracy, physical education, and music). But Plato deemed this type of education appropriate only for a narrow slice of the population whose souls destined them to become what he called "philosopher kings." What is remarkable about our education system is that for the first time in history, a country has embarked upon a publicly funded, universal education designed to make philosopher kings (and queens) *out of every citizen*. Ours is an immensely ambitious and admirable educational project.

Five Basic Problems with Current Elementary Standards

There are many virtues to the intellectually challenging Platonic state and national standards we use in elementary education. My senior elementary teacher colleagues tell me many stories of the "old days" before the standards movement when their elementary lessons lacked a certain focus and seriousness. For example, they might spend a week or a month learning all about apples: drawing apples, reading stories about apples, eating apples, measuring apples, and visiting an apple farm. All of this was at times enjoyable, but the teachers note a certain superficiality and arbitrariness about the endeavor. Our current standards add organization, purpose, and clarity to lessons that can often wander off without them.

Standards also enable teachers to present knowledge and skills in a step-wise manner one year upon the next so that by the time students reach fifth or sixth grade, they have the necessary background knowledge to perform the more complex operations which are taught there and in the grades beyond. Teaching with standards is also measurable, enabling teachers to see which students have learned what was taught and which need more instruction. They are also often benchmarked across the state, nation, or even the globe so that meaningful comparisons can be made between students in different schools, districts, states, and nations. We can thus see clearly who is excelling and who is being "left behind."

At the same time, there are problems with the use of college prep standards in elementary education. Specifically, the state and national standards that comprise the current elementary curriculum in the United States lack a larger coherence, have been formulated in an undemocratic way, focus too much on college and jobs, do not work for all students, and rely far too heavily on teachers and schools for their success.

An incoherent curriculum. Most academic curricula strive for what they call "coherence." They seek to connect particular standards with an integrated vision of the "big ideas" and "essential questions" within a discipline. For example, an essential question from the *Common Core* in Math is, "What can be quantified?" An essential question in English/Language Arts is, "How is written language different from spoken language?" These big questions are designed to sit at the heart of an academic unit or entire grade level. Teachers are urged not to present the particular standards of their lessons in isolation, but to bring them into the context of these larger and more essential questions. We had a special section at the top of our lesson plan template just for these "essential questions." Further, teachers are also urged to help students see the progression of their learning, how previous lessons are built upon and connected to later lessons. Each lesson a teacher teaches must be tangibly connected to prior learning and big questions in the discipline.

This type of "coherence" is surely a good thing, but there is an even larger kind of coherence that is often ignored. The attempt at coherence described above seeks to make connections *within a single academic disci-*

pline. We invite the student to connect today's lesson on counting to ten to the larger question of what can be quantified. This is all to the good, but recall young Jeffrey's earlier question that went to the heart of *why he needed to do Math at all*. Students constantly wonder not about how this lesson is connected to larger questions within the same discipline, but about why they are doing this discipline at all, even why they are in school in the first place. The problem is that all the lessons and academic subjects children get in school do not cohere around a larger purpose and vision of a future outside of school. As I mentioned in previous chapters, besides the vague and uninspiring "readiness" for college and a high-skilled career (whatever that means to a five- to ten-year-old child), our academic standards are completely lacking an overall vision of purpose and an adventurous course to get there.

Undemocratic process. As I have shown in this chapter, the people's elected officials and their appointed representatives have been deeply involved in the formation of the current elementary curriculum. In this sense the process has been "democratic." While the people's representatives have been in charge, the way the curriculum has been developed and implemented does not reflect a wholesale investment or buy-in from the society at large. Most parents and community members are completely in the dark about what is in their children's curriculum, why it is there, and how it was formulated. There has also been almost no input in this process from parents and local communities. Does the community feel like the standards are theirs? Do they feel a sense of pride and ownership? In this sense, the development and implementation of the elementary academic standards have been undemocratic.

As an example, witness the massive political backlash to the implementation of the *No Child Left Behind Act* (2001). Teachers, parents, and the larger public bristled at the incessant testing of standards which were often experienced as alien to the community and imposed upon them from above. After more than ten turbulent years of this controversial law, it was finally replaced by the *Every Student Succeeds Act* (2015) which attempted to limit the federal role in K-12 education. Or witness the rebellion to the implementation of the *Common Core State Standards* (2009), which reached into the 2012 and 2016 U.S. Presidential elections. A quote from then candidate Senator Ted Cruz crystalizes the defiant sentiment, "We should repeal every word of Common Core....Education is far too important to have it governed by unelected bureaucrats down in Washington…" (Andrew, 2015). Given the public resistance that formed after the details of the *Common Core State Standards* became clearer to the public, 12 states introduced legislation to block implementation, and four states which initially adopted the *Common Core* repealed and replaced it.

I am not maintaining that this "anti-national standards" position is prudent or wise. I simply point to the fact that far too many people did not feel the requisite sense of ownership for initiatives like these to succeed. This is because the curriculum was formulated by academics and other educational professionals who are often out of touch with and do not enlist the support of the families of the children they try to educate. Further, the top-down approach to the formation of educational standards stifles the development of initiatives at the state and local levels, which include more than 16,000 separate school districts. The issue before us now is that we have a universal college prep curriculum in every state for a society who may not want it or cannot all do it.

Skewed priorities. Having standards in education is good thing. I am all for them. But why these particular standards? Should K-12 education be all about college- and career-readiness? More importantly, should *elementary school* be devoted to college- and career-readiness? What about democracy, discussion, and public speaking? What about industry, self-knowledge, emotional intelligence, and relationship skills? What about physical fitness and health? A rampant educational capitalism has driven the formulation of elementary standards to date, crowding out all other, equally worthy goals.

Not working for everyone. I said earlier that the United States has embarked upon the most ambitious and admirable educational project in human history: a publicly funded, universal education system designed to make philosopher kings (and queens) out of every citizen. Our expectations for all students are extremely high and we are determined not to "leave any child behind" in reaching these lofty goals. The question is whether this project is wise. You noticed in Miss Thomas' class that about six of her 27 students are routinely doing well across the different subjects with the challenging material she presents them. About 12 get by with differing levels of mediocrity, and about 8–9 struggle mightily and seem to take up most of her time. This percentage breakdown generally obtains not just in one lesson or subject, but all of them. (I address in a later chapter the behavioral problems and classroom disruptions students who are academically behind can cause.)

The Platonic curriculum is working for some, but not nearly all students. Who is "left behind"? It is not just some African Americans and

English-language learners, but also many boys, practical kids who do not like school and would rather be doing something with their hands or bodies, some students diagnosed with learning disabilities, as well as very gifted students. One of the central questions plaguing society and the schools for the past few decades is what to do about the fact that this curriculum is not working for everyone, that there is a vast "achievement gap" separating the academically successful from the academically struggling (Taylor, 2006). We think if we just keep pushing this rigorous curriculum year after year with enough talented teachers and engaging techniques, it will somehow catch fire in these struggling or disinterested students.

Overburdened teachers. Many problems in education can be traced back to the disconnect between what I am calling the Platonic curriculum and an Epicurean society. As I have tried to show, ours is a curriculum formulated by academics to prepare students for college and a highly intellectual profession. This is where the jobs of the future are judged to be. We are no longer educating students to be plumbers or electricians, soldiers or shopkeepers. Nor are we educating students to be excellent and engaged citizens who can speak publicly in an eloquent way, read information, or problem-solve through the democratic process.

Let me take a closer look at the differences between Platonic and Epicurean mindsets. By *Platonic* I mean activities that stress abstraction, classification, discerning patterns, categories, and forms. It involves manipulating symbols such as words and numbers in your mind without visual support. These are the skills essential for college admissions and are measured by the SAT and other national assessments. By "Epicurean" I refer to ideas inspired by the Greek philosopher Epicurus (341–270 BCE) who argued that delighting in various physical and mental pleasures is the highest good in human existence. An Epicurean approach to life seeks to enjoy it, to be financially successful, to have good friends, and fine foods, a satisfying marriage and sex life. If one reads, writes, and thinks from an Epicurean point of view, it must have some practical or material advantage.

Epicureanism forms the basis of the educational capitalism I discussed in previous chapters. Many of my college students adopt the Epicurean mindset in their college education. They take only those courses which have an immediate application to their future career and are baffled why anyone would ever take a course like Chinese Architecture or Romantic Poetry which does not have a clear connection to career development. A Platonic approach seeks to understand life to its depths, which Plato thought entails a certain detachment from material things, and a modest mode of living. A Platonist seeks understanding and learning for its own sake; an Epicurean seeks understanding and learning for some material or emotional purpose.

As I mentioned in the discussion of educational capitalism, the dominant ethos of our society looks to education in an Epicurean way. This ethos wants schools to help kids get good jobs and make comfortable incomes so they will be happy later in life. Real learning and understanding are subordinate to the payoff which education is promised to bring. But the standards and the school curriculum reflect a decidedly Platonic orientation. One learns to conduct science experiments to gather information, one derives the measure of the angles of a polygon for understanding, and one reads literature to better know what it means to be a human being. High-paying jobs and college admissions in our country are based on high-level cognitive skills which are not developed by pursuing pleasure and the senses. They are not achieved by subordinating learning to any other end but learning. Parents often want their children to enjoy material advantages and a high-paying job without fully understanding or being willing to do the highly intellectual work required to attain them. American schools thus embody an odd tension between a Platonic and an Epicurean vision of life.

What happens as a result of this confusion is that students spend a few hours each day in highly literate and numerate activities, working to achieve deeply Platonic ends, and then return to a family, neighborhood, and image-based culture which does not do much to support it, and in some cases works to undermine the academic learning achieved during the day. For example, studies show in the summer after third grade, students lose 20% of their gains in Reading over the school year and 27% of their gains in Math (Cooper, Nye, Charlton, Lindsay, & Greathouse, 1996). Why does this happen? The curriculum of today's schools does not reflect the actual desires and aspirations of most of the surrounding society, but are alien and often directly opposed to what goes on at home and the wider culture. As the subtitle of this chapter indicates, we have a Platonic curriculum operating in an Epicurean culture.

This disconnect leads to what Sahlberg (2015) calls the "myth of the great teacher" (pp. 136–137). According to this myth, all it takes is a few talented and committed teachers to swoop in and magically turn any student around, regardless of the student's talents, background, motivation, character, and level of family support. Think of movies like *Dead Poet's*

Society, *Mr. Holland's Opus*, or *Stand and Deliver* which perpetuate this myth. By a long shot, schools and teachers are not as magical as they are portrayed in these films. They cannot be expected to do all the labor of teaching. It simply will not work.

THREE POSSIBLE SOLUTIONS

I will discuss more detailed solutions to the problem of the disconnect between a Platonic curriculum and an Epicurean society in Chap. 13. For now, I want to introduce a few basic ideas for further consideration. I believe that before we can begin to solve any problems in education, we must come to appreciate the vast chasm between the Platonic and Epicurean societies, and how this disjunction is at the root of so many problems in contemporary education. Once we appreciate the scope of this issue, we can begin to think about what to do about it. From my perspective, we can try one of three things.

Option 1. The first option is to keep the college prep standards we have now and continue to expect that all American children will eventually achieve them to proficiency (given, it is argued, increased educational funding and the right kinds of teacher accountability systems). If we take this option, which it appears likely, many things will need to change for it to have a fighting chance. Instead of only relying on teachers and schools for education's success, we need to facilitate a wholesale social investment in the Platonic educational project. The successful achievement of the large set of Platonic learning outcomes we have arrayed for our children to learn over 13 years of K-12 education requires more than just a few hours at school each day, but must be encased within a familial and social context which is driven constantly toward abstraction and higher order thinking. Recall the ELA standard where the child must abstract the topic of an entire story. A topic is a "formal" reality that one does not directly find in the content of the story, but is inferred as a conceptual reality. Or recall the grouping of objects by category in the Math lesson. "Round things" is a higher order concept that one does not see with one's eyes, but knows with one's mind.

My dissertation advisor Irving Sigel (1970) sees the development of abstraction not as an innate process but as a function of two important components: (a) the cognitive demands placed on the addressee (the child) as a function of what he calls the "distancing strategies" of the addressor (the parent or teacher), and (b) in terms of the mental activities which are then set in motion by said distancing acts. The child's ability to think abstractly is directly related to what he or she is regularly asked to do by others. Sigel has separated these distancing strategies, or ways of talking to children, into three levels, each of which varies in terms of the amount of distance the child is prompted to take from his or her immediate situation in answering the question. *Level 1* distancing strategies make mental demands for associations, visual observations, or routinized information. Minimal demands are placed on the child to separate him/herself from the immediate environment. *Level 2* distancing strategies make demands to classify and to relate disparate events. Here, cognitive demands force a transcendence of the immediate environment, but *visual objects* still form the basis for the mental operations to be performed. *Level 3* distancing strategies make demands upon the child to engage in causal inferences, to predict outcomes, to employ hypothetical reasoning, to transform from one symbolic medium to another. *Level 3* distancing strategies serve to facilitate the child's ability to conserve meaning, abstract, and think in non-present, non-visible terms. These operations are the ones most often utilized in school learning activities.

The Platonic curriculum relies almost exclusively on Level 2 and 3 modes of talking to a child. For example, "How are these objects like these objects," or "What do you think would happen if we put the warm water in the cold water?" However, if the only place a child is getting Level 2 and 3 distancing is at school, the developmental effects are minimal. Several studies report that the frequency of Level 2 and 3 distancing acts at home significantly affects the child's ability to engage in representational thinking at school (Labrell, Deleau, & Juhel, 2000; McGillicuddy-De Lisi, Johnson, & Sigel, 1979; Sigel, Stinson, & Flaugher, 1991). Specifically, children's school performance in mathematics and reading is correlated with parental use of Level 3 distancing strategies at home (Powell & Peet, 2008; Sigel, 1986).

This research supports the notion of looking at the child's total "distancing environment" rather than just the school. The nature of discourse practices at home matter as much or more than those at school. Level 1 distancing strategies employed frequently at home, for example, "Sit down," "What is that," "Don't talk with your mouth full," actually function as *depressors* of representational performance (Sigel et al., 1991). The Platonic curriculum cannot succeed without massive amounts of social support. Things at home will need to change for many children to be academically successful.

It is a serious question whether our ambitious, universal Platonic curriculum can thrive in a nonintellectual culture, whether everyone wants to or even can succeed in college or a high-skilled job. If we want this curriculum for everyone, then we need to go much more "all in" than we have at this point. We have tried to do it on the cheap by not calling for wholesale family changes, placing all the heavy lifting on the teachers. In addition, for the Platonic curriculum to work for all, children must be asked to demonstrate an inner resolve and determination to learn and be part of a Platonic culture. If the kids or families do not really want to be fundamentally changed by this curriculum—and that is what it calls for—I cannot see how it will work.

Option 2. A second option is to change the academic standards we have now either by decentralizing them, which will allow for more state and local flexibility to meet the different needs in locality's particular circumstances, and/or to make the standards much more technical and much less academic than they are now, to begin to prepare students for the real jobs that exist in the world rather than for college. Being able to get into college, or even graduating from college, has very little to do with "career-readiness" (Caplan, 2018). Much of the college curriculum is in the liberal arts tradition and stresses broad learning and intellectual development rather than vocational training. College professors are academics who are deeply immersed in the inner workings of the discipline they teach. Save for a few courses and majors like business or education, college students are learning to be academics as well. They do not prepare you for actual careers. Our K-12 college prep curriculum does the same Platonic thing our colleges do. It is not preparing students for jobs by any stretch of the imagination. If what the public really wants is training for real jobs, why not toss the abstract Platonic curriculum and do just that?

Option 3. A third option, and the one which I prefer, is to admit we start college and high-skilled career preparation much too early in a child's school career. From this perspective, elementary school should be redesigned to teach all students a basic package of numeracy, literacy, physical fitness, arts, and citizenship skills in elementary school which would be encased within a larger context of adventure, high purpose, and self-discovery. Rather than pushing them toward college in elementary school, we would work to help them to love learning, enjoy reading, participate constructively in the community around them, work cooperatively with others on solving real problems in the world, speak well, make cogent arguments in writing, know who they are and what they believe, and care for their bodies and the natural world around them. Under this vision, the elementary school system would be redesigned not to push all students to college, *but to enable them to participate in democracy and a mature adult life*. I will explore this option in much more detail in Chap. 13.

What You Can Do
For elementary education to work, it requires full "buy-in" from all of society's stakeholders. Here is a list of things to consider as a parent or citizen to help make that happen.

1. Start to see yourself as the primary educator in your child's life. Your primary responsibility is to your child's *mind*, not only his body. This is easy to forget as we tend to their many physical and behavioral needs.
2. Do not burden the teacher with all the instructional work in your child's education. Whenever possible, use level 2 and level 3 distancing strategies at home.
3. Devote yourself to help your child discover his or her calling in life. Believe that he or she has one. Resist the popular notion that you can shape children into what you want them to be. Sooner or later, they will be exactly who and what they are anyway. We might as well make it as painless as possible and avoid all the unnecessary damage that our own restrictive hopes and dreams cause them.
4. Stop worrying so much about your child's future. Focus on what is important in life, what will truly lead to happiness. This is not college, and it is not money (Seligman, 2002). Resist the allure of educational capitalism. School should help develop the child's soul and intellect. He or she should be excited to go to school, learn to love reading, thinking, writing, and learning. As the grades proceed, he or she should gradually become a more competent speaker, reasoner, and writer, as well as more competent to engage with others in democratic bodies and group problem-solving. Over the elementary years, a clearer vision of him or herself in the adult world should develop which fills him or her with some excitement. "I'm going to be a ___."
5. Get involved with the civic and educational issues going on around you. Do not leave all the work to others, including the "experts." They are not that smart, and they do not have nearly as much influence on your child as you do. The development of your child's mind is far too important to take a passive role and leave to educational experts.

References

Andrew, Z. (2015, March 15). *Ted Cruz on common core and education* [Video File]. Retrieved from https://www.youtube.com/watch?v=4cIHThvgeMc&feature=youtu.be

Bloom, B. S., Krathwohl, D. R., & Masia, B. B. (1956). *Taxonomy of educational objectives: The classification of educational goals.* New York, NY: David McKay Company.

Burks, B. A., Beziat, T. L. R., Danley, S., Davis, K., Lowery, H., & Lucas, J. (2015). Adapting to change: Teacher perceptions of implementing the common core state standards. *Education, 136*(2), 253–258.

Caldas, S. J., & Bankston, C. L., III. (1999). Multilevel examination of student, school, and district-level effects on academic achievement. *Journal of Educational Research, 93*(2), 91–100.

Caplan, B. D. (2018). *The case against education: Why the education system is a waste of time and money.* Princeton, NJ: Princeton University Press.

Cherry-McDaniel, M. (2014). Coming full circle: A young teacher's journey with the standards movement. *The English Journal, 104*(2), 93–98.

Common Core State Standards Initiative. (2019). Development process. Retrieved from http://www.corestandards.org/about-the-standards/development-process/

Cooper, H., Nye, B., Charlton, K., Lindsay, J., & Greathouse, S. (1996). The effects of summer vacation on achievement test scores: A narrative and meta-analytic review. *Review of Educational Research, 66*(3), 227–268.

Glaus, M. (2014). Teacher perspectives and classroom changes during the standards movement. *The English Journal, 104*(2), 48–53.

Kozol, J. (1991). *Savage inequalities: Children in America's schools.* New York, NY: Crown Publishing.

Labrell, F., Deleau, M., & Juhel, J. (2000). Fathers' and mothers' distancing strategies towards toddlers. *International Journal of Behavioral Development, 24*(3), 356–361. https://doi.org/10.1080/01650250050118349

McGillicuddy-De Lisi, A. V., Johnson, J. E., & Sigel, I. E. (1979). The family as a system of mutual influences: Parental beliefs, distancing behaviors, and children's representational thinking. In M. Lewis & L. A. Rosenblum (Eds.), *Child and its family* (pp. 91–106). New York, NY: Plenum Press.

Miyamoto, K. (2008). The origins of the standards movement in the United States: Adoption of the written test and its influence on class work. *Educational Studies in Japan: International Yearbook, 3,* 27–40.

Perie, M., Baker, D. P., & Bobbitt, S. (1997). Time spent teaching core academic subjects in elementary schools: Comparisons across community, school, teacher, and student characteristics [PDF File]. Retrieved from National Center for Education Website: https://nces.ed.gov/pubs/97293.pdf

Plato. (1987). *The republic* (D. Lee, Trans.). New York: Penguin Classics. Original work published 380 BCE.

Powell, D. R., & Peet, S. H. (2008). Development and outcomes of a community-based intervention to improve parents' use of inquiry in informal learning contexts. *Journal of Applied Developmental Psychology, 29*(4), 259–273. https://doi.org/10.1016/j.appdev.2008.04.007

Roscigno, V. J. (2000). Family/school inequality and African-American/Hispanic achievement. *Social Problems, 47*(2), 266–291.

Sahlberg, P. (2015). *Finnish lessons, 2.0.* New York, NY: Teachers College Press.

Seligman, M. E. P. (2002). *Authentic happiness: Using the new positive psychology to realize your potential for lasting fulfilment.* New York, NY: Free Press.

Sigel, I. E. (1970). The distance hypothesis: A causal hypothesis for the acquisition of representational thought. In M. R. Jones (Ed.), *Miami symposium on the prediction of behavior, 1968: Effect of early experience* (pp. 99–118). Coral Gables, FL: University of Miami Press.

Sigel, I. E. (1986). Early social experience and the development of representational competence. In W. Flower (Ed.), *Early experience and the development of competence: New directions for child & adolescent development* (Vol. 32, pp. 49–65). San Francisco: Jossey-Bass.

Sigel, I., Stinson, E. T., & Flaugher, J. (1991). Socialization of representational competence in the family: The distancing paradigm. In L. Okagaki & R. J. Sternberg (Eds.), *Directors of development: Influences on the development of children's thinking* (pp. 121–144). Hillsdale, NJ: Lawrence Erlbaum Associates, Inc.

Taylor, R. D. (2006). *Addressing the achievement gap: Findings and applications.* Greenwich, CT: Information Age.

Tyre, P. (2009). *The trouble with boys: A surprising report card on our sons, their problems at school, and what parents and educators must do.* New York, NY: Harmony.

U.S. Department of Labor. (1999). *Skills and tasks for jobs: A SCANS report for America 2000* [PDF File]. Retrieved from https://wdr.doleta.gov/opr/FULLTEXT/1999_35.pdf

CHAPTER 8

Just Wastin' Time

You have been at the school now for almost five hours. As you sit in the back of the classroom, you think back on your day so far. There has been drama, excitement, and a healthy dose of boredom. You have witnessed joy and laughter, agony and tears, even some blood and vomit. As you reflect upon these things, you notice a large pad of paper on an easel up in the front corner of the classroom. The teacher and the children have referred to it throughout the day. It contains some very important information indeed: the daily schedule. Miss Thomas' second-grade schedule looks like this:

8:00–8:10—Unpack, restroom break
8:10–8:45—Morning Math, check binders, wake-up work
8:45–10:25—Reading & Writing (ELA)
10:25–11:00—Guided reading/Independent Reading/RTI
11:00–11:30—Science (M & W) or Social Studies (T & Th)
11:30–12:10—Lunch/recess
12:10–12:25—Read aloud
12:25–12:55—Tier 2 Math/Guided Groups/RTI
12:55–1:55—Math
1:55–2:45—Specials (Music, Art, or PE)
2:45–2:55—Pack up/clean up
2:55–3:00—Dismiss walkers
3:00–3:05—Dismiss bus riders

Principals typically expect teachers to post their daily schedule for all students to see. As I mentioned in Chap. 4, teachers have surprisingly little flexibility over their own school day. Most are told when and for how long to teach Math, English/Language Arts, Science, and Specials. The daily schedule organizes the major components of both the student's and the teacher's day. The typical school day consists of the core subjects of the curriculum that are taught in "lessons" of 45- to 100-minute periods, along with "mini-lessons" with small group work, seatwork, or guided practice, which are typically done in 20- to 30-minute periods. In between, there are bathroom breaks, lunch, Specials (Physical Education [PE], Music, Art), and recess.

If you have a child in school, "the schedule" is one of the first things you might get from the teacher at the beginning of the year. Most classrooms also have a big clock on the wall, so the children become very aware of the schedule and the overall rhythm of the day. For many children, the schedule provides a structure and stability to what can be a chaotic inner and outer world. Many come to resent even slight departures from the schedule. I have been reminded many times by a fastidious student that my Social Studies lesson was four minutes too long and was eating into the Math period that was scheduled to follow. And do not even try to cut into recess or PE with a long lesson. You will have a mini-rebellion on your hands!

If you are observing a classroom rather than teaching one yourself, you become very sensitive to how much time students spend on things other than learning or instruction. In Miss Thomas' class, for example, this would include the two students you watched poking at each other and silently laughing during independent writing, the 20-minute bathroom break where you walked the entire class down the hall to the restroom and water fountain, the student who was nodding off to sleep during the entire 35-minute period of independent math work, the altercation between two students squabbling over the same square of carpet for read-aloud for the past three days, or the intercom announcement pulling a student from the room for a doctor's appointment. The thing that shocks you at first about elementary schools is what a large percentage of the day involves students' spending time doing things other than instruction and how many students who do not pay attention to the instruction that is offered. As the chapter subtitle indicates, for a good part of the elementary school day, students are "Just Wastin' Time."

The Different Kinds of Wasted Time

To explain what I mean by "wasted time," I define a few terms. *Non-academic time* is when a teacher does something with students other than learning or academic instruction (Rosenshine, 2015). This includes time spent on transitions between periods, time giving extended instructions for tasks or procedures, time spent lining up, getting jackets, taking jackets off, coming in and sitting down, waiting for help from the teacher, time spent checking homework, managing behavior problems, as well as other time-consuming interruptions like visitors, special announcements, and assemblies. Some non-academic time is intentionally built into the student's school day. I refer to this as *planned non-academic time*. There is also a good bit of non-academic time, like behavior problems or student daydreaming, that is not scheduled or planned for. I call this *unplanned non-academic time*.

As an aside, teachers sometimes refer to *non-instructional time* as the time they have outside of the classroom during the normal school day to plan for lessons, grade papers, and communicate with parents. They typically have this time to themselves while their students are receiving instruction from someone else (like the Music teacher). This is non-academic time *for the teacher*. This is not the kind of non-academic time I mean. I use the term non-academic time to refer to periods of time where there is no formal instruction, group, or independent work presented to the student.

Another important term is *student engagement* (see Dykstra Steinbrenner & Watson, 2015). Engagement is when a student or group of students are actively or passively participating in the learning tasks the teacher has given them (Gettinger & Seibert, 2002). For example, if I am reading a story to the children, students are "engaged" if they are quietly listening, paying attention, and sitting in their place. During a math lesson, students are "engaged" if they are doing their work quietly or in a group, listening to the teacher, asking or discussing relevant questions.

Non-academic time and student engagement are finite periods that can be measured with a stopwatch. I conducted the following experiment over two separate one-month periods. I observed a first-grade class for one month and then a third-grade class for another month. I was in the class for the whole school day during this time. I clicked a hand-held timer whenever anyone in the classroom, even a single student, did something where they were learning. I define learning liberally here as engaging in an activity where one is thinking or acting in a new way and is practicing some new thought or action that one has recently acquired. I turned the timer off when all students in the classroom were engaged in a non-academic activity or when they were disengaged from learning or instruction due to distractions, chaos, or interruptions.

There were days in my first-grade group where the learning time was as low as 52 minutes out of the entire 390-minute day. For third-grade, learning time went as low as 58 minutes. These were not terribly chaotic and undisciplined classrooms. Some days the learning time was closer to three hours (46% of the school day), but I *never* got above three hours in any school day for any grade where I did this study. Keep in mind, I am talking about three hours where *anybody* in the room of 25 students was learning. What this means is that for the rest of the school day (56%), *nobody* in the class was academically learning at all. A sad and secret fact of elementary school life is that much of the school day is simply wasted time. This is true for all elementary schools, but some are much worse than others.

WHERE DOES THE TIME GO?

Up to this point I have dealt mainly in anecdotes. Non-academic time and student disengagement have been formally studied by scientific researchers. These data allow us to draw even more valid and reliable conclusions about the use of time in elementary school. In order to establish a baseline, I first consider how much time students spend in school each day. Estimates vary, but grades 1–4 spend an average of 32 hours in school per week, or 6 hours, 24 minutes per day (Perie, Baker, & Bobbitt, 1997, p. 7; Rosenshine, 2015). This would look like a school day that started at 8:00 a.m. and finished at 2:25 p.m., or started at 8:30 a.m. and finished at 2:55 p.m. Of course, some schools go longer, and some go shorter.

Given the need for transitions (e.g., getting out books and materials, moving from the carpet to desks and back, lining up to go to different rooms, walking down the hall), time for recess, lunch, snacks, bathroom breaks, specials, and assemblies, the whole six-and-a-half-hour school day cannot be completely devoted to instruction and academic learning. Estimates vary here again, but on average the grades before fourth-grade schedule about 4.9 hours of the school day for academic instruction (Benavot, 2007). Upper grades schedule a little more time for instruction, about 5.2 hours of the school day (Benavot, 2007). What this means is that about 22% of the school day is *designed* to be devoted to non-academic tasks. Right off the top, students lose about 1 hour and 24 minutes of the 6 hours and 24 minutes of their school day to *planned* non-academic activities. That leaves about 5 hours per day scheduled for academic instruction, independent work, and group learning.

A teacher can schedule five hours per day of academic instruction, but this does not mean she will actually teach for that long, or that students will learn for this scheduled amount of time. How much of a teacher's planned academic time actually goes to learning or instruction? Several studies (e.g., Anderson, 1984; Borg, 1980; Rosenshine, 2015) indicate the average teacher spends between 20% and 23% of the five hours of scheduled instructional time on non-academic activities such as dealing with student behavior problems, giving extended instructions, gathering lesson materials, collecting completed work, passing out work to be completed, fielding class interruptions such as students entering or leaving the room to work with resource teachers, waiting for computers that will just not boot up, waiting for the class to return late from their PE class, or waiting for a student who needs to change his clothes because he had an "accident" on the way to bathroom. This kind of time is what I mean by unplanned non-academic time. The average teacher will lose between 60 and 70 minutes of instruction to these distractions. In poorly managed classrooms, which have been estimated to be as many as 50% of elementary classes (Smith, 1998), or in classrooms with disruptive students, which comprise as many as 40% of elementary classes (Taie & Goldring, 2017), unplanned non-academic factors can consume as much as 40% or more of instructional time (Smith, 1998, p. 12). What this means is about one half of all elementary classrooms lose as many as two hours a day of scheduled academic time.

As an example, consider the flow of the day so far in Miss Thomas' second-grade class. The children arrived between 8:00 and 8:10 a.m., unpacked their things, and completed a "Morning Math" worksheet at their desks until 8:45 a.m. About one half of the class did not do the sheets at all during this time, but arranged items in their desks and book bags, doodled, sharpened pencils, ate their snack, went to breakfast, got water, or went to the bathroom. About one-quarter of the students found the sheet too easy and completed it in about two minutes. The other quarter found the sheet much too hard and stared blankly at it for 35 minutes. The schedule also called for homework checks during this time. The children were to have their notebooks open and out on their desks. Only about one-third of the group had their work out. But it did not matter, since Miss Thomas needed this time to get her day's lessons organized, rapidly answer nine to ten parent e-mails, deal with missing students from a late school bus, and get her attendance and lunch choice lists ready.

The morning bell sounded at 8:45 a.m. and the hum of noise subsided a bit. Students stood and said the Pledge of Allegiance. They then listened to various announcements from the principal. They sang their morning song together, an adaptation of Bruno Mars' *24K Magic*. Miss Thomas then addressed something that happened in class yesterday. Someone had stolen a pack of gum from her purse. She was very upset about it and strongly encouraged the culprit to step forward. She waited for several minutes, but nobody did.

Of course, none of this was on the daily class schedule. By now it was 9:00 a.m. According to the schedule, Reading & Writing was to have started at 8:45 a.m. Fifteen minutes of planned instructional time has already been lost to unplanned activity. Miss Thomas then went over the morning schedule. She informed the class that for their Reading & Writing lesson, they would review the story they read aloud yesterday about the upcoming Thanksgiving holiday, color a festive meal on a paper plate, and write an invitation to a holiday gathering to their friends. They would also "read around the room," a process, Miss Thomas explained, in which pairs of students walk around the room reading other students' written invitations. They then role-played this procedure a few times by getting up and walking around the room, simulating reading their neighbor's work. Finally, she told the students if they were done reading everyone's invitations, they were to read posters and other printed materials on the classroom walls.

These extended instructions lasted until about 9:20 a.m. Another 20 minutes of planned instructional time was lost. Miss Thomas then did a "mini-lesson" for ten minutes on how to write an invitation. She wrote her own invitation for the class on a large pad of paper and then invited the children to re-read the Thanksgiving story at their desks and write their own invitation using the format she used in the mini-lesson. Some independent student seatwork then began. Several students could not find their books and asked if they could go to their bags to find it. A few students looked over the story at their desks, but most focused immediately on the crayons and markers and started the coloring activity on the paper plates.

After about ten minutes of this independent work, six children got up from their desks, gathered some items, and left the room for small group reading instruction with the resource teacher. They interrupted Miss Thomas because several of the students needed some textbooks that were behind her desk. The resource teacher and Miss Thomas chatted for a few minutes about a student in the resource group who was having some problems at home. Miss Thomas then pulled together her own small "Response to Intervention" (RTI) reading group of six to work with her at a table near her desk shortly after that at 9:45 a.m. About one half of the class remained at their desks unsupervised. About one half of them made furtive attempts to write an invitation. The remainder quietly talked to each other or colored their holiday plates. A few started to ramble around the room reading posters.

At 10:00 a.m., Miss Thomas sent the first small group back and called a second reading group to her desk. She noticed several students were off-task at their desks and so had to stand up, repeat her original instructions, and try to get students who were off-task back to their work. This took her about ten additional minutes. You also wandered around the students' desks and tried to work with some of the remaining students in the room who were struggling or asked for help. Miss Thomas worked with the second group of readers at her desk for another ten minutes. She then stood up and refocused those in the larger group who were off-task for the remaining five minutes of the lesson.

It was 10:25 a.m. when the scheduled Reading & Writing period was over. By that point, students had been at school for over two hours. During this first 145 minutes of the school day, the first 60 minutes was lost to unpacking, busy worksheet tasks, announcements, and classroom rituals. When the Reading & Writing lesson finally started at 9:00, 15 minutes of the lesson was already lost to non-academic business. Twenty-five minutes of the remaining 85 minutes of the scheduled lesson were taken up by extended teacher instructions and classroom management. Though 100 minutes was scheduled for Reading & Writing, it was physically possible for students to do just 60 minutes of academic learning. Forty percent of *planned* instructional time was spent on non-academic tasks. Nobody could academically learn during this time. I should note that Miss Thomas' classroom is not a "bad" or atypical classroom by any means. This 40% figure does not include the many students who did not fully engage or engage at all in classwork during the 60 minutes that were available to them for learning. That is a separate category I will consider in a moment.

Several factors can cause the average amount of time wasted on unplanned non-academic activities to be even greater than the national average of 20–23%. Research shows if a classroom contains a higher percentage of "at-risk" students, that classroom will spend a greater proportion of its day on non-instructional activities compared to students with fewer students at-risk. Stichter, Stormont, and Lewis (2008) have shown that teachers in Title 1 schools spend more scheduled time in non-instructional activities (45–50%) than their non-Title 1 counterparts (20–23%). It should be noted that 57% of all public schools receive Title 1 funds (U.S. Department of Education, 2018). Further, teachers in Title 1 schools have a significantly higher percentage of their students entering and leaving their classrooms during scheduled periods of instruction to work with resource, special education, and English as Second Language teachers. Recall Miss Thomas' Reading & Writing lesson where several students had to cut their work short and leave right in the middle of the lesson to go work with another teacher in another room. Another factor that adds to the amount of unplanned non-academic time is disruptive or aggressive student classroom behavior, which I will consider in a later section of this chapter.

We began this discussion with the baseline planned instructional time figure of five hours per school day. We lose an average of one hour and five minutes (20%) of these five hours to the various "unplanned" non-academic activities. This leaves about 3 hours and 55 minutes (61%) of the average 6-hour and 24-minute school day for actual learning and instruction. However, you can see from the example of Miss Thomas' class that even though there is a fixed period scheduled for "Reading & Writing," many individual students are using a good portion of their Language Arts time doing other things besides reading and writing. Many can get through the day doing almost nothing at all. So, how much of the roughly four hours of academic time do students actually spend "on task," and how much do they use it for something else?

Time-Off-Task

If you have spent any time observing an elementary school class, you quickly learn that scheduling time for instruction does not guarantee that students will engage the lesson or learn anything from it. Students are "off task" during instruction for a variety of reasons (see Lee, Kelly, & Nyre, 1999). The lesson could be too hard for them or too easy, the children may not be interested in the topic of the lesson, the teacher may be doing all the talking and not allowing the students to practice, the children could be tired, upset from something else going on, daydreaming, passing notes to each other, engaging in more serious behavioral infractions, or being distracted by those infractions.

I have already shared my anecdotal observations that some students spend a surprisingly small percentage of scheduled instructional time "on task" and learning. A few students are on task almost all the time. Others are on task for bits of time and move back-and-forth between being on- and off-task. Still others are doing other things most of the time while the teacher is teaching. Obviously, the degree to which a student is either actively or passively engaged with instruction is essential to learning. Without academic engagement, students cannot benefit from instruction (e.g., Gettinger & Seibert, 2002; Singh, Granville, & Dika, 2002). The crucial question is, what percentage of the 3 hours and 55 minutes of academic time are students on-task and engaged in learning? In answering this question, we need to look at two different types of off-task behavior: student disengagement and disruptive behavior.

Student disengagement. Student disengagement is a bit harder to measure than planned instructional time. You can just look at the schedule of the school day or time the teacher while she teaches to get an accurate measure of planned or actual instructional time. With student engagement, on the other hand, the researcher must "get down on the ground" and measure whether students are really paying attention to instruction and doing the work being asked of them. This is a little more difficult, but not impossible to measure. Engagement varies considerably from student to student. Rosenshine (2015) observed that on average, students are engaged in elementary classroom lessons for about 73% of instructional time. In real hours, this amounts to between 60 and 75 minutes of disengagement for each student every day. For the less engaged student, time spent on task amounts to as little as 0–25% of academic time. For the more engaged student, engagement can run as high as 90% of instructional time. Of course, these figures assume a relatively quiet and orderly class. Student daydreaming and disengagement from instruction is a fairly low-impact behavior problem as it does not necessarily distract other students or impede the teacher's ability to teach. High-impact disruptions is another issue that I turn to now.

Disruptive behavior. Thus far I have not considered the thorny issue of student misbehavior. It is a huge issue in all schools and a major stressor in the lives of teachers (Demir, 2009). During the 2015–2016 school year, 43% of teachers either "agreed" or "agreed strongly" that student misbehavior interfered with their teaching (Taie & Goldring, 2017). In a study of 55 fifth-grade teachers, observations revealed an average of between 35.81 and 102.62 rule-challenging behaviors from students per hour of class time (Owens et al., 2018). Instructional time lost to non-learning activities like disruptive behavior and the spectacle caused by it can be quite large in some schools and classrooms (Aronson, Zimmerman, & Carlos, 1999).

We can divide disruptive behavior into two types: moderate-impact disruptions and aggressive/antisocial disruptions. Moderate-impact misbehavior includes not following classroom rules and procedures, wandering around the room, talking out of turn, and interrupting another student's work (Briesch, Briesch, & Chafouleas, 2015). Research shows that moderate-impact disruptive behavior (as well as student disengagement) occurs quite frequently in elementary classrooms (Postholm, 2013). Teachers find these behaviors as among the most persistent and difficult to manage. It was, perhaps, my single greatest struggle as a new elementary teacher.

Aggressive and antisocial behavior is less frequent, but it does occur in certain schools and classrooms at extremely high rates. These behaviors include walking out of the classroom, shouting at the teacher or other students, loudly arguing with the teacher or other students, cursing the teacher or other students, hitting the teacher or other students, throwing things, or moving furniture around (Sun & Shek, 2012). In the 2015–2016 school year, 10% of elementary teachers reported being threatened with violence by their students, and 3.9% reported being physically attacked (National Center for Education Statistics, 2018). When this kind of behavior occurs, it can prevent most students in the room from learning for long pockets of time.

Why Is so Much Time Lost?

There are several factors responsible for the lost time in elementary classrooms. Some, like time to take off your jacket, are inevitable and cannot be prevented. But others can be controlled or reduced. I discuss the time-draining factors by organizing them into three categories depending upon where the factor derives: from the teacher, from the student/family/society, and from the Administration. Each of these factors needs to be studied in much greater detail to determine the precise contribution of each in different kinds of geographical regions and school settings. I will address specific things each party can do to improve student time on task in Chap. 13 and list here only the general factors.

Teacher-related factors. Several factors related to the teacher have been found to contribute to time-off-task in elementary classrooms. If the teacher has poor classroom management skills, this can contribute heavily to lost learning time (Brophy, 1996; Doyle, 1986). *Classroom management* concerns the repertoire of strategies a teacher uses to increase students' cooperation and engagement and decrease both moderate and high-impact disruptive behavior (Bluestein, 2011). In addition, teachers who present lessons in a cut-and-dry fashion without a lot of adventure, relevant examples, time for hands-on practice, and even physical movement can also struggle to keep otherwise engaged students on task (Downer, Rimm-Kaufman, & Pianta, 2007; Lekwa, Reddy, & Shernoff, 2019).

Student/familial/social factors. Other factors pertain more to the student's state of mind and disposition in class and are difficult to mitigate no matter how talented the teacher or engaging the lesson is (Kholisiyah, Rukayah, & Indriayu, 2018). Sleep deprivation (Williams, 2017), problems at home (Shamama-tus-Sabah & Gilani, 2011), diet, exercise, vision, medical issues, psychological disorders, aptitude, character, self-esteem, interests, and motivation are huge factors determining how much or how little a student will engage and learn in school.

Administration-related factors. The Administration's choice to pursue a challenging college prep-for-all curriculum has seriously impacted many students' ability to adequately perform and engage with school. The Administration is also involved with the determination to place students of greatly differing abilities in the same classroom and insist that a single teacher teach them all at the same time. This situation can waste an immense amount of time as the teacher must tend to often radically different student needs and problems and prepare a host of leveled materials for the different students in the room. Administrative policies that tolerate inappropriate and disrespectful behavior also cause a huge drain of time from academic instruction. Many requirements for tiered interventions in an "RTI," along with data gathering and assessment from targeted students, also take time away from general classroom instruction.

How Lost Time Negatively Impacts Teacher and Student

Teachers spend 9–16 hours each week on school-related tasks outside the classroom. These activities include mentoring students after school or during lunch, tutoring, having meetings with parents, preparing their lesson plans, grading papers and homework, attending staff meetings, team meetings, and various school events. The time teachers spend outside the classroom has steadily increased over time. In 1987–1988, teachers spent 1.8 hours per day (9 hours per week) doing school tasks outside the classroom. In 1990–1991, this number increased to 2 hours per day/10 hours per week. In 1993–1994, the figure went to 2.5 hours per day or 11.6 hours per week. Today that figure is close to 3.1 hours per day or 15.5 hours per week (Perie et al., 1997, p. 7). Teachers' workweek also went up from 40 hours in 1987–1988 to 53 hours in 2011–2012 (Strauss, 2012).

Time spent doing things in the classroom besides teaching is directly tied to teacher job retention and satisfaction. If you have many demands and objectives you need to achieve, but then must constantly deal with setbacks, obstacles, interruptions, and failures, it begins to erode your enthusiasm. Achieving some measure of success at your job comes to feel impossible. Teachers get into the field to teach, but find they spend much of their professional time doing paperwork, dealing with student misbehavior, writing lesson plans, administering assessments, tutoring students who are grade levels behind, all while being criticized (and even threatened with firing) for not achieving more learning objectives in the classroom. This is a sure recipe for burnout (Demir, 2009; Mitani, 2018).

Wasted classroom time is not fun for most students either. In the 2016 *Gallup Student Poll*, 25% of elementary students report either not being engaged (18%) or actively disengaged (8%) in school. By the time students reach 11th grade, 35% report being not engaged, and 34% report being actively disengaged in school (Calderon & Yu, 2017). In another national poll, only 40% of teachers believe the majority of students at their schools are "highly engaged and motivated" (Education Week Research Center, 2014). So, when your child comes home from school and you ask him, "what did you do today?" and he says "nothing," perhaps this is fairly close to the truth.

What You Can Do
Many of the issues described in this chapter relate to internal dynamics of the school rather than the wider public. However, there are still important things that parents and the wider community can do to address them.

1. Volunteer your time as much as possible to help in the classroom. Most teachers need a lot of help, but are reluctant to ask. If you are there to help supervise a larger group while the teacher works with a smaller group, it can make a huge difference in terms of what she will be able to do in the classroom. Teachers are talented, but they only have two hands.
2. Respect the teacher's time. Do not clutter her e-mail, text, or voicemail with irrelevant questions or requests. It takes a lot of time for teachers to answer these messages, and they usually make a point of getting back to you promptly. Minimize classroom interruptions for doctor's appointments, do not plan a vacation during times when school is in session, and send all paperwork back. You cannot imagine the time these kinds of things can cost a teacher.
3. Help your child with his or her homework every night. It is part of your responsibility as a parent. Find out what he or she needs to do and help him or her do it. The more your child uses time at home to learn and practice what is covered in class, the less time the teacher will have to spend in class going over it again and taking away from the next, more complicated aspect of the lesson. Teachers spend far too much time catching up unprepared students.
4. If your child misbehaves at school, believe the teacher that it is true. It is likely far worse than what she reports. If your teacher tells you of behavioral infractions at school, please discipline the child at home for it as well. If a child talks back to a teacher and then goes home and plays on his phone for the rest of the night, he learns there are really no consequences for his bad behavior. However, if he knows you have the teacher's back, it will make her life a world easier.
5. Do whatever you can to advocate for two certified teachers in every classroom. The current arrangement of one per room is

(continued)

(continued)

unworkable. Too many important educational tasks fall through the cracks and too many students' educational needs are ignored under this system.
6. As much as possible, minimize drama and family dysfunction at home. I realize some of this is out of people's hands, but it really is a great gift to a child if he or she can come home to a safe and peaceful environment to decompress and prepare for the next school day. Your drama affects your children far more deeply than you realize. Children bring all this anxiety to school and it limits their own learning if they are distracted and daydreaming. And it makes their own and other students' learning next to impossible if they are acting out.
7. Ensure that you follow recommended guidelines for the number of hours your child needs to sleep each night. It is typically much more than you think. Children need much more sleep than adults to grow physically and cognitively. Ensure they get regular meals and snacks. Missing just one meal can shut a child's cognitive functioning down almost completely. About 30–60 minutes of vigorous exercise is also needed for every child each day. There is a deep connection between a healthy body and a healthy mind. Severely limit or eliminate screen time. There is no way a book or a lecture can compete with material on an iPad if that is all the child is used to seeing. The more screen time a child has, the more it begins to transform his or her cognitive functioning in a way that makes the abstract operations of school seem difficult and alien.

References

Anderson, L. W. (Ed.). (1984). *Time and school learning: Theory, research, and practice*. New York, NY: Routledge.

Aronson, J., Zimmerman, J., & Carlos, L. (1999). *Improving student achievement by extending school: Is it just a matter of time*. San Francisco, CA: WestEd.

Benavot, A. (2007). Instructional time and curricular emphases: U.S. state policies in comparative perspective. In C. E. Finn Jr. & D. Ravitch (Eds.), *Beyond the basics: Achieving a liberal education for all children* (pp. 149–185). Washington, DC: Thomas B. Fordham Institute.

Bluestein, J. (2011). *Classroom management*. Thousand Oaks, CA: Corwin.

Borg, W. R. (1980). Time and school learning. In C. Denham & A. Lieberman (Eds.), *Time to learn* (pp. 33–72). Washington, DC: National Institute of Education.

Briesch, A. M., Briesch, J. M., & Chafouleas, S. M. (2015). Investigating the usability of classroom management strategies among elementary schoolteachers. *Journal of Positive Behavior Interventions, 17*(1), 5–14. https://doi.org/10.1177/1098300714531827

Brophy, J. (1996). *Teaching problem students*. New York, NY: The Guilford Press.

Calderon, V. J., & Yu, D. (2017, June 1). Student enthusiasm falls as high school graduation nears. *Gallup*. Retrieved from https://news.gallup.com/opinion/gallup/211631/student-enthusiasm-falls-high-school-graduationnears.aspx?g_source=link_NEWSV9&g_medium=TOPIC&g_campaign=item_&g_content=Student%2520Enthusiasm%2520Falls%2520as%2520High%2520School%2520Graduation%2520Nears

Demir, S. (2009). Teacher perceptions of classroom management and problematic behaviors in primary schools. *Procedia—Social and Behavioral Sciences, 1*(1), 584–589. https://doi.org/10.1016/J.Sbspro.2009.01.105

Downer, J. T., Rimm-Kaufman, S. E., & Pianta, R. C. (2007). How do classroom conditions and children's risk for school problems contribute to children's behavioral engagement in learning? *School Psychology Review, 36*(3), 413–432.

Doyle, W. (1986). Classroom organization and management. In M. C. Wittrock (Ed.), *Handbook of research on teaching* (pp. 392–431). New York, NY: Macmillan.

Dykstra Steinbrenner, J., & Watson, L. (2015). Student engagement in the classroom: The impact of classroom, teacher, and student factors. *Journal of Autism & Developmental Disorders, 45*(8), 2392–2410. https://doi.org/10.1007/s10803-015-2406-9

Education Week Research Center. (2014). *Findings from a national survey: Engaging students for success* [PDF File]. Retrieved from https://www.edweek.org/media/ewrc_engagingstudents_2014.pdf

Gettinger, M., & Seibert, J. K. (2002). Best practices in increasing academic learning time. In A. Thomas & J. Grimes (Eds.), *Best practices in school psychology IV* (pp. 773–787). Washington, DC: National Association of School Psychologists.

Kholisiyah, R. N., Rukayah, & Indriayu, M. (2018). Achievement motivation analysis of outstanding students in learning writing at primary schools. *International Journal of Educational Methodology, 4*(3), 133–139.

Lee, S. W., Kelly, K. E., & Nyre, J. E. (1999). Preliminary report on the relation of students' on-task behavior with completion of school work. *Psychological Reports, 84*(1), 267–272. https://doi.org/10.2466/PR0.84.1.267-272

Lekwa, A. J., Reddy, L. A., & Shernoff, E. S. (2019). Measuring teacher practices and student academic engagement: A convergent validity study. *School Psychology, 34*(1), 109–118.

Mitani, H. (2018). Principals' working conditions, job stress, and turnover behaviors under NCLB accountability pressure. *Educational Administration Quarterly, 54*(5), 822–862. https://doi.org/10.1177/0013161X18785874

National Center for Education Statistics. (2018). Indicator 5: Teachers threatened with injury or physically attacked by students. Retrieved from National Center for Education Statistics Website: https://nces.ed.gov/programs/crimeindicators/ind_05.asp

Owens, J. S., Holdaway, A. S., Smith, J., Evans, S. W., Himawan, L. K., Coles, E. K., ... Dawson, A. E. (2018). Rates of common classroom behavior management strategies and their associations with challenging student behavior in elementary school. *Journal of Emotional & Behavioral Disorders, 26*(3), 156–169.

Perie, M., Baker, D. P., & Bobbitt, S. (1997). *Time spent teaching core academic subjects in elementary schools: Comparisons across community, school, teacher, and student characteristics* [PDF File]. Retrieved from National Center for Education Website: https://nces.ed.gov/pubs/97293.pdf

Postholm, M. B. (2013). Classroom management: What does research tell us? *European Educational Research Journal, 12*(3), 389–402. https://doi.org/10.2304/eerj.2013.12.3.389

Rosenshine, B. V. (2015). How time is spent in elementary classrooms. *Journal of Classroom Interaction, 50*(1), 41–53.

Shamama-tus-Sabah, S., & Gilani, N. (2011). Household chaos, attention and school problems in primary school children. *Journal of Behavioural Sciences, 21*(1), 68–79.

Singh, K., Granville, M., & Dika, S. (2002). Mathematics and science achievement: Effects of motivation, interest, and academic engagement. *The Journal of Educational Research, 95*(6), 323–332. https://doi.org/10.1080/00220670209596607

Smith, B. (1998). *It's about time: Opportunities to learn in Chicago's elementary schools. Improving Chicago's schools.* Chicago, IL: Consortium on Chicago School Research.

Stichter, J. P., Stormont, M., & Lewis, T. J. (2008). Instructional practices and behavior during reading: A descriptive summary and comparison of practices in title one and non-title elementary schools. *Psychology in the Schools, 46*(2), 173–183. https://doi.org/10.1002/pits.20361

Strauss, V. (2012, March 16). Survey: Teachers work 53 hours per week on average. *The Washington Post.* Retrieved from https://www.washingtonpost.com/blogs/answer-sheet/post/survey-teachers-work-53-hours-per-week-on-average/2012/03/16/gIQAqGxYGS_blog.html

Sun, R. C. F., & Shek, D. T. L. (2012). Student classroom misbehavior: An exploratory study based on teachers' perceptions. *The Scientific World Journal, 2012,* 1–8. https://doi.org/10.1100/2012/208907

Taie, S., & Goldring, R. (2017). Characteristics of public elementary and secondary school teachers in the United States: Results from the 2015–16 national teacher and principal survey. First look [PDF File]. Retrieved from https://nces.ed.gov/pubs2017/2017072rev.pdf

U.S. Department of Education. (2018). Improving basic programs operated by local educational agencies (Title I, Part A). Retrieved from https://www2.ed.gov/programs/titleiparta/index.html

Williams, L. (Ed.). (2017). *Sleep deprivation: Global prevalence, dangers and impacts on cognitive performance.* New York, NY: Nova Science Publishers.

CHAPTER 9

No Child Left Behind?

The end of your visit to Miss Thomas' class draws near. During the last hour of the school day, she sits the group down in a circle on the carpet and talks about "the test" coming up in a few weeks. She reviews a PowerPoint slide with the title, "Tips for the Test." She reminds the students, "Remember, not reading the instructions carefully is the biggest mistake students make, so what are we going to do?" The students chime in unison, "Read the instructions!" They have heard this presentation before. She then tells them, "The second biggest mistake is pacing. A lot of kids think finishing the test first means they are the smartest. But what does it mean?" "You were probably not careful!" they all say again in unison. "Correct," Miss Thomas replies. "When you rush," she continues, "you lose focus, and are more likely to get the question wrong." She then reminds them, "The night before the test, be sure to…" They immediately respond, "Get a good night's sleep!" The class has practiced this lecture well. "Correct," Miss Thomas says. "And on the morning of the test?" The class responds, "Eat a good breakfast!" "Perfect!" Miss Thomas finishes. "And remember these are just tests, there is no reason to worry about them." The class responds with its final chant, "Yes, Miss Thomas."

The last part of the day involves a whole school assembly to "celebrate student learning." You walk down the hall with the class to the auditorium. Hundreds of students are already sitting on the dimly-lit gym floor. Dance music is playing through the speakers of a DJ set up on the side of the stage. It is "DJ Jack," the husband of the Assistant Principal, Mrs.

Daniels. Streamers hang from the ceiling. The stage is decorated with banners made by the students which bear slogans like, "The Eagles Soar," "Don't Stress, Just Do Your Best," or "Today You Will Glow When You Show What You Know." There is even a *Star Wars*-themed banner reading, "May the Scores Be with You."

As your class takes its seat on the floor, a giant eagle in a costume like a mascot from a football game comes out of nowhere and furiously runs up and down the aisles, giving high-fives to the kids, and dancing to the music. The children are transfixed. The eagle then goes up to the stage holding hands with a fourth-grade student who carries a microphone. The lights dim and the music suddenly changes to "Uptown Funk" by Bruno Mars. The student breaks into a rap song with lyrics she wrote about how to do well on the test, "I'm too smart/Called a police and a fireman/I'm too smart/Make a teacher wanna retire man/I'm too smart." The principal comes to the stage when the student finishes her song, and the crowd breaks into a sustained applause. She thanks the fourth grader for her "fabulous rhymes," and then talks to the eagle about the fact that there is a test coming up next week. "And you know my Eagles are just gonna soar on their scores! Are we gonna soar, Eagles?" she asks the crowd. They yell with a weak, "Yeah!" She responds, "I can't hear you!" And the kids yell louder, "Yeah!" She then calls several students to the stage and recognizes them for their work this month in English or Math. They are given gift certificates to a local pizzeria. The Eagle then starts throwing t-shirts out to the crowd. The principal ends her time on the stage by reminding the kids once again not to worry or stress about the test. They then enjoy another song from DJ Jack before lining up to go back to their classrooms.

As you walk back with the students, Miss Thomas talks to you about what just happened. "We never used to do stuff like this, but last year's test results were pretty low. Parents were mad, and some students transferred to other schools, which cost the school a lot of money." She tells you that last May the faculty had a retreat with a consultant hired by the district to discuss "strategies" and "best practices" to improve school-wide test performance. They came up with a plan which includes doing "fun school events" a few times each year to reward students' hard work and to get ready for the big day. Miss Thomas whispers she does not enjoy all the hype around the test and wishes the school would have focused on smaller classes so she could give struggling students more individual attention. She would also prefer to get students' families involved with supporting children's learning at home and over the summer. "But that," she says in a resigned tone, "would cost some *real* money." She wonders about all the time she spends on test prep in class because students will often get an improved test score at the end of the academic year only to return after a long summer having forgotten most of what they learned. Though the school has been doing this new program for over a year, Miss Thomas says it seems like the same group of students do very well on their tests, the same group does poorly, and most struggle in the middle, often a year or two behind their grade level. You recall your own childhood in elementary school. It may be difficult for you to remember even taking a standardized test, much less having a DJ and prizes to celebrate it. How did we get to where the test has become such a big deal?

A Brief History of Standardized Tests

The history of standardized testing in elementary school closely mirrors the "standards movement" discussed in Chap. 7. If we change the curriculum to teach explicitly articulated and measurable standards, it makes sense that we would also "assess" the degree to which students can demonstrate those standards. A "standardized test" assesses the different standards covered in the curriculum over one or more academic years. Sometimes "benchmark" standardized tests are given each month or several times over an academic year to assess how well students are progressing toward their end-of-year standards. At the end of the year, there is also a "summative" standardized test from the state which assesses all the standards covered that year. These tests can take several days to administer.

Flattau et al. (2006) chronicle an evolving movement in U.S. public schools toward increased standardized testing which formally began in 1958 with the *National Defense Education Act* (NDEA). As a reaction to the 1957 Russian launch of Sputnik, the NDEA offered large sums of federal money to schools which encouraged students to study science, computers, math, and foreign languages. Between 1958 and 1967, standardized tests given to elementary and middle school students increased from 10 million in 1958 to 45 million in 1967. Standardized testing also increased in high school during this time from 45% of students tested in 1958 to almost 100% in 1967 (Flattau et al., 2006). Testing slowly became the primary, though not the only, way to determine whether schools were teaching and students were learning what they were supposed to.

In 1965, Congress passed the *Elementary and Secondary Education Act* (ESEA) as part of Lyndon B. Johnson's celebrated "War on Poverty."

This first-of-its-kind law gave the federal government new power to direct federal dollars to the most economically disadvantaged children in order to equalize funding disparities between wealthier and poorer schools. This law has been reauthorized 8 times since 1965, including in 1994 as the *Improving America's Schools Act* (IASA). IASA mandated that states test students in grades 3 through 12 on the standards articulated in *Goals 2000* or an equivalent. Recall that *Goals 2000* included having children leave the 4th, 8th, and 12th grades with "demonstrated proficiency" in English, mathematics, foreign languages, civics, geography, economics, the arts, and history. States receiving federal grants were mandated not only to test but also to define what making "adequate yearly progress" meant in their schools and districts. "Progress" came mainly to mean student performance on standardized tests in the listed academic subjects. Schools were held accountable by law for their test results and were mandated to articulate improvement plans in the face of any poor test scores. IASA also provided extra funding to help economically disadvantaged and historically marginalized students meet any achievement gaps.

The Elementary and Secondary Education Act (ESEA) of 1965 was reauthorized again in 2002, but this time as the infamous *No Child Left Behind Act* (NCLB). NCLB built on *Goals 2000* and incentivized more than ever before the national effort already underway toward standardization of the curriculum, equality in performance between advantaged and disadvantaged students, and a more rigorous college prep curriculum. Though Congress recently replaced NCLB with the *Every Student Succeeds Act* (ESSA) in 2015, I consider NCLB the culmination of the standards and assessment movement in U.S. education. I therefore focus much of my attention in this chapter on NCLB.

Under NCLB, states were required to test students not just in 4th, 8th, and 12th grade, but *each year* in Reading and Math in grades 3 through 8, and once more in high school. Schools were also mandated to report their results in a brand-new way. Not only would they report test results for the whole school or grade level, but they were required to issue separate reports on the performance of various "marginalized groups," including special education students, racial minorities, English learners, and children from low-income families. Before NCLB, schools could "aggregate" their test performance data by averaging scores of all students in a grade or school together. When schools do this, higher performing students mask the scores of lower performing students. Imagine I have five students in my Math class. Their standardized test scores are as follows: 100, 90, 70,

50, and 40. My average score would be a 70, which is likely at the "proficient" or "adequate" level. When I aggregate these test results, I would report my class as "proficient" in Math, but this would hide the two students who are quite behind the other students in the room. NCLB forced schools to "disaggregate" their performance data so any disparities between groups would be clearly visible for all to see.

NCLB also set ambitious performance goals for all schools. States would be expected to have *all students*, even those from marginalized groups, at the "proficient" level on state tests by the 2013–2014 school year (ten years from NCLB's passage). Since most schools started around the 35% proficiency level in 2002, this represented quite a heavy lift. Each state was free to decide its own standards within the federal framework, to define what "proficiency" meant, and to develop which assessments to use to determine proficiency. NCLB also stipulated that all teachers were to be "highly qualified" by holding a state teaching certificate and a bachelor's degree in the subject they taught. It also required that these "highly qualified" teachers be spread evenly through all schools in a district, rather than concentrated in just the wealthier ones.

One of the most notable aspects of NCLB was the mechanism borrowed from IASA known as "adequate yearly progress" (AYP). AYP is an accountability measure intended to keep schools on track toward their stated performance goals. Under the provisions, if a school missed the state's proficiency goals for two or more years for all students or *even a subgroup*, it would be labeled as "not making adequate yearly progress," and subject to various punishments, including having to offer free tutoring to struggling students, allowing students to transfer to a better-performing school in that district, being turned into a charter school, being taken over by the state, or being shut down completely. For a variety of obvious reasons, schools were desperate to stay off this "naughty list," which was made public each year to eager parents and administrators. While ESEA and its progeny directed federal dollars toward reducing gaps in performance between advantaged and marginalized groups, NCLB was the first law to formally require that schools close achievement gaps by sanctioning schools that failed to reduce them. NCLB sought to end the unacceptable practice of ignoring, hiding, or ineffectively addressing poor academic performance from children year after academic year.

Among the many remarkable features of this landmark law, NCLB held schools accountable for their test results using the same standards as all other students across the state. The reason NCLB did this was to close the unacceptably large achievement gaps between black and white students, English learners and native speakers, as well as rich and poor schools. It sought to stop allowing states and districts to use one set of standards (usually lower) to assess poor or minority students, and another to assess students from affluent or non-minority backgrounds. Under NCLB, *all students* would be held to the same performance standards regardless of race, ethnicity, or family income. This facet of the law is what led some to call NCLB "the most progressive development in K-12 education since *Brown v. Board of Education*" (Jellig, 2013).

Common Critiques

NCLB was a bi-partisan political triumph in 2002. The bill was coauthored by liberal Democratic Senator Edward "Teddy" Kennedy and signed by the "compassionate conservative" Republican President George W. Bush. It received 381 out of 434 votes in the Republican-controlled House of Representatives and 87 out of 100 votes in the Democratic-controlled Senate. Since that time, however, there has been overwhelming backlash and protest from students, parents, teachers, principals, politicians, educational professionals, and researchers. For example, Barnes and Slate (2013) charge that NCLB has "drastically changed the climate and culture of public education by utilizing high-stakes standardized test scores as the primary measure of student learning" (p. 3). They say these tests, and the "punitive accountability measures" that come with them, "…are detrimental to student learning, closing the achievement gap, lowering the dropout rate, increasing graduation rates, and preparing students for access to and success in academic endeavors beyond high school" (p. 3). Barrels of ink have spilled from the pens of parents and educational researchers on the evils of NCLB and standardized testing more generally.

Criticisms of NCLB can be grouped into those which oppose the act on philosophical grounds and those which point to alleged practical failures. At the philosophical level, many critics have balked at what they see as too much Federal involvement in K-12 education and a concomitant loss of state/local control (see Berlak, 2005). Other critics allege NCLB's emphasis upon yearly Math and English testing narrows the curriculum and results in teachers spending less time teaching "non-tested" subjects like science, social studies, foreign languages, music, art, and physical education (e.g., Dee & Jacob, 2011; McMurrer, 2007). They charge this focus on just a few highly tested academic subjects has also led many schools to limit recess time or to eliminate it completely (Henley, McBride, Milligan, & Nichols, 2007). Some have pointed to various adverse effects of this change of focus, including making school tedious and boring, and even causing kids to gain weight because of less time in Physical Education (PE) and recess (see Anderson, Butcher, & Schanzenbach, 2017).

Another common criticism is that NCLB leads to an overreliance upon standardized testing in education, making test scores the only data that matter, and poisoning the educational climate with an unnecessary "high-stakes atmosphere" (Barnes & Slate, 2013, p. 3). Further, some suggest there are other ways of measuring learning than standardized tests (Amrein & Berliner, 2003), or that some students (particularly racial minorities and English learners) do not perform well on standardized tests because of cultural bias in the test and/or a lack of test-taking skills (Arbuthnot, 2011; Harris, Smith, & Harris, 2011). Some suggest that NCLB's reliance upon teachers and schools to close achievement gaps ignores underlying problems of poverty which are largely responsible for those achievement gaps in the first place (Breunig, 2014).

At a practical level, critics of NCLB point to the fact that in each of the 13 years since its passage, Congress never once provided more than half of the promised additional Title 1 funding earmarked to help underperforming students and schools. This led many to the conclusion that NCLB merely raised standards and accountability, but did not provide schools with the tools to address the problems of student underperformance (see Noddings, 2013). Noddings (2013) writes, "simply stating what students must know and be able to do is not enough to ensure the desired outcomes" (p. 29). Given this inadequate funding, the pressure to perform, and the real threat of firing or school closure, many teachers, schools, and districts took counterproductive (e.g., "drill-and-kill" and "teaching-to-the-test") and even illegal measures (Jacob & Levitt, 2003; Merwin, Perry, & Pell, 2012) simply to boost test scores rather than improve student learning.

In addition, critics charge the enforcement mechanisms of NCLB, which were initially presented with much bluster, were never really applied. Many states simply ignored NCLB's requirement that "highly qualified" teachers be evenly spread within a district between economically advantaged and disadvantaged areas. Facing massive district protest and panic, the U.S. Department of Education almost immediately allowed states to apply for waivers from NCLB's rigorous accountability standards. Many of these waivers, for example, permitted schools to focus on individual student "growth" from one year to the next rather than hold all students to the same standards of academic progress. In the case of my five-student Math class, my school would have two years under NCLB to get the students who earned 40s and 50s on their assessments *all the way up to 70*, or else be deemed "not making AYP." But if my school principal obtains a waiver to get out from under this requirement, I would now be judged on how much progress my students made on test scores from year to year. If a student's score increased from 40 to 43 in one year, this would be counted in the school's favor, even though the student is far below the level of proficient. The problem with this type of waiver is that it allows the achievement gap to persist over time.

There were also a host of other criticisms based on the unintended consequences of NCLB. Critics suggested the law was causing teachers, parents, and students a great deal of unnecessary anxiety. Many teachers will tell you horror stories of the student in their class who vomited or fainted on the morning of the test (Cheek, Bradley, Reynolds, & Coy, 2002). The evaluation of teachers based on student test scores, it was argued, also led to massive teacher frustration and burnout, causing many to simply leave the field (Barrett, 2009; Mitani, 2018). States also devised many loopholes to their assessment systems that effectively rendered NCLB's accountability requirements meaningless. For example, many schools implemented a practice called "triaging" in which they focused an inordinate amount of energy on students who were near the proficiency level and ignored those who were above or very behind (see Neal & Schanzenbach, 2010). There was also a practice known as "strategic staffing" in which more effective teachers were placed in tested-subjects and less effective teachers in non-tested-subjects (see Grissom, Kalogrides, & Loeb, 2017). Others charged that schools unnecessarily suspended poorly performing students to boost test scores (Figlio, 2006) or abused special education categories to hide poor results by administering a different (easier) assessment (Figlio & Getzler, 2002).

I do not have sufficient space to address all of the criticisms of NCLB, so will organize my response into three major categories: criticisms based on things that are just not in the law, criticisms which are on point, and criticisms which are off base.

Criticisms of things not in the law. First, many of the criticisms of NCLB are about problematic things going on in schools, but these things are not caused or required by the law. Instead, they occurred as a result of panicked, unethical, or misinformed interpretations of what NCLB's requirements were. For example, there was nothing in the law that required instructional time to become so top-heavy toward Math and English. The architects of NCLB correctly determined that performance in Math and English in the K-12 years is predictive of college success in a way that performance in social studies, or art, or PE is not. Consider the subjects assessed on the SAT test as a simple example. There is no PE or art component. Math and English were stressed in NCLB because those subjects form the heart of the rigorous, college prep curriculum all states have adopted for their students. The fact that schools inordinately focused on these subjects was not necessarily because these were the only subjects assessed under the law, but because student performance in these subjects was so dreadfully poor. Since the achievement situation was so bad, most schools found they needed a large amount of instructional time to try and make these deficits up. Instruction in other subjects often went by the wayside. Further, if NCLB required the testing of even more subjects, schools would have had to scramble even more than they already did to achieve proficiency in these additional subjects.

There is also nothing in the law which required the U.S. Department of Education to immediately grant states waivers from the law's rigorous sanctions and accountability measures or to unevenly apply the requirements for highly qualified teachers. The fact that it did so is no flaw of the law, but a failure of executive authority. In addition, there is nothing in the law that required teachers to "drill and kill" students, "teach to the test," or deliver an excessive amount of "benchmark tests" each month. *NCLB required one annual test.* Some studies indicate that students in the United States are not tested very much at all compared with students in other countries (Barshav, 2015). I suggest this "too much testing" critique is vastly overstated. If students were doing well on these end-of-year tests, schools would never have had to implement all the additional benchmark testing to ensure they made the long, step-wise journey to proficiency. This is not a flaw in the law, but a reflection of how poor student achievement is.

Similarly, there is nothing in the law which required schools to devise all manner of administrative tricks, even to cheat to boost test performance. Again, the fact that so many schools and districts felt they needed to do these things is not a defect of the law, but a reflection of the fact that student performance in the tested-subjects was so poor, and that some administrators and teachers had poor ethical character. At the end of the day, if children were acing their end-of-year state standards tests, nobody would have had a problem with NCLB.

On-point criticisms. Other criticisms of NCLB are directly on-point and I say, "guilty as charged!" For example, NCLB relied completely on teachers and schools to boost academic performance, ignoring factors like family involvement in education and poverty which have as much or more of an impact on educational performance as teachers do. Without a concerted, national approach to poverty, simply holding schools to rigorous educational initiatives is ineffective and possibly counterproductive. NCLB also should have had requirements for parental involvement in schooling, but lawmakers were worried about losing lawsuits over the matter. It was also highly unfortunate, tragic even, that Congress did not provide adequate funding for tutoring and extra help for underperforming students. It is to Congress' great shame that they did not, but again, the provision of funding was part of the law. In the end, teachers were left to provide all the academic improvement in NCLB and were blamed when students underperformed. The problem with NCLB is not evaluating students by standardized test performance, but expecting teachers to be the ones responsible for all the learning.

Misguided criticisms. Other criticisms of NCLB are just misguided. For example, the notion that the Federal government should have *no* role in K-12 education ignores both case law and the Constitution. NCLB was explicitly designed to enable children from disadvantaged backgrounds to have the same access to quality schools as those from advantaged backgrounds. The individual states were failing to ensure that all children had the same access to quality schools. This is a civil rights issue, which puts it squarely into Federal territory. NCLB did not mandate what should be taught in schools, but that all students should be able to attend a quality school with a quality teacher no matter where they live, and that all students should be held to the same performance standards. Dealing with educational inequality is exactly what the Federal role in public schools should be under the 14th Amendment and general welfare clauses of the Constitution. As I will try to show, the real problem people had with NCLB was not the tests or the Federal role in education, *but the poor scores on these tests.* To make this case, I make a close examination of the test results when NCLB was first implemented.

The Real Reason Why NCLB Caused So Much Trouble

NCLB suggested the National Assessment of Educational Progress (NAEP) should be used to evaluate whether the law was working or not. The NAEP is a Congressionally-mandated initiative administered by the U.S. Department of Education. It is an assessment of what students know in the major subjects of mathematics, reading, writing, and science, plus art, civics, economics, geography, technology, and U.S. history for the grades after elementary school. In 2003, the year after NCLB started, only 31% of the nation's fourth graders was "proficient" in Math and only 30% in Reading (National Assessment of Educational Progress, n.d.-a). The scale for Reading and Math ranges from 0 to 500 points. The performance gap between white and black fourth-grade students on the NEAP in Math was 27 points (243 vs. 216) and 31 points (229 vs. 198) for Reading (National Assessment of Educational Progress, n.d.-b). The achievement gap was a few points smaller in 2003 between white and Hispanic, and white and disability. There is also a smaller, but still significant performance gap in 2003 between students who were eligible for free lunch and those who were not. In 2007–2008, a few years after NCLB's passage, the overall percentage of public schools identified as failing to make AYP for one or more years based on test scores was *35% of all public schools.* Some states had as many as 80% of their schools and some with as few as 7% not making AYP (Congressional Research Service, 2009).

I vividly recall the protest and the panic during those first years after NCLB was "rolled out" from Washington. It was chaotic and stressful for everyone involved. I sat in trainings and meetings where there was shouting, crying, and misunderstanding all around. The communication was sometimes very poor, and many teachers were inadequately prepared by their districts and principals for the requirements of this law. At the same time, I could not shake the nagging sense that much of the hysteria was simply overblown. I saw the tests which were causing all the controversy. I thought they were quite reasonable and accurately reflected what we were teaching the children all year. They did not seem unfair or biased in any way. All manner of accommodation was provided to students with special needs and everyone was given ample instruction during the year on the mechanics of taking these tests. The problem was that principals and teachers knew many of their students were going to do terribly on these tests and all the world would soon know it. This is exactly what happened. Everyone was now looking for someone to blame.

I realize many people feel passionately about this "testing" issue and that my defense of standardized tests is out of step with what is often written by educational researchers. Before you throw the book against the wall in disgust, take a breath. Forget all you have heard about "standardized testing" and "teacher accountability," and just take a good, honest look at the tests for yourself. After that, look at the list of standards students are expected to learn in a given grade level. When I do this, what I see is that for the most part state standardized tests accurately and fairly assess how well students know the elements of the rigorous, college prep curriculum I discussed in Chap. 7. It is not that the tests are hard or unfair, *it is that the curriculum is hard*. The curriculum was designed to be challenging and to prepare children for college and a high-skilled career in a way no curriculum had ever before. While not all people enter college or a high-skilled career by a long shot, we now expect all students to be "proficient" in a college prep curriculum! If we insist on a college prep curriculum for all students, then yearly assessment is required since so many students fall behind so early. We must have a reliable way to identify who these students are so we can get them the help they need.

End-of-year state assessments are competency tests, not intelligence tests. While IQ measures how capable a child is to learn in general, competency tests measure what a child has actually learned in particular. This is an important difference. When a child does poorly on a competency test, it usually (though not always) means the child does not know or has not learned what is being asked in the question. It is very rare that a student does poorly on a standardized test and then demonstrates these competencies in real life. I will consider a few examples from the third-grade test from my own state's *Georgia Milestones* exam, formerly known as the *Criterion-Referenced Competency Test* (*CRCT*) exam. All test items come from the state practice guide which contains sample questions from past exams (Georgia Department of Education, 2018). Miss Thomas' second-grade students will take this test next year. The following is an item from the Reading test:

> Ashley plays basketball well, but Tina is _____. Which word BEST completes the sentence?
>
> A. gooder
> B. more good
> C. better
> D. best

The question is designed to assess Georgia standard ELAGSE3L1g, which expects that students will be able to "Demonstrate command of the conventions of standard English grammar and usage when writing or speaking" including the ability to "Form and use comparative and superlative adjectives and adverbs, and choose between them depending on what is to be modified." Recall teachers are given these standards by the state or district, and spend most of their class time teaching them throughout the school day. Miss Thomas likely had students write this standard down, and she explicitly devoted many lessons and practice sessions to this standard.

What does it mean that more than half of Georgia's third graders do not know the correct answer is "C?" What other way is there to interpret choosing a wrong answer than that a student does not know this convention of English grammar? Do we believe a student might choose "gooder" as the correct answer on this test and then in his or her own writing and speaking in daily life use comparative adverbs correctly? Surely some students might be having a bad test day or are terribly anxious, but 55%? It is more likely that getting this question wrong indicates many more grammatical errors the student likely makes in real life.

Later in this same exam, students read a four-paragraph informational essay on tortoises from the Galapagos Islands. The essay is about how the tortoise population has been endangered, and how government efforts to increase their numbers have been succeeding. The question reads:

Which sentence BEST states the main idea of the passage?

A. Though Galápagos tortoises used to live only on some islands, they are now found in many places.
B. People are helping the Galápagos tortoises in many ways so that the number of tortoises is going up.
C. Removing goats from the islands of Galápagos tortoises has helped increase the food supply for tortoises.
D. Galápagos tortoises and turtles are similar, but turtles have not experienced as many problems as tortoises.

The standard assessed in this section of the exam is Georgia standard ELAGSE3RI2, "Determine the main idea of a text; recount the key details and explain how they support the main idea." Again, Miss Thomas and other teachers have been teaching and practicing this standard for months, if not years. They have read countless essays and responded to numerous analytical prompts about determining the main idea and supporting details.

The correct answer is "B." Incorrect answer choices have information that is either not in the essay or is a mentioned detail extraneous to the essay's main point. Again, I do not know how to construe a wrong answer choice as indicating anything other than the fact that the child does not yet know how to read a passage of text to be able to decipher its main idea. They may be poor readers and do not take much from the passage at all. Or they may recall key details, which is good, but they confuse these details with the larger point. The inability to perform this task will have negative ramifications for next year when the class moves on to more complex skills that are based on this competency.

I provide one more example from the Reading portion of the *Milestones* test. After answering a few more multiple-choice questions about the tortoise passage, the child is then given a lined test booklet and these instructions, "Explain how the author uses cause and effect to connect ideas in paragraphs 3 and 4. Use details from the article to support your answer. Write your answer on the lines of your answer document." This question is designed to assess Georgia standard ELAGSE3RI8, "Describe the logical connection between particular sentences and paragraphs in a text (e.g., comparison, cause/effect, first/second/third in a sequence)." Students have learned and practiced this standard over and over in class. It is not new information by any means. A model answer found in the study guide looks like this, "The author uses cause and effect to show how people have changed the number of tortoises on the island. Paragraph 3 shows how people caused the number of tortoises to go down. It says people brought goats to the island, and the goats ate all the grass that the tortoises normally ate. Also, sailors ate the tortoises. Paragraph 4 shows the effects of people taking away the goats and bringing more tortoises to the island. The effect is there are now more tortoises on the island than there have been in the last 40 years" (Georgia Department of Education, 2018).

The teacher has likely taught this style of analytical writing, modeled this standard in her own writing in front of the class, and had the students practice it themselves on numerous occasions. But on the test, more than half of students respond with an answer that looks like this, "This article talks about tortoises on islands. They are not happy. Tortoise numbers grow and change all the time. Many people are very worried." Students would not receive any points for an answer like this because it addresses neither cause and effect nor paragraphs 3 and 4. Low scores on these items are not just "scores on standardized tests," but clear and convincing data that the student does not demonstrate the knowledge and skills that have previously been taught.

I consider a few more examples, but these come from the Math portion of the same third-grade *Milestones* test. Students are given a question like this:

An equation is shown. 8 × ? = 64. What is the missing number that makes the equation true?

A. 8
B. 9
C. 56
D. 72

This question is designed to assess Georgia standard MGSE3.OA.4, "Determine the unknown whole number in a multiplication or division equation relating three whole numbers using the inverse relationship of multiplication and division." As much as critics charge that standardized tests merely assess "rote information," this question demands that students go beyond mere memorization of multiplication algorithms to deeper concepts. The correct answer is "A." What could it mean that a student would select "72," or "9," or "56" other than that this student does not fully understand multiplication?

Another item has the students respond to this question:

Solve. 724 + 152 =

A. 776
B. 875
C. 876
D. 975

This item is designed to assess Georgia standard MGSE3.NBT.2, "Fluently add and subtract within 1000 using strategies and algorithms based on place value, properties of operations, and/or the relationship between addition and subtraction." The question does not ask the student to "carry," but it tests whether they properly can line up the numerals in a three-digit number so as to correctly perform addition on it. What would getting this item wrong mean other than that a child cannot fluently add numbers within 1000 and does not understand place value? And what will it mean for next year when they start to add numbers within 10,000?

As I discussed in Chap. 7, in the years leading up to NCLB, all states developed and adopted a challenging K-12 college prep curriculum filled with standards like the ones I just described from Georgia. This college prep curriculum begins as early as Kindergarten. In NCLB, Congress required that in ten years, all children must be "proficient" in their own state's college prep standards, usually by earning a 70% on state standardized tests (along with other measures). But the results turned out to be a disaster for many students and schools. Some entire schools and some students within most schools did very well on these tests. At the same time, many schools, and many students within most schools did very poorly on these tests. Instead of addressing this gap in achievement, states swept their problems under the carpet by watering down their tests or seeking waivers for failing to make AYP. The strict accountability provisions of NCLB were diluted each year after the law's passage and never really given a chance to succeed. By mid-2012, more than half the states had obtained waivers, so most of the country did not operate under the NCLB the way it was written. Its political support had completely hemorrhaged.

Life After NCLB

In 2015, Congress passed the *Every Student Succeeds Act* (ESSA) to replace what had become the wildly unpopular NCLB. ESSA was an attempt to deal with the political backlash from NCLB by rolling back the federal role in K-12 education and its stringent accountability requirements for poor academic progress. ESSA keeps some important things from NCLB. For example, ESSA still requires academic testing of students one time per year in reading and math, and requires the public reporting of disaggregated data. It still seeks to close achievement gaps and promises (woefully inadequate) funding to do so.

Unfortunately, ESSA removes the NCLB goal that every student in every school be proficient in reading and math. It extols the virtues of *UDL*, or *Universal Design for Learning*, a problematic teaching model which I will discuss in the next chapter. It allows the use of other tests to assess academic performance in addition to state tests and considers other factors besides math and reading test scores in evaluating schools. For example, in addition to standardized tests, ESSA now also allows the use of English-language proficiency test scores, high school graduation rates, a state-chosen academic measure for grade schools (like "growth" in reading or math scores), and a "school-quality factor" like Kindergarten readiness, school climate and safety, or chronic absenteeism to assess how well schools are educating students. These are all much weaker measures of student knowledge than competency test scores.

Perhaps most importantly of all, under ESSA there are now no penalties for schools whose students who fail to reach proficiency. Instead, these schools are granted more funding and told to develop a "plan to improve." ESSA also effectively hands oversight authority back to the state governments which NCLB and the original ESEA of 1965 sought to regulate due to their proven inability to deal with large achievement gaps. ESSA keeps the same high academic standards and yearly assessment requirements, but removes NCLB's strict accountability measures and sanctions. It is therefore a serious concern that the unacceptable performance of millions of students will continue unaddressed for many more years to come.

As worrisome as this all is, it is a testament to NCLB's lasting impact that today we debate *how* schools must demonstrate the academic performance of their students rather than *whether* they should. We can surely quibble over whether the changes brought by ESSA are improvements in how to demonstrate academic performance. I think they are not, but we shall see. At least we all now expect schools to show evidence that all students are learning what is being taught. Despite the many noble intentions of NCLB, our schools today are in many important ways no better than they were in 2002 when the law was first passed. The achievement gap today is more (see Hanushek & Raymond, 2005) or less (see Dee & Jacob, 2010) exactly where it was in 2002. In 2017, only 35% of schools was proficient in Reading (up from 30% in 2003). Only 40% of schools was proficient in Math (up from 31% in 2003). These are marginal increases for sure, *but far from the 100% proficiency required by the original NCLB law*. In 2013, the achievement gap between black and white on the NEAP in Math was 26 points (it was 27 in 2003) and 26 points for Reading (it was 31 points in 2003). Disparities between other identified groups are similar. Ironically, nearly a generation of students has literally been "left behind" as we have idly bickered over the federal role in education and standardized tests. Far too many students do not learn the literacy and numeracy skills of the college prep Platonic curriculum. Of course, some are doing just fine, go to college, and/or succeed in a high-skilled career. But many do not despite more than a decade of college prep classes.

Why does this underperformance problem persist? Rather than blame bad teachers or society, there are a few explanations which are closer to the mark. First, getting underperforming students the help they need is a huge and expensive undertaking, requiring far more than high standards and inadequate federal dollars for extra help. It would include much smaller classrooms, at least two qualified instructors per room, tutoring, and even summer school for some students. This would be extremely expensive, and the public does not seem ready for that price tag. Second, addressing the achievement gap must involve other "stakeholders" besides the schools and teachers. These parties include families, parents, neighborhoods, and the students themselves. It is possible to hold states accountable for poor test performance without blaming teachers and schools. We must widen the net of accountability. These additional stakeholders are the ones who can help put a serious dent in chronic problems of student misbehavior, low academic engagement and motivation, poor attitude, and lack of support of academic activity in the student's life outside the classroom. We have tried to hold schools and teachers accountable for low test scores, but we have not yet developed the courage to demand accountability from families and neighborhoods. There are programs underway to increase family and community engagement, but these initiatives lack any meaningful consequences for failing to comply.

Finally, the achievement gap problem persists because we avoid having the conversation about whether the rigorous, college prep curriculum we have developed for the K-12 grades is appropriate for all students, whether all students want to attend college, or can succeed in college if they do enroll. When I consider the high school dropout rates, low college graduation rates, surveys on children's attitudes toward school, common behavior problems in school, students who consistently underperform and earn low assessment scores, I am prompted to wonder whether the hyper Platonic curriculum we have set up for nearly all elementary students works for all of them. Perhaps an entirely different approach to the curriculum is in order. As noble as our college prep-for-all educational project is, we must think long and hard about whether it is the only or best approach for all. Should we continue to push the Platonic curriculum all through middle and high school until underperforming students are old enough to drop out and leave in humiliation? Or might we consider a variety of educational goals for the multiplicity of students who take widely different paths in life.

What You Can Do
No parent wants their child to be "left behind." But things only look this way when we have just one road to success. Not attending college or succeeding in the college prep curriculum is not necessarily to be "left behind." If a child has discovered what he or she loves and learns how to do it in school, perhaps this is complete success. There should be many ways to succeed in school, not just one. Here are some things to do to lessen the pressure on our children to see their success in life in terms of whether they are "ahead" by going to college or "behind" by doing something else.

1. Regularly check your child's state standardized test performance measures. Review the disaggregated test results from your school as well. Take each year's results as a gauge of your child's readiness for college.
2. Low test scores may be a sign of a poor teacher or even a poor school. It may also reflect too much time your student spent disengaged from class, not enough time spent doing homework, and too much time engaging video games or other screen devices. Persistently low scores that cannot be chalked up to a bad teacher or bad day may be a sign that your child is not interested in (or good at) the Platonic aspect of the curriculum.
3. I believe many children are called to other life paths which are not academic or intellectual, and do not involve college. These are to be celebrated as much as we celebrate college. We must expand the definition of "success" to include all different types of jobs, blue collar and white collar.
4. If you want your child to go to college, it is important to realize it will require a lot of work not only on the teacher and school's part, but on your child's and your part as well. Unless college prep learning is supported at home, it will not happen for most children merely from attending school. What this means is that you must help your child prepare for school each evening as well as for the state tests at the end of the year. Your school provides many resources to do this. Use them.
5. Show your child in tangible ways that you value school by attending all parent-teacher conferences and if you can,

(continued)

(continued)

Parent-Teacher Association (PTA) meetings. Volunteer for a school event at least once per year. Ask to see all homework assigned for the next day. Read to your child at night.

6. Help the state and federal government make every school equal in quality. Support candidates who support *state*, rather than local funding of schools. There is no way for schools to provide equal education if half the funding for schools comes from local property taxes. For example, the Chicago Ridge School District spends an average of $9794 per pupil per year, while Rondout District 72 less than an hour north spends $28,639 per pupil per year (National Public Radio, 2016). This is a typical scenario. All education monies should be put into a single state pot and then divided equally per pupil among the various districts no matter how affluent or impoverished. This is a hugely unpopular proposal that will require struggle and political courage, but it is the right thing to do.
7. Support smart and effective anti-poverty programs at the federal, state, and local level. In addition, work to create a climate to ensure that manufacturing and other high-skilled jobs which do not require college are not sent overseas. This may entail paying more for certain products, enacting tariffs, or paying higher taxes, but it is far better than having an economy where the only jobs are either those which require college or low-skilled retail work.

References

Amrein, A. T., & Berliner, D. C. (2003). The effects of high-stakes testing on student motivation and learning. *Educational Leadership, 60*(5), 32–38.

Anderson, P. M., Butcher, K. F., & Schanzenbach, D. W. (2017). Adequate (or adipose?) yearly progress: Assessing the effect of "no child left behind" on children's obesity. *Education Finance and Policy, 12*(1), 54–76.

Arbuthnot, K. (2011). *Filling in the blanks: Standardized testing and the black-white achievement gap*. Charlotte, NC: Information Age Publishing.

Barnes, W., & Slate, J. R. (2013). College-readiness is not one-size-fits-all. *Current Issues in Education, 16*(1), 1–12.

Barrett, B. D. (2009). No child left behind and the assault on teachers' professional practices and identities. *Teaching and Teacher Education, 25*(8), 1018–1025. https://doi.org/10.1016/j.tate.2009.03.021

Barshav, J. (2015, December 7). Education myth: American students are overtested. *The Hetchinger Report.* Retrieved from https://hechingerreport.org/24830-2/

Berlak, H. (2005). From local control to government and corporate takeover of school curriculum: The no child left behind act and the reading first program. In H. S. Shapiro & D. E. Purpel (Eds.), *Critical social issues in American education: Democracy and meaning in a globalizing world* (3rd ed., pp. 267–285). Mahwah, NJ: Lawrence Erlbaum Associates Publishers.

Breunig, M. (2014, August 22). Michelle Rhee's real legacy: Here's what's most shameful about her reign. *Salon.* Retrieved from https://www.salon.com/2014/08/22/michelle_rhees_real_legacy_heres_whats_most_shameful_about_her_reign/

Cheek, J. R., Bradley, L. J., Reynolds, J., & Coy, D. (2002). An intervention for helping elementary students reduce test anxiety. *Professional School Counseling, 6*(2), 162–164. Retrieved from https://www.gadoe.org/Curriculum-Instruction-and-Assessment/Assessment/Documents/Milestones/Study-Resource%20Guides/GM_GR03_Study_Guide_7.5.18.pdf

Congressional Research Service. (2009). Adequate yearly progress (AYP): Implementation of the No Child Left Behind Act. Retrieved from https://www.everycrsreport.com/reports/RL32495.html

Dee, T. S., & Jacob, B. (2011). The impact of No Child Left Behind on student achievement. *Journal of Policy Analysis and Management, 30,* 418–446.

Figlio, D. N. (2006). Testing, crime and punishment. *Journal of Public Economics, 90*(4), 837–851. https://doi.org/10.1016/j.jpubeco.2005.01.003

Figlio, D. N., Getzler, L. S. (2002). *Accountability, ability, and disability: Gaming the system.* National Bureau of Economic Research Working Paper 9307 [PDF File]. Retrieved from https://www.nber.org/papers/w9307.pdf

Flattau, P. E., Bracken, J., Van Atta, R., Bandeh-Ahmadi, A., de la Cruz, R., & Sullivan, K. (2006). The National Defense Education Act of 1958: Selected outcomes [PDF File]. Retrieved from https://www.ida.org/idamedia/Corporate/Files/Publications/STPIPubs/D-3306.pdf

Georgia Department of Education. (2018). Georgia milestone assessment system: Study/resource guide for students and parents grade 3. Retrieved from https://www.gadoe.org/Curriculum-Instruction-and-Assessment/Assessment/Documents/Milestones/Study-Resource%20Guides/GM_GR03_Study_Guide_7.5.18.pdf

Grissom, J. A., Kalogrides, D., & Loeb, S. (2017). Strategic staffing? How performance pressures affect the distribution of teachers within schools and resulting student achievement. *American Educational Research Journal, 54*(6), 1079–1116.

Hanushek, E. A., & Raymond, M. E. (2005). Does school accountability lead to improved student performance? *Journal of Policy Analysis and Management, 24*(2), 297–327.

Harris, P., Smith, B. M., & Harris, J. (2011). *The myths of standardized tests: Why they don't tell you what you think they do.* Lanham, MD: Rowman & Littlefield Publishers.

Henley, J., McBride, J., Milligan, J., & Nichols, J. (2007). Robbing elementary students of their childhood: The perils of no child left behind. *Education, 128*(1), 56–63.

Jacob, B. A., & Levitt, S. D. (2003). Rotten apples: An investigation of the prevalence and predictors of teacher cheating. *The Quarterly Journal of Economics, 118*(3), 843–877.

Jellig, J. (2013, November 12). In defense of NCLB: One school's journey toward intentional practice. *Education Week.* Retrieved from https://www.edweek.org/ew/articles/2013/11/13/12jellig_ep.h33.html

McMurrer, J. (2007). *NCLB year 5: Choices, changes and challenges: Curriculum and instruction in the NCLB era.* Washington, DC: Center on Education Policy.

Merwin, E., Perry, J., & Pell, M. B. (2012). [Interactive map of school districts with suspect test scores]. *Suspect scores, substantiated cheating.* Retrieved from https://www.ajc.com/news/special-reports/suspect-scores-substantiated-cheating/0bX3nYl6hOxX9uCC96uymK

Mitani, H. (2018). Principals' working conditions, job stress, and turnover behaviors under NCLB accountability pressure. *Educational Administration Quarterly, 54*(5), 822–862. https://doi.org/10.1177/0013161X18785874

National Assessment of Educational Progress. (n.d.-a). State performance compared to the nation: Grade 4 reading 2003 [Interactive map and data set]. Retrieved from https://www.nationsreportcard.gov/profiles/stateprofile?chort=1&sub=RED&sj=&sfj=NP&st=AP&year=2003R3

National Assessment of Educational Progress. (n.d.-b). Which student groups are making gains? [Data and results for mathematics 4th grade]. Retrieved from https://www.nationsreportcard.gov/reading_math_2013/#/gains-by-group

National Public Radio. (2016, April 18). Why America's schools have a money problem [Radio broadcast and article]. Retrieved from https://www.npr.org/2016/04/18/474256366/why-americas-schools-have-a-money-problem

Neal, D., & Schanzenbach, D. W. (2010). Left behind by design: Proficiency counts and test-based accountability. *Review of Economics and Statistics, 92*(2), 263–283.

Noddings, N. (2013). *Education and democracy in the 21st century.* New York, NY: Teachers College Press.

CHAPTER 10

I'm Five Teachers at Once!

About 45 minutes is left in the school day. The test assembly really threw Miss Thomas' schedule off, so instead of her scheduled Physical Education class, she had to adjust by assigning 25 minutes of independent reading. "Take out your pleasure reading book and go to your reading spot," she tells the students. "OK? You have 10 seconds." She counts down, "10, 9, 8…" She reminds the students as they scamper to their desks, "Be sure to pick a 'just right book.'" She whispers to you that many students tend to pick big thick books for independent reading to impress their neighbors. But the books are often far too difficult for them. A "just right book" is one color-coded to the student's Lexile reading level.

You are impressed with how quickly the students settle into their reading spots. Some lay on the floor with their books. Some go to a corner. Others sit quietly at their desks. As you wander around the room, what strikes you at first is the wide variety of reading levels in this single second-grade class. Some students deftly read the 766-page *Harry Potter and the Order of the Phoenix*, a book on a sixth-grade reading level. Others struggle mightily with *Pete the Cat*, a book on a Kindergarten level. Still others are right at grade level, carefully reading *Dog Man* or *Amelia Bedelia*.

You quietly mention to Miss Thomas the wide range of abilities in the room. She says, "Yeah, we used to track the students into different class sections when I first started here, but now they want us to teach all the kids in the same room at the same time. It's like they expect me to be five teachers at once!" She mentions she recently got "dinged" on her evaluation by the principal for not "differentiating" her lesson enough to accommodate her students' varying abilities and learning styles. Now that she mentions it, you recall Miss Thomas' Math lesson from earlier in the day. It was quite different from your own memories of elementary school. You recall your teachers standing in front of the room, explaining a concept or operation in a "lecture," and then inviting students to practice the skill themselves. Miss Thomas, on the other hand, briefly introduced her Math lesson on comparing fractions, mentioned a few ideas and operations, but then broke the group into six rotating "centers." At one center, students watched a video from Khan Academy on comparing fractions, another center made graphs representing different fractions, another read the section from their textbook on fractions, another completed sample fraction problems on a worksheet, and still another sat at a table and listened to Miss Thomas teach about how to compare fractions. Students rotated centers every 15 minutes over the 90-minute period. This way of teaching is all part of what is known as "differentiation" or "differentiated instruction" (DI).

Much of the public has never heard of differentiation, but it is absolutely huge in educational circles. DI was taught as the preferred pedagogical method in all my education classes. I was required to take a whole class on differentiation called "The Differentiated Classroom." My college had mandatory special trainings for us pre-service teachers on differentiation which were conducted by various experts. There was a whole section on differentiation in the lesson plan template we had to use to construct all the lessons we taught in our placement schools (more than 50 total lessons).

When you get to your fieldwork in teaching, you learn that most principals, districts, and administrators expect that teachers will "differentiate" their lessons. I learned in my senior capstone seminar for education majors that when you are interviewing for teaching positions, questions about differentiation are the ones most frequently asked. You are given a real-world classroom scenario during your job interview and asked how you would "differentiate the lesson" for the diverse learners in the room. A quick and informed answer is obviously preferred. Full-time teachers must submit evidence of differentiation in the lesson plans they hand into their principals each week. And when teachers are observed and evaluated by principals and other administrators, differentiation is a crucial factor upon which they are evaluated.

What Is DI?

Tomlinson and Allan (2000) define differentiation as "a teacher's reacting responsively to a learner's needs" (p. 4). Consider the opposite of differentiation: a teacher instructs all her students with the same lesson, uses the same teaching materials, presents the same learning tasks, and then uses a single paper-and-pencil assessment for students to show what they know. When we "differentiate" a lesson, we respond to students' needs by varying what we teach (the content), how we teach it (the process), and what we ask students to do to demonstrate they know what we have taught (the product).

The first step in differentiating a lesson is to consider the different abilities, cultural histories, learning styles, and interests of all the students in the room. Johnny is a visual learner. Carlos has not yet mastered reading. Joyce likes to move around. Juan's family does not speak English at home. Jiahua has recently immigrated from China. Billy loves to play baseball. Juila is into Minecraft. When we differentiate, we modify our lesson to meet the many individual differences present in the classroom. We do this by varying our instructional strategies, the materials we use to teach, the tasks we ask students to perform, the learning environment, the emotional climate of the room, and the assessments we eventually use for students to demonstrate what they know, understand, or can do as a result of our teaching.

Consider the English/Language Arts lesson Miss Thomas taught earlier in the day, where students read a narrative about the Thanksgiving holiday. Instead of a lesson that asked all students to engage in the same classroom learning task, say doing a worksheet on outlining an essay, Miss Thomas' "differentiated" approach encouraged students to choose different learning tasks to practice their new knowledge. Some students were able to work with the storyline in a writing project, others were able to act out what they were learning in the story in a skit or role-play, while still others could draw timelines and make diagrams on a storyboard. Miss Thomas differentiated her learning environment by seating students who like to work in groups together in a circle, those who prefer solitary desk work seated alone, and those who need one-on-one attention next to her at her desk. At the end of the unit, Miss Thomas will allow students to choose how they are evaluated on their learning. Some will complete portfolios of their work, others will complete an end-of-unit project, others will work together in groups to compose a skit to show what they know, and still others will take a traditional paper-and-pencil exam.

It is clear to anyone facing a room full of children that they are all different. Some are interested in sports; some like anime movies. Some read at a sixth-grade level; others at a Kindergarten level. Some need to move around as they learn, while others can sit still and listen for hours. We try to adjust and meet students where they are because we teach *people*, not lessons. But Miss Thomas' quip about feeling like "five teachers at once" has a lot of truth in it. Rather than separate students of different abilities into separate classrooms, or what educational researchers call "homogeneous groups," differentiation seeks to reach students of differing interests and abilities by keeping them all together. This expresses a commitment to equality and avoids the purported negative effects of "tracking."

A Sympathetic Critique of DI

I have observed and used differentiation in a myriad of settings. I have listened to countless veteran teachers tell me what they think about the way differentiation is used in today's classrooms. These experiences have left me with some basic questions about DI which should at least temper the enthusiasm so many in the academy and the Administration have for it. While the basic principles and values behind differentiation make great sense, how far can a teacher bend in a wide-ability classroom before she starts to break? When we tailor our lesson to student interests, and vary our learning tasks and assessments, does it really enhance student learning? When might it be better to expect students to accommodate to a lesson rather than expecting the lesson to accommodate the student?

Flimsy empirical support. One of the most basic problems with differentiation as it is practiced in today's elementary schools is that it is hardly ever questioned by those in power. In all my years in elementary education, differentiation was never once held up for critical scrutiny by any of my professors, textbooks, supervising teachers, or school principals I worked for. At the same time, I never once saw any convincing data supporting differentiation or met an actual teacher who proclaimed its practical riches. All the fierce advocates were consultants, administrators, or researchers who had long-since left real classrooms. When a movement is taught and practiced without critical examination, when it promises big gains at almost no cost, and when it is met with rolled eyes from real teachers, it has "educational fad" written all over it.

The field of education is highly prone to the fads and fashions of the day. Administrators pick up ideas and new approaches at conferences where they are pushed by publishers, consultants, and book companies who want to sell the latest educational products to school districts. These expensive new packages are often backed up by flashy "data" and "empirical research." Though some of these fads have some educational value, they typically promise great rewards at very little cost. This high-reward-low-cost tune is music to the cash-strapped administrator's ear.

Once adopted by a critical mass of fellow administrators, the fad takes the educational world by storm. Sometimes wholesale changes are made to the entire school system. From my study of educational history, a fad tends to last between five and ten years. Once it collapses—and it always does—you never see it again. Fads in the history of education are like the bell-bottom jeans and lava lamps we have tucked deep in our attics. When we stand over the dusty boxes and look at them from the vantage point of history, we cannot believe how they ever could have been so popular. When I was a child in elementary school, the educational fad of the day was the "open classroom." This was a school that minimized the presence of walls, which were believed to prevent teachers from working collaboratively and to inhibit children's ability to learn in ways that suited their individual interests. All the schools were "open" when I grew up; they literally had no walls. After this fell out of fashion, administrators had to put up cubicles and makeshift walls in open classrooms, since entire buildings had been constructed without any boundaries. How many schools are "open" today? Before this, it was the "New Math," "Reform Mathematics," "Block Scheduling," "School-Based Management," the "Self-Esteem Movement," "Gifted Education," and so on. I imagine in ten years we will be saying, "Can you believe we were that into differentiation?"

For a movement to have such widespread administrative buy-in, you would think there was a mountain of supporting evidence behind it. But that is not the case with differentiation. By my count, there are only a handful of positive studies, and the data are hardly overwhelming. One commonly cited study to support the benefits of DI is Lewis and Batts' (2005) report on a North Carolina elementary school which began a school-wide differentiation program in response to poor 1998 test results. It is not clear from the study exactly what this "program" consisted of, but it appears to include using multiple teaching strategies in the classroom, varying group configurations depending on the students or the lesson (e.g., whole group, small groups, pairs, or independent work), emphasizing student strengths rather than deficits, recognizing different learning styles, considering student interests, and being clear with students about what is expected of them for a particular assignment.

Before starting differentiation, Lewis and Batts (2005) report that students had a proficiency rate of 79% on state end-of-grade tests. By national standards, this is more than two times the national proficiency average, hardly "poor" performance. In 2003–2004, after five years of differentiation, 94.8% of students scored at the proficient level, a 15-point increase. This "study" comes from a magazine article, not a peer-reviewed academic journal which has much higher quality control. It is highly anecdotal, contains no details about exactly what was implemented in the school, the characteristics of the students, and it has no control group. Plus, some of the things evaluated as part of the differentiation program, like being clear with students about what is expected of them for an assignment, are not an essential part of differentiation. We also do not know what else was implemented at the school during this five-year period which may have accounted for the test score increases. For example, the school may have implemented a discipline or expulsion program which skewed results, could have hired a team of talented teachers, started a tutoring program, and so on (see Fahey, 2000, for a similarly flawed and frequently cited anecdotal report).

Perhaps most importantly, Lewis and Batts (2005), and almost all other empirical studies of differentiation, do not examine differentiation's core claim: that differentiation is a better way of educating students of differing abilities than tracking them into different rooms for all or part of the day. A true control group would have separated students of similar abilities into separate rooms and compared their learning to students who remained in the "differentiated classroom." We also cannot tell from this study if differentiation made a difference with students of differing abilities because the results are all aggregated into the global 15-point increase. Perhaps the gifted students alone increased their scores and the average or struggling students did not.

Other studies cited in support of differentiation either lack or have misleading control groups. Baumgartner, Lipowski, and Rush's (2003) work is a frequently cited example in support of the effectiveness of DI. This study is an unpublished Master's thesis which examined a "differentiated instructional program" to boost reading performance in elementary and middle school students. Teaching strategies included student choice of learning tasks, flexible grouping, access to a range of texts rather than just one, and student-selected reading times. The authors report students receiving differentiated instruction improved their reading skills and attitudes toward reading, though no statistics are provided. We can therefore not tell how large these effects are. The study also does not compare DI to another intervention or to a control group of students who received no intervention or a different intervention. It is therefore impossible to determine if it was DI which improved reading skills and attitudes or whether the improvement was simply the result of getting some special, individual attention in the classroom, which then increased student motivation.

Similarly, in an often-cited study of 31 math teachers and 645 students, Tieso (2005) found that differentiated instruction kept high-ability students challenged in heterogeneous classrooms (as opposed, I assume, to separating them into their own classroom). These high-ability students who were taught using a differentiated approach demonstrated significantly higher scores on the post-tests than did the high-ability students taught using the textbook curriculum and whole-group instruction alone. But these are improvements compared to students who received no special instruction or ability grouping at all. These control students sat in large groups, were given no choice of what to read or do, were told when to read, had limited access to interesting texts, and did not interact with other students of similar abilities. It is hardly surprising that students in the experimental group showed some improvement given what they were able to do, but this comparison is not relevant to the argument about DI. The alternative to DI is not to teach all students the same way, but to separate them even further into ability groups in different rooms with different instructors (for similar studies which demonstrated positive effects of DI compared to misleading control groups, see Förster, Kawohl, & Souvignier, 2018; Ocampo, 2018; Valiandes, 2015; Mastropieri et al., 2006).

Many other studies cited in support of differentiation do not actually examine differentiation. For example, Odgers, Symons, and Mitchell (2000) employed various problem-solving tasks to "differentiate" science instruction in two mixed-ability classrooms. One set of prompts asks that students "bring prior knowledge" to the solution of the classroom tasks; the other group was not asked to do this. While having students bring prior knowledge, reflect upon, and evaluate their learning is pedagogically effective, it is not differentiation. Similarly, Gamoran and Weinstein (1998) examined differentiated instruction by looking at conditions such as small class size, extra resources, intellectual support, and commitment. They claim these factors have a significant effect on student achievement. This may be so, but none of these factors is about differentiation.

Nonexistent or irrelevant psychological categories. A second problem with DI is that it encourages teachers to categorize students based on popularized ideas like "learning styles" and "multiple intelligences" which may not actually exist, or if they do, are not helpful in making school-related material more accessible to students. Differentiated instruction most frequently asks teachers to address students' "preferred ways of learning" or "learning styles." *Learning styles* are defined as the different ways students approach the same leaning task. For example, some students tend to draw out the visual component of a lesson, while others focus on the auditory, or the kinesthetic, impulsive, reflective, right brain, or left brain component (see Keefe, 1979). The idea is that if Sally is a "visual learner," she will respond best when information is represented in diagrams or graphs. She will struggle if a teacher is merely lecturing without visual support since she will attend to what she sees (the teacher moving) rather than what she hears (the important spoken information). Sally will learn best if she can use pictorial forms to process and represent what she is learning (rather than writing with notes). The assumption is that a learning style is a relatively permanent preference for processing information in a particular way. The key point in the context of education is not only that students have these ingrained styles, but that teaching them in a way that accords with this style will lead to improved learning (e.g., Sims & Sims, 2006). Confidence in the educational benefit of learning styles is ubiquitous among administrators. Despite this widespread belief, there is not a lot of evidence for the existence of learning styles (see Geake, 2008; Lilienfeld, Lynn, Ruscio, & Beyerstein, 2010; Pashler, McDaniel, Rohrer, & Bjork, 2008; Rohrer & Pashler, 2012).

Further, the reliance on learning styles in the classroom may actually inhibit students' learning (Dandy & Bendersky, 2014; Pashler et al., 2008; Riener & Willingham, 2010; Willingham, Hughes, & Dobolyi, 2015). These potential harms include the "pigeonholing" of learners according to dubious assessments and shaky criteria. The label works to become a self-fulfilling prophecy with potentially debilitating effects. A "kinesthetic learner" for example, may not pursue tasks which do not accord with what the teacher has told them is their learning style (e.g., learning music or reading a book). Other possible dangers include wasting valuable teaching time and resources tailoring how we teach to these alleged preferences which may not yield many positive results. It also runs the risk of creating expectations of teachers by students and parents since the teacher is seen to somehow possess the key to the student's mind.

Another thing teachers are asked to do in DI is to consider the fact that students have multiple intelligences rather than just one. Multiple intelligence is often confused with learning style. While learning style refers to how a student approaches a learning task, *multiple intelligence* refers to different intellectual abilities, for example, interpersonal, musical, or linguistic (see Gardner, 2011). The theory of multiple intelligences comes mainly from the work of Harvard University psychologist Howard Gardner. Gardner (2011/1983) originally identified seven intelligences: spatial, linguistic, logical-mathematical, musical, bodily-kinesthetic, interpersonal, and intrapersonal. More recently, he added naturalistic intelligence as an additional intelligence (Gardner, 2006). You will find this theory in almost any textbook on elementary or secondary education.

Though its existence is questioned by some researchers (e.g., Waterhouse, 2006), there is more empirical support for the existence of multiple intelligence than there is for learning styles (Shearer & Karanian, 2017). However, when you take a close look at them, only a limited number of these eight intelligences are applicable to the school setting, and more generally, to later adult life. Murray (2008) notes that bodily-kinesthetic, naturalistic, and musical intelligence are important abilities to have in fewer than 100,000 total jobs in the United States. While they surely enrich adult life, and should be supported by the schools, these three intelligences do not comprise the core function of the education system, which mostly involves spatial intelligence, logical-mathematical intelligence, and linguistic intelligence. Murray (2008) calls these three intelligences together "academic ability" (p. 25). Academic ability is central to the Platonic curriculum, as it is integral to college readiness and high-skilled employment. The other intelligences simply are not.

While the Platonic curriculum does not explicitly address interpersonal and intrapersonal intelligence, these two abilities are surely necessary in adult life. They are indirectly developed in many schools through character education, team sports, clubs, and the normal problem-solving and decision-making procedures which most teachers must utilize in the classroom. They are not directly assessed by the state in any formal way and so tend not be a central focus in the classroom (other than in sorting out behavior problems and student conflicts). I will discuss this issue in more detail in Chap. 14, but I believe intrapersonal and interpersonal intelligence should become a much larger part of the formal school curriculum than it presently is.

While it may be true that we all have these eight intelligences, they are not equally important to adult life or success in school. A teacher's awareness and use of these eight abilities are therefore of limited value in an enterprise which is devoted to advancing academic ability through the Platonic curriculum. Perhaps more importantly, it is extremely rare for students to be highly developed in one intelligence and poorly developed in others. High intelligence tends to cluster and cross several intelligences at once. Thus, students who are high in musical intelligence, for example, also tend to be high in mathematical ability. In the rare case of the student who is of very high intelligence in music and very low intelligence for mathematics, using music to teach mathematics would not be effective, since these are distinct intelligences. We may ask the musical genius to write about music in an essay, but crafting the text will utilize his linguistic, not his musical intelligence. Consequently, the elementary school would not be the ideal forum to cultivate this child's high musical intelligence.

One of the problematic influences of the focus on multiple intelligence in DI is to foster a widespread belief among teachers that "every student is good at something." Thus, when a student performs poorly in Math or Reading (as they often do), the "differentiating teacher" will go on the hunt for that one area where the child is allegedly "gifted." As humane and compassionate as this belief is, there appears to be no empirical support for the claim that a child who is below average in one intelligence will have an equal chance of being above average in one of the other seven intelligences. As Murray (2008) writes, "The truth that people may possess many different abilities is unthinkingly transmuted into an untruth: that everyone is good at something, and that educators can use that something to make up for other deficits" (p. 29). It is simply not true that all children learn in different, but equally gifted ways and that all we teachers need to do is discover that special ability, that "inner giftedness" which resides in every child and then draw it out. Statistically speaking, most children are below average in all eight intelligences together (Murray, 2008, p. 32).

What do learning styles and multiple intelligences mean in the context of the Platonic curriculum, which primarily focuses on academic ability? To explore this question, let us go back to the lesson and test items from Chap. 8 which dealt with drawing out the main idea of a multi-paragraph essay. The ability to read a multi-paragraph essay and then to draw out the main point of the piece is a highly abstract cognitive-linguistic operation which does not depend on any sensory modality. If we have already decided that Billy is a "visual" learner and Kenia is an "auditory" learner, we may be tempted to allow Billy to watch a video on the story or to allow Kenia to hear the story read on an audiobook. The other students who do not have these "learning styles" may be asked to read the passage in the traditional way (and will likely benefit from that). Billy and Kenia, on the other hand, are now prepared to answer questions about the passage, but they have not learned to read it and will suffer when they are asked to do so again with an unfamiliar passage on their standardized tests.

Let us assume further that Billy and Kenia are struggling to read, understand, and draw out the main idea of the passage. They may be getting low scores on the pre-assessments we give them. We may conclude this task focuses on "linguistic intelligence," and that Billy and Kenia are both not "high" in that area. Billy has higher "musical intelligence," while Kenia is higher in "kinesthetic intelligence." Because of this rather unhelpful information, we now become a little less worried about their failure to adequately read the passage. We may even allow Billy to listen to a rap song which contains the theme of the passage and then write his own rhymes instead of reading and writing about the informational essay. Or we allow Kenia to watch an interpretive dance on the theme of the passage and construct her own response through movement. We may feel we have been accommodating and "student-centered" here, but at the end of the day, each student has not actually mastered the standard.

A preference to have information presented in a sensory modality or to utilize nonacademic intelligences can easily become a bad habit that is reinforced by a teacher's constant focus on learning styles or multiple intelligence. When anyone learns abstract cognitive and linguistic operations, they need the aid of concrete examples. Ideally, the teacher will use sensory examples to teach an abstract skill, but will eventually "remove the training wheels" as it were, and expect the student to perform the operation without examples or concrete support. The focus on learning styles and preferred intelligences can wind up simply affirming the student in their current modality-preference or ability, rather than challenging them to stretch and do things differently than they may prefer or are used to. And what message do we teachers send when we are the ones always doing the accommodating? What is wrong with asking Billy to become less visual when he reads? Asking Kenia to become less auditory?

Borders on tracking. As mentioned earlier, when DI is implemented in today's schools, teachers are typically required to keep all students of varying abilities together in the same room and "differentiate" a single lesson, rather than separating the students into different "tracks" or "homogeneous groups" where they receive instruction in separate rooms at their ability level. "Within-class grouping" or "ability grouping" is often promoted as a way of dealing with the often-vast diversity in a single classroom, while avoiding the potentially negative effects of tracking (Chorzempa & Graham, 2006). Schools currently shy away from different rooms for different abilities because it is believed it will hurt child's feelings or create negative stigmas. But no matter how subtly you do it or cutely you name the ability groups, children know right away who is in the "high" group and who in the "low." While there are surely some benefits to keeping all students in the same room, within-class grouping also has its own negative effects.

Depending on the ability range in the class, within-class grouping can seriously dilute instruction, mask persistent student underperformance, and/or fail to adequately challenge high-performing students. Consider this scenario from Miss Thomas' Science lesson earlier in the day on the digestive system. The standard of the lesson was, "Construct an argument that plants and animals have internal and external structures that function to support survival, growth, behavior, and reproduction." Miss Thomas started this lesson off by reading the whole class a short informational text aloud about digestion. She then showed a brief video and did a bit of lecture on important terms and concepts. The differentiation started after that. She broke the class into four ability groups (Knights, Bears, Astronauts, and Ghosts). She then gave each group different texts and projects to complete based on their abilities. She gave the Bears (the "highest" performing group) complex texts to use for their work, a detailed diagram of the digestive system which they were to complete together as a group, and then a writing prompt where each student was to explain how food is processed by the human body. She gave the Astronauts (the "lowest" performing group) a single easy text for their work, an extremely simple picture to complete together as a group, and a worksheet (not an essay) dealing with the way food is processed by the human body.

The Bears learned such terms as anus, bile ducts, colon, esophagus, small intestine, rectum, duodenum, gallbladder, liver, pancreas, stomach, trachea, and upper gastrointestinal (GI) tract. They explained how each of these parts works together in digestion and so mastered the standard. The Astronauts, on the other hand, worked only with the terms mouth, stomach, and anus. They used these words to fill in blanks on a diagram sheet and did not explain how they all worked together. This "differentiated" lesson pretends it is the same lesson, teaching the same standard to the whole group, but it is not. It is basically "tracking" in a single room and a terribly inefficient way of dealing with children of different abilities. For the low-ability group, the students' work does not come close to meeting the standard. Over time, this will increase rather than decrease achievement gaps.

Differentiation is supposed to use different instructional modalities to achieve the *same learning goals*, not use different modalities to reach different goals. Recall the original intention of the *Elementary and Secondary Education Act* (ESEA) (and the *No Child Left Behind Act* [NCLB]) was to hold all students to the same standards and insist they all achieve them. Under the law, we are not supposed to differentiate the *curriculum*, but our *instruction* of a single curriculum. In practice, however, the curricular goals often change under DI. Actual standards are unrecognizable between ability groups, as was evident in Miss Thomas' Science lesson. One group is at best "beginning" to approach the standard, and another "exceeds" it.

All classrooms have some children who achieve learning goals more quickly and easily than others. The assumption we must make under ESEA and NCLB (and *Every Student Succeeds Act*) is that everyone is equally able to meet the standards, just that some lack the background knowledge, or the material is presented in an alien learning style, or struggling students need to relearn concepts they have forgotten or never learned adequately. The point is *struggling students need more time than the rest of the group*. The tragedy is that most schools are not able to vary learning time. We have 55 minutes scheduled for Math and then we all move on as a group. The students who need more time do not get it at all, or they only get a fraction of the time they need. Some may get a little extra time for Math or Reading with a specialist, but this will come at a cost of their being "pulled" from other instruction, and is usually for 25 minutes two times per week. Despite vastly different abilities, students are forced to learn what they can under DI in the time allotted to the whole group. The Bears master the duodenum and the process of digestion; the Astronauts have a diffuse conception of the stomach and move on to the next subject frustrated and behind.

Further, students in Miss Thomas' class behaved themselves and worked independently in their ability groups. I have not even considered the many classrooms where students, particularly underperforming students, act out during instruction and do not work well together in ability groups. Those students require a much larger share of the teacher's attention and tend to take it away from students who are doing what they are supposed to do. A few children can easily prevent the entire class from moving at a reasonable pace through the material.

Stresses teachers out. Just how far must a teacher go with DI? Does she create 25 different lessons for 25 different students? The demands of DI that teachers assemble several different sets of materials for each lesson they teach can complicate their already stressful work to the point of insanity. It took Miss Thomas over an hour just to find appropriate activities for the four different groups in her Science lesson on the digestive system. And this was just part of a single 30-minute lesson. Imagine what she must do for the other 4–5 hours of her lessons. I have experienced myself and seen exasperated teachers desperately search for materials that suit each student's or group's interests, learning style, or ability. With so many different ability levels to teach in the same classroom, teachers can find it extremely difficult to offer a focused lesson for each child or ability group. What is worse, when teachers go to all this trouble, it does not lead to overwhelmingly improved outcomes. This combination of upward demands from administrators for increased preparation resulting in limited downward benefits for students is the recipe for teacher burnout (Fernet, Chanal, & Guay, 2017). DI in the modern context contributes to a powerful and seductive romantic image of the teacher who can somehow, if she just works hard enough, reach all students of all abilities. This image is unsustainable.

Less Noble Reasons for Using DI

One would expect that in any group of similarly aged children, there will be diversity of ability, interest, and focus. But in many elementary classrooms, the ability range is unmanageably large. Petrilli (2011) notes that by fourth grade, public school students who score within the top 10% of students on the National Assessment of Educational Progress read at least six grade levels above those who score in the bottom 10%. These achievement scores are normally distributed, meaning that 10% or more of children in a given classroom are on a sixth-grade reading level and 10% or more on a Kindergarten level. How could *anyone* deal with this? Petrilli (2011) points to the even more common spread between students in the

25th and 75th percentiles which are at least three grade levels. One group of students is reading for complex plot lines and the other is still working on decoding words. You simply cannot effectively teach students of such wide abilities with the same lesson. The lesson will be incoherent. In the context of this unacceptable achievement gap, differentiation functions as a management trick that hides the problem of too much intellectual diversity in the same room. Differentiation helps administrators avoid the political hot potatoes involved with really tackling this problem of so many children not meeting their grade level standards.

How did the performance gap get so big that by third or fourth grade where such administrative tricks are even necessary? This is a very complicated question for sure, but one major factor is the promotion of students to the next grade level without proven demonstration that they have met that grade's standards. This is commonly called "social promotion" (McCombs, Kirby, & Mariano, 2010). For example, in the 2008–2009 academic year, just over 3% of first-grade students was retained (Warren & Saliba, 2012). Retention rates for all other grades following first grade falls below 3% and hovers between 2% and 2.8%. Roughly 2.8% of all elementary students is retained, and this despite an average of 60% or more of students who do not earn a "proficient" score on their grade level standard examinations.

There is some research suggesting that retention might "scar" children socially and emotionally (Anderson, Jimerson, & Whipple, 2005; Andrew, 2014) and that it does not necessarily lead to higher rates of graduation (Allensworth, 2005). This is not, however, an argument to keep doing what we are doing. By passing so many academically underperforming children in first–third grade to the next level, we have created a situation in which the intellectual spread is so large in many upper-level elementary classrooms as to be unmanageable for the teacher. It leads to a ridiculous amount of make-up work teachers must do with students to remediate deficits from prior grades, and it gives the child the sense that academic accomplishment can be achieved without stamina and determination. Contrary to the research on the negative effects of retention, there is also research indicating that retaining underperforming children in third grade makes it more likely they will succeed in later grades compared to their cohorts who are not retained (e.g., Edwards, 2016; Lorence, 2014). I will discuss this retention problem in more detail in Chap. 14, where I consider the proposal to do away with age-based grade levels entirely and replace them with skill-based "gates" in which students could stay for more extended periods of time until they mastered the standards contained in them.

From what I can tell, so-called high-stakes tests at the elementary level are really only high stakes for the teachers, not the students. Teachers are often held accountable for low scores and can even be dismissed after continued student underperformance. But with enough parental protest and sympathetic administrators, a child who essentially "fails" his report card for the year or does not earn a "proficient" score on the end-of-year tests can still find his way to the next grade. Ask any teacher about this problem and she will fill your ears with shocking stories.

Differentiated instruction as it is practiced today surely has some positive attributes. It enables teachers to be engaging, flexible, student-centered, and creative. But it offers these benefits so long as the intellectual range of the classroom is kept small and manageable. Many experts recommend keeping class sizes no larger than 20 to realize the full promise of DI (Sparks, 2015). In the face of large classrooms, vast achievement differences, and wide-ability classrooms, differentiation is mostly a disaster. Differentiated instruction is no solution to the achievement gap the way it is practiced today. If schools want to close achievement gaps, they must do several things, and DI is the *least* of them. First, schools must commit to teaching everyone the full curriculum, not watered-down standards. Second, schools must figure out a way to get struggling students the significant extra instructional time they need without taking time from the other students. These include the following: (a) separating some students for all or part of the day, (b) providing extra help/tutoring before or after school, (c) extending the school day, week, or year, (d) investing heavily in early education, and (e) insisting on high levels of school involvement and academic support from families, along with changed discursive practices at home. And third, schools must be more willing to retain students for failing to make adequate progress or to end the practice of age-based grades entirely. To be honest, politicians and administrators do not like the way any of these initiatives look because they are either expensive, controversial, or require time and effort on the part of stakeholders other than teachers. So they ignore what would really put a dent in the problem and assume instead that if a teacher properly "differentiates her lessons," it will somehow get students up to grade level.

What You Can Do
To make the achievement of grade-level standards more possible for today's classroom teachers, there are a number of things you can do to help:

1. Educate yourself on the state-level standards for each grade. Ensure that you are doing as much as you can at home to help your child's teacher with this herculean task. For small children, this means at least 30 minutes of reading at home each night, limited screen time, and frequent practice of mathematical operations and algorithms.
2. If your child is struggling to meet grade-level standards, do all you can to minimize distractions and drama in his or her life which could be compromising educational success. Work with the school to get the child as much extra time and help with missed standards as possible. This may include summer school, tutoring at school if it is available, and doing extra work at home. If the child has an undiagnosed disability, work with the school to see it is attended to. If there are behavioral factors impeding academic progress, do what you can to support the school's discipline policies at home. A child should not be able to wreak havoc on the school all day and then return home to enjoy all his or her privileges.
3. As hard as it may be for you and the child, sometimes grade retention is the best option. It should surely occur much more than the 2.8% of students it does now. It is incredibly difficult for a child in fourth grade to make up skills and information that were not learned in earlier grades. They cannot cover that material anymore in the classroom. Students who are promoted and are unprepared just dig themselves into a deeper hole as time goes by. Being in a giant hole is much more frustrating and humiliating than being a year or two older than one's classmates. It is also generally not useful, productive, or accurate to blame the teacher or the school for your child's failures. The more quickly your child learns to take responsibility for his or her own educational progress, the better you and your child will be in the long run.

References

Allensworth, E. M. (2005). Dropout rates after high-stakes testing in elementary school: A study of the contradictory effects of Chicago's efforts to end social promotion. *Educational Evaluation & Policy Analysis, 27*(4), 341–364.

Anderson, G. E., Jimerson, S. R., & Whipple, A. D. (2005). Students' ratings of stressful experiences at home and school: Loss of a parent and grade retention as superlative stressors. *Journal of Applied School Psychology, 21*(1), 1–20.

Andrew, M. (2014). The scarring effects of primary-grade retention? A study of cumulative advantage in the educational career. *Social Forces, 93*(2), 653–685.

Baumgartner, T., Lipowski, M. B., & Rush, C. (2003). *Increasing reading achievement of primary and middle school students through differentiated instruction* (Masters dissertation). Retrieved from https://eric.ed.gov/contentdelivery/servlet/ERICServlet?accno=ED479203

Chorzempa, B. F., & Graham, S. (2006). Primary-grade teachers' use of within-class ability grouping in reading. *Journal of Educational Psychology, 98*(3), 529–541.

Dandy, K. L., & Bendersky, K. (2014). Student and faculty beliefs about learning in higher education: Implications for teaching. *International Journal of Teaching & Learning in Higher Education, 26*(3), 358–380.

Edwards, A. M. (2016). *The impact of social promotion on the academic performance of students in South Carolina: A forensic multi-year approach* (Doctoral dissertation). Dissertation Abstracts International Section A: Humanities and Social Sciences, 76(8-A). Retrieved from http://gateway.proquest.com/openurl?url_ver=Z39.88-2004&rft_val_fmt=info:ofi/fmt:kev:mtx:dissertation&res_dat=xri:pqm&rft_dat=xri:pqdiss:3662532

Fahey, J. (2000). Who wants to differentiate instruction? We did.... *Educational Leadership, 58*(1), 70–72.

Fernet, C., Chanal, J., & Guay, F. (2017). What fuels the fire: Job- or task-specific motivation (or both)? On the hierarchical and multidimensional nature of teacher motivation in relation to job burnout. *Work & Stress, 31*(2), 145–163. https://doi.org/10.1080/02678373.2017.1303758

Förster, N., Kawohl, E., & Souvignier, E. (2018). Short- and long-term effects of assessment-based differentiated reading instruction in general education on reading fluency and reading comprehension. *Learning and Instruction, 56*, 98–109. https://doi.org/10.1016/j.learninstruc.2018.04.009

Gamoran, A., & Weinstein, M. (1998). Differentiation and opportunity in restructured schools. *American Journal of Education, 106*(3), 385–415.

Gardner, H. (2006). *Multiple intelligences: New horizons*. New York, NY: Basic Books.

Gardner, H. (2011/1983). *Frames of mind: The theory of multiple intelligences*. New York, NY: Basic Books. Original work published 1983.

Geake, J. (2008). Neuromythologies in education. *Educational Research, 50*(2), 123–133.

Keefe, J. W. (1979). Learning style: An overview. In *NASSP's Student learning styles: Diagnosing and prescribing programs* (pp. 1–17). Reston, VA: National Association of Secondary School Principals.

Lewis, S. G., & Batts, K. (2005). How to implement differentiated instruction? Adjust, adjust, adjust. *Journal of Staff Development, 26*(4), 26–31.

Lilienfeld, S. O., Lynn, S. J., Ruscio, J., & Beyerstein, B. L. (2010). *50 great myths of popular psychology: Shattering widespread misconceptions about human behavior*. New York, NY: Wiley-Blackwell.

Lorence, J. (2014). Third-grade retention and reading achievement in Texas: A nine year panel study. *Social Science Research, 48*, 1–19. https://doi.org/10.1016/j.ssresearch.2014.05.001

Mastropieri, M. A., Scruggs, T. E., Norland, J. J., Berkeley, S., McDuffie, K., Tornquist, E. H., & Connors, N. (2006). Differentiated curriculum enhancement in inclusive middle school science: Effects on classroom and high-stakes tests. *Journal of Special Education, 40*(3), 130–137. https://doi.org/10.1177/00224669060400030101

McCombs, J. S., Kirby, S. N., & Mariano, L. T. (Eds.). (2010). *Ending social promotion without leaving children behind: The case of New York City*. Santa Monica, CA: RAND Corporation.

Murray, C. (2008). *Real education: Four simple truths for bringing America's schools back to reality*. New York, NY: Three Rivers Press.

Ocampo, D. M. (2018). Effectiveness of differentiated instruction in the reading comprehension level of grade-11 senior high school students. *Asia Pacific Journal of Multidisciplinary Research, 6*(4), 1–10.

Odgers, S., Symons, A., & Mitchell, I. (2000). Differentiating the curriculum through the use of problem solving. *Research in Science Education, 30*(3), 289–300.

Pashler, H., McDaniel, M., Rohrer, D., & Bjork, R. (2008). Learning styles: Concepts and evidence. *Psychological Science in the Public Interest, 9*(3), 105–119.

Petrilli, M. J. (2011). All together now? *Education Next, 11*(1). Retrieved from https://www.educationnext.org/all-together-now/

Riener, C., & Willingham, D. (2010). The myth of learning styles. *Change, 42*(5), 32–35. https://doi.org/10.1080/00091383.2010.503139

Rohrer, D., & Pashler, H. (2012). Learning styles: Where's the evidence? *Medical Education, 46*(7), 634–635. https://doi.org/10.1111/j.1365-2923.2012.04273.x

Shearer, C. B., & Karanian, J. M. (2017). The neuroscience of intelligence: Empirical support for the theory of multiple intelligences? *Trends in Neuroscience & Education, 6*, 211–223. https://doi.org/10.1016/j.tine.2017.02.002

Sims, R. R., & Sims, S. J. (2006). *Learning styles and learning: A key to meeting the accountability demands in education*. New York, NY: Nova Science Publishers.

Sparks, S. D. (2015, January 28). Differentiated instruction: A primer. *Education Week*. Retrieved from https://www.edweek.org/ew/articles/2015/01/28/differentiated-instruction-a-primer.html

Tieso, C. (2005). The effects of grouping practices and curricular adjustments on achievement. *Journal for the Education of the Gifted, 29*(1), 60–89.

Tomlinson, C. A., & Allan, S. D. (2000). *Leadership for differentiating schools and classrooms*. Alexandria, VA: Association for Supervision and Curriculum Development.

Valiandes, S. (2015). Evaluating the impact of differentiated instruction on literacy and reading in mixed ability classrooms: Quality and equity dimensions of education effectiveness. *Studies in Educational Evaluation, 45*, 17–26. https://doi.org/10.1016/j.stueduc.2015.02.005

Warren, J. R., & Saliba, J. (2012). First through eighth grade retention rates for all 50 states: A new method and initial results. *Educational Researcher, 41*(8), 320–329. https://doi.org/10.3102/0013189X12457813

Waterhouse, L. (2006). Multiple intelligences, the Mozart effect, and emotional intelligence: A critical review. *Educational Psychologist, 41*(4), 207–225. https://doi.org/10.1207/s15326985ep4104_1

Willingham, D. T., Hughes, E. M., & Dobolyi, D. G. (2015). The scientific status of learning styles theories. *Teaching of Psychology, 42*(3), 266–271.

CHAPTER 11

The Incredible Bending School

Your visit to the school is almost through. Miss Thomas rings a little bell to announce that independent reading is now over, "Please return your books and get ready for dismissal." While the students were reading, several staff members entered the room and left bags of groceries on the desks for about five children in the class. The children now busily pack the food into their book bags. There were also small frozen turkeys placed on two other students' desks for the upcoming Thanksgiving holiday. Miss Thomas mentions the food is for the families of seven poor or undocumented children in her room. A few years ago, the school decided to create a program to do what it could to help these families out.

As you think about it, one striking thing from your day at the school is just how much the school does for students, families, and the wider community which go well beyond classroom instruction. The school provides students free transportation to and from the building, including special transportation for students with disabilities. The school feeds students breakfast and lunch, often at free or reduced prices. In many cases, the school gives students snacks throughout the day, often purchased with the teacher's own money (along with weekend groceries at compassionate schools like Miss Thomas'). Some schools run thrift stores to provide clothing. Schools have full- or part-time nurses who deliver medication, tend to injuries, and monitor children's many chronic health issues such as allergies, asthma, and diabetes. Schools provide physical, occupational, and speech therapies. The school also provides mental health services in the form of school counselors, psychologists, and social workers.

In addition to all this, schools provide various educational support services for students who are English-language learners. You noticed there was a group of children who were "pulled" from Miss Thomas' class to work with the English to Speakers of Other Languages (ESOL) counselor in the period before lunch, as well as during several classes throughout the day. Come to think of it, you saw kids pulled from the classroom all day long. This is because children who are significantly behind academically, or who have been diagnosed with a behavioral, emotional, physical, or learning disability are entitled to various "special" educational services designed to accommodate their needs and give them the support they require to do grade-level work. During Math, some of the lower performing students were pulled to work with a Math Specialist. During Reading, a lower performing group and a "gifted" group were pulled to work with two different Reading Specialists. Various children were also pulled from instruction throughout the day to work with the school counselor for behavioral, emotional, and psychological problems. Miss Thomas also provided special "Response to Intervention" (RTI) instruction herself to several different groups of struggling students throughout the day.

Miss Thomas quietly complains to you that all the kind-hearted services society wants to provide children often fall on the teacher's and the cash-strapped school's shoulders. She tells you about the paperwork and data gathering she must do each day for the three children who have an "RTI" in her room, as well as what she must do for the four students who have an "Individualized Education Program" (IEP). These additional tasks can cost her between two and five hours per week. She says other teachers, who have more students with an RTI, 504, or IEP, can spend as many as one to two hours per day on them. "What look like great ideas to the politicians and administrators become just 'one more thing' I can't do properly in my already impossible day." Just as Miss Thomas feels like "five teachers at once," so the school is stretched, doing many things besides education. It is a restaurant charged with feeding people two meals a day, a social service agency sending food and groceries home, a day care center providing "aftercare" services, a recreation center providing sports leagues and clubs, a theater production company providing plays and concerts, a counseling center dealing with children's emotional problems, a medical clinic conducting vision tests, dental exams, and obesity screenings, as well as a special education center that diagnoses learning disabilities and provides special instruction for students who cannot learn as well in their own grade-level classrooms.

This chapter outlines the various special education and non-academic services that our elementary schools provide and explores how this role has slowly expanded over time. I conjure the image of the school as a circus contortionist, bending her body in unnatural and possibly painful ways. When schools overextend themselves the way they currently do, the price is declining student learning, stressed out teachers, and a passive dependency on the part of children, parents, and the public at large. To put it plainly, we Americans expect far too much from our schools, and we expect more and more of them with each passing year. When we do not get the results we want, we become frustrated and blame the schools, never asking the important questions: Are schools the best vehicles to provide the many services we ask of them? Have we created an impossible series of tasks for schools to perform? Have we provided adequate support and funding for all the things we require schools to do? And are there things we ask schools to do which we should do ourselves? I realize even raising these questions is controversial and unpopular, but it must be done.

Reasonable Special Education and Non-Academic Services

While the school's primary function is the education and intellectual development of children, there are surely other services it must provide in order to be able to perform this educational role. I call these *reasonable special education and non-academic services*. Some reasonable (and legally mandated) special education accommodations make it possible for students to learn who otherwise would not because of a diagnosed disability, for example, providing large print for a student with a visual impairment. Other reasonable non-academic services compromise, but do not fundamentally damage, the school's educational mission. I discuss a few major instances.

Transportation and grounds. Running a school bus system is a huge and costly non-academic enterprise for a school or district. Nationally, a little over half of public students use this service at a cost of almost $1000 per year, per student transported (National Center for Education Statistics, n.d.). Children must get to school somehow. Many families live too far away, do not have transportation, or must go to work. They cannot be expected to provide their children transportation to school themselves. It does not make a lot of sense to me to have another agency besides the school district handle this function, particularly since the process is so intimately interwoven with the daily rhythms of the school. The same is the case with building and grounds. Schools need to be clean and safe. Buildings need to be in good repair. As with transportation, it makes good sense for the school district to be responsible for providing janitorial and physical plant services. Of course, the public does not factor in these costs when it considers and votes on "education spending," thinking it is only paying for teachers, buildings, and books.

A lean administration. As I mentioned in Chap. 4, it makes some sense to have a lean level of Administration to handle issues of insurance, physical plant, transportation, pensions, salaries, benefits, hiring and firing, personnel disputes, employee training, maternity/paternity leave, scheduling, community outreach, and compliance with state and federal laws. As I mentioned in that chapter, there are far too many layers of Administration in the current school system, but some Administration is surely necessary.

Counseling and nursing care. Children get cuts, bruises, and bloody noses every day. Others have feeding tubes, medicine, or asthma inhalers which must be administered and monitored at school for the child to be able to safely learn. Therefore, depending on the size of the school, having a full- or part-time nurse is reasonable and sometimes legally required. At the same time, a small counseling staff is necessary to work with some children who have difficulties at home, conflicts with other students, or behavioral problems which are interfering with their schooling. There are also state-mandated classes at each grade level which must be conducted by certified counselors. Of course, there is a limit to how many conditions counselors can and should be treating in the school. Facilitating mental health is not the primary mission of the schools.

Special education and other accommodations. Students who are English-language learners should receive at least a year of special assistance in making the transition to reading and speaking in English. Other students struggle to meet the state-level standards of learning in their grade. They do not have a diagnosed disability, but are at high risk of falling significantly behind. Some tutoring, extra help, and even an RTI are appropriate in these cases. (I realize RTI is technically not considered "special education," but it is nonetheless a "special" set of things a teacher or specialist must do to support a child's learning.) For students who have a diagnosed disability which inhibits them from meeting grade-level standards, an IEP is reasonable (and legally mandated) as well. While lawmakers and members of the Administration are seemingly oblivious to the significant costs to the teacher of implementing these often onerous accommodations, the requirements to provide accommodations to meet grade-level standards are themselves reasonable.

However, I show in the next section that an IEP and other special educational measures are only reasonable when they are standards-based and require the school to give the child only those accommodations to help him or her meet grade-level standards. Unless a child has a severe cognitive disability, an IEP cannot introduce a different, usually lower set of standards. If a child cannot meet grade-level standards because of a disability, *even with accommodations*, this creates a situation which is well outside the typical classroom teacher's (and perhaps the typical school's) ability to effectively handle.

Unreasonable Special Education and Non-Academic Services

Many of the special education and non-academic services which schools provide are not based on fiscal reality, common sense, educational research, or sane human resource allocation. I therefore consider them to be *unreasonable*. Schools currently provide a range of services which other agencies, or the people affected can provide for themselves. In addition, there are many unfunded or poorly funded state and federal mandates which may be reasonable in theory, but in the context of underfunding and the many other demands of the modern classroom, become an unreasonable burden on the teacher and the school. I point out in beginning this discussion that many current special education and/or non-academic services which I consider unreasonable are seen as legally mandated and therefore must be provided. I do not suggest that schools stop providing these services, but to advocate to change unreasonable special education laws, erroneous judicial interpretations, and unwise policy prescriptions based on these laws. Many unreasonable special education and non-academic services are not legally mandated and so could more easily be eliminated. I include a brief list of such unreasonable services below. They include food and dining services, extra-duty assignments, and what I call "extra special education."

Food and dining services. Simply put, schools should not be in the business of providing food to students. Now before you throw the book down and call me a heartless fool, please hear me out. One of the most fundamental aspects of parenthood is providing one's children food and safety. When that basic role is performed by someone else, it only weakens the parent-child bond. All parties become less of what they are. The program that is most problematic is the School Breakfast Program. The federal government spends nearly $4 billion each year to feed 11.6 million children a free breakfast (at a cost of $1.80 per breakfast). It also feeds about 800,000 children per year a reduced-price breakfast (at about $0.30 per breakfast). Around 2.2 million more children eat a full-priced breakfast at school each year at no cost to the government (Congressional Budget Office, 2015).

I am aware and saddened that millions of children are "food insecure." Government estimates are that about 13 million children in the United States (1 in 6) lives in an environment where there is consistent lack of access to adequate food (Coleman-Jensen, Rabbit, Gregory, & Singh, 2016). There are many reasons for the problem of food insecurity which are quite beyond the scope of this book to address. My point is to question why the schools are assigned the responsibility to deal with it. Schools are really only good at one thing: teaching. The many other things schools do are add-ons which they either do poorly or which siphon valuable time and resources from their more primary educational purpose. Schools are not social service agencies, restaurants, or food pantries. There are government programs (e.g., the Supplemental Nutrition Assistance Program or SNAP) whose primary function is to provide food assistance to economically disadvantaged families. There are also private assistance programs which are, admittedly, often less reliable. My argument is that families should avail themselves of these specific food assistance services rather than expecting the school to prepare and provide the food for them. If SNAP cannot cover the cost of breakfast, why not take the $4 billion spent on the existing breakfast program and send it directly to the eligible families as a grant and let the schools return to doing what they do best?

When families have food in the home, whether they earned it themselves or acquired it through assistance, they can now perform that most primary parental function: feeding one's own children. The benefits of this activity to all parties far outweigh any inconvenience of preparing the meal. On the other hand, when the school prepares and provides the food, the parent and family are robbed of this vital and precious opportunity to be with the child. It also significantly changes the relationship that parents and children have with their school. They become passive consumers of the school's many "services" rather than active members of the school community. Food provision helps create an image of the school not as a place that helps you as a parent or family member perform the educational role for which you are primarily responsible, but as a place that takes care of your children for you. It is an unhealthy image indeed.

Most importantly, breakfast should be eaten and shared in the home over the kitchen table. This is the "quality time" children and families so desperately need. People of all ages tend to eat better when they have a meal together over the table. They eat more fruits, vegetables, and other healthy foods (Jong, Visscher, HiraSing, Seidell, & Renders, 2015). Eating together also gives children the opportunity to hear and learn more words. It is associated with academic success and fewer problems at school (Fruh, Fulkerson, Mulekar, Kendrick, & Clanton, 2011). Schools serve about 2.4 billion breakfasts each year. That is 2.4 billion lost conversations over the kitchen table, 2.4 billion stories not exchanged between adults and children, 2.4 billion plans for the day not made, guidance, and encouragement not given. Even if the breakfast lasted just 10 minutes, that is 400 million hours each year that children are not spending with an adult caregiver.

I take my point about the unreasonableness of food in school to its logical conclusion. It does not seem too much to ask that parents and families pack a lunch for their child. All the school would then need to provide in the area of food service is a space in which to eat it. There would be no more need for kitchens, kitchen staff, cashiers, food deliveries, ovens, dishwashers, elaborate safety procedures, health inspectors, chefs, and nutritionists. This would represent a huge cost savings to districts. In 2014, the National School Lunch Program served lunch to about 30 million children each day at a cost of $12.7 billion (Congressional Budget Office, 2015). As with school breakfasts, if SNAP funding is not adequate to cover the cost of lunch for economically disadvantaged children, perhaps add the $12.7 billion budgeted for school lunches into SNAP (along with the eligibility requirements) and get the whole operation out of the schools. Or take the $12.7 billion and directly send it to eligible recipients as a grant. If SNAP funding is already adequate for purchases of breakfast and lunch each day for children, the almost $17 billion spent on lunch and breakfast together should be put back into education. At a rough cost of $60,000 a year per teacher for salary and benefits, that would be 283,333 new teachers we could hire. If we put all those new teachers into the 98,000 public schools in the United States, that would amount to almost three teachers per school. This would make a huge academic difference.

Imagine for a moment what would happen to a legislative proposal like mine which tried to move funding for school breakfast and lunch out of the schools and into SNAP. "Senator Dillon's proposal represents an assault on every child in this nation. We must oppose it. He seeks to deprive needy school children of a healthy breakfast and lunch. How can children learn when they are hungry? How can Dillon be so heartless?" Surely, nobody is talking about allowing kids to go hungry. The proposal is to enlist agencies other than schools to handle food assistance and preparation. When I discuss this idea of getting schools out of the restaurant business with my colleagues, many argue that we should not "punish kids for adults' bad behavior." Other colleagues tell me, "If we sent food assistance to parents as a grant, they would spend it on other things besides food. They would not feed their child in the morning or send a lunch with them to school." Underline that last sentence and read it back to yourself a few times over. Are we really in a cultural situation where 11–15 million parents and families would not use provided government assistance properly and would instead send their kids to school hungry? Can these parents not be trusted to feed their own children? If this is the case, the solution is a call to the Division of Child Protective Services, not to have the schools cook the child's meals for them.

Extra-duty assignments. The Administration does not just ask teachers to teach during their workday. In addition to their massive and exhausting teaching responsibilities, most teachers have a daily, weekly, and monthly rotation of chores which are not related to the instruction of children. These are typically called "extra-duty assignments." They include, but are not limited to, monitoring hallways, supervising study hall, doing bus duty, the carpool line, cafeteria duty, playground duty, and other such assignments. A school of a teacher I interviewed requires teachers to stand in the doorway in the morning for 30 minutes and greet students rather than preparing for their classes. They are prohibited from being at their desks during this time because the Administration decided the research showed children who were greeted in the morning performed better in school. Teachers can easily spend an hour or more per day doing such things. Official school and district policies say the teacher is expected to use her own planning time for such duties. But when is she supposed to do the planning she needs to get ready for class? The answer is at home on her off time. These extra duties are usually assigned and determined by the principal. In most schools, this duty assignment process is an extremely contentious one.

Teachers are also asked to assume longer-term duty commitments which include sponsoring a student organization, directing plays, coaching an intramural activity, sponsoring field trips, attending a school meeting (e.g., PTA and school board), dance, or sports game, and serving on a school committee. Essex (1990) notes that courts have determined that for these kinds of tasks to be legal, the duty must be professional in nature (as opposed to say, taking tickets at a basketball game), benefit students, and not take up "too much" of the teacher's time. The principal is given wide latitude in determining what is "professional" and what is not, what "benefits students," and how much extra-duty time is "too much." Many teachers, especially new or untenured ones, do not question a principal's authority or judgment here.

If the teacher has a collectively bargained agreement, many of these large and small extra duties are enumerated in her contract. If she does not have a collective contract, the duties are not enumerated and so can be subject to much more abuse. Either way, teachers can legally be asked to perform many non-instructional duties with their limited planning time. I mentioned that it is reasonable to have schools involved with transportation, but it does not seem reasonable that teachers need to be involved with bus duty. Bus drivers, parent volunteers, paid school assistants, or employed assistants of the bus company should be doing these things. I mentioned that it is reasonable for a school to provide a room for students to eat lunch, but it is not reasonable for teachers to have to use their planning time to monitor student behavior while students eat. Again, why not utilize parent volunteers or paid cafeteria workers for such matters? It is reasonable that hallways remain safe and passable. It is not reasonable that teachers are enlisted to stand for 30–45 minutes at various corners to monitor hallways. For longer-term duties, like coaching or attending a district meeting, teachers should be compensated for their time. In many districts they are, but in many more they are not.

Extra special education. When I talk to teachers, one of the biggest things they complain about is the additional teaching interventions, data gathering, paperwork, and meetings they must attend to implement mandated "special education" and other interventions. These complaints do not reflect a lack of care for these students, but express exasperation with having more assigned tasks than can be completed in a day. As I showed in the previous chapter, all teachers are asked to teach students of often widely varying abilities in the same classroom through either regular or differentiated instruction. While it is admirable that schools strive to educate all students in the same room as much as possible, there are some children who do not reach grade-level standards through typical modes of instruction because of a disability and therefore need more individualized/specialized interventions for all or part of the day. This is the essence of "special education."

If you spend just a little time in today's schools, you quickly realize there are really two separate schools in the same building: one for "typical" education and another for "special" education. Special education is run by its own rules, policies, practices, laws, and administrators. I speak with some familiarity on this topic. I am not only a child psychologist and an elementary educator, but my daughter Zoe is a person with Down syndrome and an intellectual disability. This has given me an intimate glimpse into the workings of elementary and middle school special education over the past ten years. In this section, I focus particularly upon how special education requirements impact the teacher of the typical classroom.

Special education as we know it began in 1975 when Congress passed the *Education for All Handicapped Children Act* (EHA). This landmark piece of legislation did several different things at once. First, it required that all public schools which receive federal funds provide "equal access" to education. Second, the law required schools to conduct an evaluation of children with disabilities, and with parental input, create an educational plan that would produce a learning experience that mirrored, as much as possible, the learning experience of students without a disability. Third, to empower parents, the act required school districts to construct administrative procedures for parents to dispute decisions the school made about their child's education. Finally, the act provided that students with disabilities be placed in the "least restrictive environment" (LRE). The LRE is defined as one that allows a child with a disability the largest possible opportunity to interact with students who do not have a disability. This is sometimes mistakenly called "inclusion." A separate school or classroom for students with disabilities can occur under the law, but only if a child's disability is so profound that learning goals cannot be achieved in the typical classroom.

The U.S. Congress reauthorized EHA in 1990 and changed its name to the *Individuals with Disabilities Education Act* (IDEA). IDEA developed and formalized many of the requirements of EHA, but now with the benefit of 15 years of case law and special education practice. IDEA required schools to develop an IEP to meet the unique needs of each child with a disability. ("Disability" would be defined according to federal or state standards.) IDEA also went into much more detail as to the people who must be involved with an IEP and what must be contained in it. Second, IDEA required schools to provide a "Free and Appropriate Public Education" (FAPE) for all students with disabilities in order to meet state educational standards (in conformity with the child's IEP). Additional special education costs could not be passed on to parents or families of children with disabilities. Third, IDEA reiterated and clarified the requirement that children with disabilities be educated in the LRE, receive an appropriate evaluation, and solicit parental and teacher input on all educational decisions. It also further clarified the procedural safeguards introduced under EHA for student evaluation, the formation of the IEP, and placement process in special education services.

In the years following IDEA, many expressed concerns about the growing number of students who were diagnosed with a "specific learning disability" (SLD) and then placed in special education. Children with SLDs had quickly become the largest percentage of individuals in special education (one-third of all special education students). Many argued that a good number of these students might have been kept out of special education if appropriate support and educational interventions were provided to them earlier in their educational careers (Al Otaiba, Wagner, & Miller, 2014). In response to this "wait-to-fail" issue, some procedural changes were undertaken in the early 2000s to reform the way children would be identified as having SLD (or one of the other learning disabilities). What has come to be known as "Response to Intervention" emerged as a process of providing targeted educational interventions within the typical educational environment to children who were struggling in school and who would likely be later diagnosed with an SLD (see Kappenberg & Burton, 2012). RTI specifies a series of screenings, tiered classroom interventions, and data gathering procedures. These steps are followed by a case review and assessment to evaluate the impact of these interventions and determine if formal special education services are required. While an RTI is not a formal part of special education (due to the lack of a disability diagnosis), the proscribed interventions do represent a departure for the teacher from her typical delivery of instruction, and so are "special" in the sense of being out of the ordinary.

An entire book could be written on EHA, IDEA, IEP, or RTI alone. As the parent of a child with a disability, I believe these laws and policies represent the best aspects of American compassion and a commitment to the dignity of each person. They seek to identify, protect, and serve students most at risk of struggling and failing in school. They empower parents, require schools to monitor student progress, and adjust interventions accordingly. There is much I am leaving out in my description of these highly influential laws and policies. What I am interested in is not what these laws and policies are designed to do, or the inspiring values and visions behind them, but with the practical problems that emerge for teachers who are trying to work with them in real classrooms. In this context, I identify two kinds of problems: fiscal and pedagogical.

Fiscal irresponsibility. The Federal government originally promised in EHA to cover 40% of the costs of the special education it mandated the states to provide. Due to a stiff dose of sticker shock, the law was later amended downward to provide not 40% of the actual cost of teaching special education students, but 40% of the "average per pupil expenditure" in the United States. Clearly, 40% of the cost of educating a typical student is significantly less than 40% of the cost of educating a student with disabilities. What is more, *the federal government has never met even this lower rate of funding.* Griffith (2015) points out that in the 2013–2014 school year, average spending per student was $12,057 (it was $12,526 in 2018). For the federal government to meet its 40% average per pupil promise, it would need to have provided special education funding at a rate of $4823 per student. But in 2013–2014, the federal government funded special education at a rate of $1743 per student with a disability, just 14.5% of the already low average spending per general education student (Griffith, 2015). According to a National Education Association (NEA) report, the federal contributions to special education in 2015 made up just 16% of the total cost of special education in the United States (Litinov, 2015). For the federal government to make good on its 40% average per pupil promise, it would need to provide states with $20 billion more each year of special education funding. This funding would amount to about $201,000 per public school, enough to support three full time teachers and a paraprofessional. It is hard to underestimate the practical difference to schools this full funding would make. An *IDEA Full Funding Act* or its equivalent is introduced each year in Congress to require the full 40% funding, only to go down in defeat each time.

These per pupil cost estimates to local schools and districts cited above do not include the price of lawsuits they face each year over special education issues. Given the wording of certain provisions (e.g., "free and appropriate education" and "least restrictive environment"), it is not always clear exactly what the law requires of schools. Given the uncertainty, these issues are often passed on to the courts, creating a litigious, adversarial relationship between parents and schools over special education. A typical IEP meeting for a single student can involve as many as ten or more school teachers, staff, and other professionals. If the parents have concerns, they bring a lawyer, which then requires the district to send (and pay for) one of their own. Beale (2017) notes that in 2000, school districts across the country spent $146 million in legal bills fighting parents in court over private tuition bills alone. Parents reason that if a school cannot provide an "appropriate" education for the child's disability under the law, they are entitled to send him or her to a special school and bill the district. School districts already fund over 80,000 private special education placements which cost about $51,000 a year for a day program and $105,000 a year for a residential program (Beale, 2017).

The instructional costs of special education are high. National average per pupil spending is two times higher for a student in special education compared with a student in typical education. Further, there are a large number of students with one or more of the 13 disabilities which entitle them to special educational services. According to the Centers for Disease Control and Prevention, disabilities affect one in six children (Centers for Disease Control and Prevention, 2018). In the 2015–2016 school year, the number of students served under IDEA was 6.7 million students, 13% of the public school population (National Center for Education Statistics, 2018). This number does not include those students who receive RTI services, which makes the actual number of students receiving special teaching interventions even larger. The lack of federal funding, booming numbers of students with disabilities, legal fees, private placements, and additional staff required for special education have been truly devastating to state and local public education budgets. The public has not had a frank and open conversation about special education, relying instead on the courts to set policy and spending priorities.

Pedagogical stress. Putting matters of cost aside, in this section I examine the educational benefits of the money spent on special education, along with the impact of underfunded special education requirements on the typical classroom teacher. I will argue that many accommodations and tiered interventions are difficult to effectively implement in a typical classroom, require an immense expenditure of time, do not help most of the affected students to perform grade-level work, and effectively introduce a separate (and potentially illegal) educational system into the public schools.

Difficult to effectively implement. An IEP (or an RTI report) can be as many as 30 pages long, filled with jargon, legal minutiae, and diagnostic terminology. They are extremely difficult to read and even more difficult to put into practice. Special education teacher Lacie Rader (2010) writes, "Even some of the best reports I've seen are not successful in supporting the student. A completely accurate summary of the student's ability needs and suggested tools for support can be drawn up, a meeting held and still at the end of the day the implementation of the IEP by teacher, administration, student and parents rarely occurs" (p. 83). In Chap. 10, I mentioned the serious questions I have about the viability of differentiated instruction to work in a mixed-ability group. When you make the ability spread even larger by introducing several students with an IEP and RTI, it complicates matters for the teacher even further. She will do what she is asked to do of course, just not very well. She will tread water all day long.

Time drain. Even the practical supports that can be discerned from these often inscrutable IEP and RTI plans take an immense amount of time to implement. Most classroom teachers have received only the briefest training in an RTI or IEP. I had just one class in special education, and even that discussed actual special teaching interventions for maybe an hour. Teachers commonly say they lack real strategies to support students with the practical requirements of an IEP or the interventions specified in Tier 2 and 3 of an RTI. They also say there are not nearly enough staff to support the small intervention groups required of their students with an RTI or IEP. After all, a teacher only has so many things she can do at once. Teachers also report the paperwork demands of special education are onerous. A special report issued by the Government Accountability Office in 2016 found teachers reported spending an hour or two each day dealing with the administrative tasks imposed on them by IDEA alone (see U.S. Government Accountability Office, 2016). Rader (2010) adds, "I spent more time writing IEPs and having IEP meetings than I did meeting with students and actually supporting them" (p. 83).

Ineffective interventions. All children are precious. Spending money to help struggling children achieve grade-level standards is well worth the cost. But most special education students are not meeting grade-level standards, despite our many interventions. According to the National

Center for Educational Outcomes, the achievement gap in 2006–2007 in Reading between elementary students with an IEP and students without an IEP was 31 points. Eight years later, when these same students were in high school (2014–2015), the gap was 37 points, *6 points larger*. The achievement gap in 2006–2007 in Math between elementary students with an IEP and students without was 29 points. In 2014–2015, the gap was virtually unchanged at 28 points. (Thurlow, Albus, & Lazarus, 2017). IEPs are not effectively getting students to grade level.

Data on the effectiveness of RTI approaches have not been gathered in quite the systematic way as data from students with an IEP. Despite the lack of national numbers, Reynolds and Shaywitz (2009) conclude the research cited to support the effectiveness of RTI is all based on small-scale university studies which have extreme treatment fidelity and full-scale interventions through university research and training programs which do not take place in real-world educational settings. They also note the effect sizes reported for RTI, even in these artificial environments, is not consistent or overwhelmingly strong. They conclude the existing empirical support for the effectiveness of RTI does not warrant the largescale belief in its benefits (e.g., 14 states currently mandate RTI for the identification of SLD; all states mention RTI in their regulations). Reynolds and Shaywitz (2009) claim the RTI craze is more politics and fad than sound science (see also Kavale, Kauffman, Bachmeir, & LeFever, 2008). They write, "Like much in special education, RTI is characterized by moral imperative and political activism rather than science" (Reynolds & Shaywitz, 2009, p. 134).

The purpose of IDEA is to enable all students, excepting those with the most severe disabilities, to have equal access to high-quality schooling and perform at the same level as everyone else. If they cannot do this, they are to have as much involvement with the general curriculum as possible. With billions of dollars spent and countless hours of special instructional time, these interventions have not made much of educational difference in terms of reducing the achievement gap and helping students get to grade-level performance. The long-term failure of IEPs and RTIs to close the achievement gap for many students with disabilities works to create an inferior and expensive "shadow curriculum" in the public schools, the very thing that *Elementary and Secondary Education Act*, EHA, and IDEA were designed to eliminate. Many schools use IEPs in a way that does not tie learning to grade-level standards, but significantly lowers standards. The child passes from grade to grade each year below the radar, under protection of an IEP, never getting close to grade-level work. This problem has become so serious that in 2015, the U.S. Department of Education had to issue a guidance letter to clarify that all IEPs, including those for students with specific learning disabilities, must be tied to state grade-level academic standards (U.S. Department of Education, 2015). The letter added that if a school does not tie a child's IEP to state grade-level standards, it is violating the child's right to a FAPE under IDEA. The only exception, of course, is for students with significant intellectual disabilities. These students, like my daughter, may have IEPs tied to alternate academic standards. All the others cannot.

IDEA lists 13 different disability categories under which 3–21-year-olds are eligible for services. If a child has a hearing impairment, for example, the school should provide those accommodations as to help the student to learn alongside students without hearing loss. In this regard, the school might provide personal hearing instrument like a hearing aid or tactile device, personal hearing assistance technology, a classroom sound distribution system, videophone, or alerting devices. The assumption is that the child will be able to perform grade-level work with these accommodations.

Disability categories like specific learning disability, intellectual disability, and speech or language impairment (which together account for more than half of all diagnosed disabilities) follow the same logic. The assumption is that the child can do grade-level work *if given accommodations for his or her disability*. To accommodate the disability, the teacher might provide information to the student on an audio tape, use an augmentative communication device like print output, provide special on-task prompts, present instructions orally, allow for answers to be dictated to a scribe, implement course modifications like using a computer with a voice synthesizer, allow frequent breaks while doing work, give extra time for a test, provide a space with minimal distractions, or administer a test in a private room or in smaller timed sessions over several days. The idea is that given these special provisions, the child's intellect will then be able to perform the grade-level learning task. However, if the child cannot learn at grade level *despite accommodations*, then we are dealing with a completely different scenario. If a child is unable to do grade-level work because of a disability, then the teacher or the school should not be expected to provide accommodations to achieve grade-level standards. They should provide accommodations for sure, but accommodations to meet a different, developmentally appropriate set of standards. Since these students cannot achieve grade-level standards, grade-level teachers should not be expected to provide the accommodations in their typical classrooms. This is what I mean by "extra special" education. It goes above and beyond what is intended and required by the law.

What You Can Do
One of the big things which the wider public can do to stop stretching schools beyond their capacity is to stop asking them to do so many things that are unrelated to school. To this extent, there are several items which would help to destress the bending school.

1. Eat breakfast with your kids each morning and pack a good lunch for them. Older elementary students can also learn to pack a lunch for themselves.
2. The school does not provide services to you. It helps you perform an educational function for which you as a parent are primarily responsible. Help the schools help you perform this educational task.
3. There are a variety of reasons why children fail to achieve grade-level standards. Sometimes a learning disability is behind it, but more often there is an issue of motivation, intelligence, aptitude, and interest. Learning disabilities are perhaps the most scientifically unsound and over diagnosed category of all under IDEA. Many things are now called "disabilities" which are really other kinds of problems. An accommodation cannot work if the child does not actually have a disability.
4. Special education is not about "getting services" from schools for your child but about determining and providing those accommodations that are necessary for a child with a disability to perform grade-level work. If your child cannot perform grade-level work, even with accommodation, the typical classroom is not the setting to achieve these objectives. Work to find the best path forward given your child's strengths and limitations.
5. Lawsuits are required only for the most egregious circumstances of abuse or professional malpractice. When you bring a lawyer to the school or an IEP meeting over a grade, discipline decision, or conflict with a teacher, it unnecessarily complicates life for all involved and does not help your child in the long run. Schools make all kinds of poor administrative decisions simply from fear of litigation. There is a difference between getting your way and being right. Poor administrative decisions do not help students in the end.

References

Al Otaiba, S., Wagner, R. K., & Miller, B. (2014). "Waiting to fail" redux: Understanding inadequate response to intervention. *Learning Disability Quarterly, 37*(3), 129–133.

Beale, S. (2017, August 8). America's special education mess: The system has never been grounded in fiscal reality. *The American Conservative.* Retrieved from https://www.theamericanconservative.com/articles/americas-shameful-special-education-mess/

Centers for Disease Control and Prevention. (2018). Facts about developmental disabilities. Retrieved from https://www.cdc.gov/ncbddd/developmentaldisabilities/facts.html

Coleman-Jensen, A., Rabbit, M. P., Gregory, C. A., & Singh, A. (2016). Household food security in the United States in 2015 [PDF File]. Retrieved from https://www.ers.usda.gov/webdocs/publications/79761/err-215.pdf?v=42636

Congressional Budget Office. (2015). Child nutrition programs: Spending and policy options. Retrieved from https://www.cbo.gov/publication/50737

Essex, N. L. (1990). Extra-duty assignments for teachers—A growing controversy. *American Secondary Education, 18*(4), 30–33.

Fruh, S. M., Fulkerson, J. A., Mulekar, M. S., Kendrick, L. A. J., & Clanton, C. (2011). Continuing education: The surprising benefits of the family meal. *The Journal for Nurse Practitioners, 7*(1), 18–22. https://doi.org/10.1016/j.nurpra.2010.04.017

Griffith, M. (2015). The progress of education reform: A look at funding for disabilities [PDF file]. *Education Commission of the States, 16*(1), 1–6. Retrieved from https://www.ecs.org/clearinghouse/01/17/72/11772.pdf

Jong, E., Visscher, T. L. S., HiraSing, R. A., Seidell, J. C., & Renders, C. M. (2015). Home environmental determinants of children's fruit and vegetable consumption across different SES backgrounds. *Pediatric Obesity, 10*(2), 134–140. https://doi.org/10.1111/ijpo.243

Kappenberg, J., & Burton, D. (2012). *The complete guide to RTI: An implementation toolkit.* Thousand Oaks, CA: Corwin.

Kavale, K. A., Kauffman, J. M., Bachmeir, R. J., & LeFever, G. B. (2008). Response-to-intervention: Separating the rhetoric of self-congratulation from the reality of specific learning disability identification. *Learning Disability Quarterly, 31*(3), 135–150. https://doi.org/10.2307/25474644

Litinov, A. (2015, May 9). How Congress' underfunding of special education shortchanges us all. Retrieved from National Education Association Website: https://educationvotes.nea.org/2015/05/19/how-congress-underfunding-of-special-education-shortchanges-us-all/

National Center for Education Statistics. (2018). Children and youth with disabilities. Retrieved from National Center for Education Statistics Website: https://nces.ed.gov/programs/coe/indicator_cgg.asp

National Center for Education Statistics. (n.d.). Fast facts: Transportation. Retrieved from https://nces.ed.gov/fastfacts/display.asp?id=67

Rader, L. (2010). Special education is broken. *Journal of the American Academy of Special Education Professionals*, 81–88. Retrieved from https://eric.ed.gov/?id=EJ1137129

Reynolds, C. R., & Shaywitz, S. E. (2009). Response to intervention: Ready or not? Or, from wait-to-fail to watch-them-fail. *School Psychology Quarterly*, 24(2), 130–145. https://doi.org/10.1037/a0016158

Thurlow, M. L., Albus, D. A., & Lazarus, S. S. (2017). *NCEO report 405: 2014–15 publicly reported assessment results for students with disabilities and ELs with disabilities*. Retrieved from National Center on Educational Outcomes Website: https://nceo.info/Resources/publications/OnlinePubs/report405/default.html

U.S. Department of Education. (2015). Significant guidance document [PDF File]. Retrieved from https://www2.ed.gov/policy/speced/guid/idea/memosdcltrs/guidance-on-fape-11-17-2015.pdf

U.S. Government Accountability Office. (2016). *Special education: State and local imposed requirements complicate federal efforts to reduce administrative burden* [PDF File]. Retrieved from https://www.gao.gov/assets/680/674561.pdf

CHAPTER 12

Look Not to the Stars

The final bell is about to ring in the end of your school day. How do you feel? Are you exhausted? Exhilarated? Worried? Happy? You probably feel all these things at once. When the dust settles, one of the things you might notice is how strange it is that you, a layperson, are even sitting in a classroom involving yourself in instruction. You have been in the school building all day long, and you have not seen a single member of the community doing anything other than helping with copies or picking a child up early for a doctor's appointment. The thing that is not a big part of the public schools is the public!

Unless you work in a school, you would probably never find yourself in there for part of the day, much less the whole day. Scarcely anyone from the community, even parents, sits in a classroom or is involved with the school's educational mission. When the public does enter the classroom, it is the occasional parent coming in briefly to read a story and then leave, volunteer to help the teacher staple reading packets, chaperone a field trip, have lunch with their child, or attend a parent-teacher conference, but very rarely are parents or community members involved in anything academic at the classroom level or in formulating educational standards at the district, state, or national level.

The wall separating the classroom and the public is quite high. I do not know exactly how this wall got there or how it can come down, but it is a real problem. Part of the issue is that schools and teachers often do not reach out and ask. I had two children go through two different public elementary and middle schools over a 15-year period. I have a Ph.D. in child psychology and elementary teaching certificate. Never once was I asked to visit the class or asked for my input on an educational matter. It was very clearly communicated to me that this was just not my turf. I understand this resistance on some level. Many parents can be unhelpful, bossy, or babying of their children. Children can be distracted with parents or other volunteers in the room. Parents or other family members can seriously interfere with the teacher's routine with pop-in visits and calls. After all, the teacher is the one on the hook for any deficiencies, not the parent. Why would she want to waste any of her limited instructional time on other parties in her room? Many teachers will privately tell you they do not appreciate when parents visit and experience many parents as having to deal with another child in their room. A great deal of work needs to be done to help teachers feel less defensive and more welcoming of parental involvement. Some of this work must surely be done by parents who are often quick to blame teachers for any perceived deficiencies in their children, for poor grades, and behavioral infractions.

But these barriers should ultimately be of no consequence. The schools are *our schools* after all, not the teacher's or the principal's. For whatever reason, we have allowed a situation to develop where a great wall of separation not only stands between the public and the schools but continues to grow. The blame ultimately lies with us, the public. *We are the problem*: parents, students, and citizens. "The fault, dear Brutus, is not in our stars, but in ourselves, that we are underlings" (*Julius Caesar*, 1.2.135). When I step back from today's elementary schools, I see an over-managed, underfunded institution trying to do far too much. And I see families and other members of the public doing far too little. Schools can only work effectively if they assist parents and the wider community *in what they are already doing to educate their children*. Parents shoulder the primary educational role for their children. If families are not also educating their children, the public education project will fail. Teachers and principals are just hirelings. But does it feel this way to you? Do you feel in charge of your child's education? More often than not, it seems our teachers and schools are the only ones doing any intellectual work with children. We have allowed this vital task to be overtaken by experts and managers. We need to reclaim it. *Public* schools mean not only that our schools are paid for by the public, but that the school's functioning is the public's responsibility. Rather than teachers or schools being the only ones who need to change to make education better, I argue that *we* need to change, and change in a big way.

A Picture of Contemporary Parental Engagement

Family and parental engagement in schooling is a highly researched and often controversial topic. I cannot hope to summarize all the relevant literature here, but paint the briefest portrait of what parents, families, and neighborhoods currently do to support and involve themselves in elementary and other kinds of public education. *Parental engagement* in education is defined as those attitudes and behaviors families exhibit that contribute to a child's academic success (Fantuzzo, McWayne, Perry, & Childs, 2004). Research suggests this parental engagement can occur in a variety of places, such as the home, the school, and the wider community (see Kohl, Lengua, & McMahon, 2000). Research paints a mixed picture of parental engagement. Parents care about their child's education, but for the most part do not devote nearly enough time to the right kinds of school initiatives. I look specifically at both sides of the divide: the school side and the parent side.

At a general level, the school communicates with parents and keeps them abreast of things that are going on there. About nine in ten parents during the 2015–2016 school year said they received e-mail, memos, newsletters, or notices addressed to "all parents" from their child's school. The information is often not as personalized and specific as it needs to be. Just 62% of parents report receiving notes or e-mail from the school or a teacher about their own child (National Center for Education Statistics, 2017). Although schools sponsor various programs open to parents, and invite parents to attend them, parents do not always come. School events that promise interaction with the child's teacher draw more parents than those that exhibit student shows, performances, or demonstrations of student work. Parents attend conferences with their child's teacher much more than any other kind of school event like an open house, back-to-school night, an arts or sports event. Fifty-seven percent of public elementary schools reported that "most or all" parents attended scheduled parent-teacher conferences (National Center for Education Statistics, 1996a). This is the highest attended event, but note that more than 40% of parents do not attend it. What is more, teachers almost uniformly tell you the parents who do not attend these meetings are the ones who most need to attend. Several teachers told me they wished that parent attendance at conferences could be tracked with student grades so that people could see how closely they correlate.

Parent attendance at school events varies across different school demographics. For example, the Southeast, where I live, reports significantly less parental involvement in school events than other regions of the country. About 60% of schools in all other regions report that parent participation in school events is "very high," while in the Southeast, only 20% of schools report this number. Depending on the region, anywhere from 40% to 80% of schools report low to average parental attendance at school events. Another robust difference in parent attendance at school events is related to the poverty status of the school. Specifically, as the poverty status of the school increases, parent attendance decreases. Seventy-two percent of low-poverty schools report that "most or all" parents attend the school open house, while 48% of schools with moderate poverty, and 28% of schools with high poverty report these high rates. Similar inverse relationships are reported when the percentage of minority students at the school is high. Schools with minority enrollments of less than 5% report levels of parent attendance at all events are twice as high compared to schools with minority enrollments of 50% or more (National Center for Education Statistics, 1996b).

Of course, parental engagement in schooling goes much deeper than attending school meetings or functions, though attendance at such things is a strong indicator of deeper parental involvement. Fantuzzo et al. (2004) found that when parents engage in activities at home like reading to a child, helping a child with schoolwork, organizing the home environment to support learning, modeling intellectual activities at home, talking to children about the importance of school achievement and success, or communicating in an intellectually stimulating way, it is a stronger predictor of end-of-year academic success than mere parental engagement at school functions (attending meetings, school events, volunteering in the classroom). Parents engage in these deeper level activities far less frequently than they attend school functions. Just 53% of parents read every day to their children between the ages of three and five. This already low figure drops even more as children get older. Just 38% of families read to their children between the ages of six and eight at least five days a week (Scholastic Publishing, 2018, p. 58). Children in families with incomes below the poverty line are much less likely to read aloud to their children every day than parents in families with incomes at or above the poverty line (Scholastic Publishing, 2018).

Further data on deep parental engagement are distressing. Half of parents admitted their children's homework was often too difficult to help them with, and 21.9% said they were too busy to help their kids with homework at all (National Center for Family Literacy, 2013). Children under eight spend an average of 2 hours and 15 minutes per school day passively watching a tablet or TV screen (Common Sense Media, 2017). U.S. adults spend about 10 hours and 39 minutes each day to consuming media, which includes tablets, smartphones, personal computers, video games, and TVs. (The Nielsen Company, 2016). We adults are often terrible models for engaging in intellectual activity.

Barriers to Parental Engagement

Low levels of parental engagement are a complex problem with several causes. Researchers find the most common reasons parents give for low school engagement is lack of time (see Holliday, 1986; Spoth & Redmond, 2000). Parents may have a baby or toddler at home or have a work schedule that conflicts with school events. Mendez (2010) found that half of parents from low socioeconomic backgrounds reported work conflicts as the main reason for low engagement, along with concerns about transportation (13.9%), being too tired (12.4%), and having night classes (11.4%). Other factors parents raise include their own feelings of inadequacy around school matters, feeling like being involved would "overstep their bounds," and the fact that some children resist their efforts to become more involved in school. Some schools also have a culture and organizational structure that parents feel is not inviting to them and does not lend itself to parent-school collaboration. Finally, many parents are simply confused about what goes on at school. For example, Barbarin et al. (2008) present results from a large and ethnically diverse group of pre-kindergarten parents. Though families were willing to help, most conceived of school readiness as involving children's knowledge and memorization of information such as letters, numbers, and other objects to the exclusion of higher-order cognitive abilities stressed in most classrooms. So, when these parents do help, it can be counterproductive to the teacher's larger educational aims.

Why Parental Engagement Matters

The research is overwhelmingly consistent on the fact that parental involvement in their children's education is correlated with higher levels of academic achievement. By studying a group of children over time, Reynolds, Mavrogenes, Bezruczko, and Hagemann (1996) show that parental engagement in school activities when children are very young positively affects the child's readiness and acclimation to elementary school later (see also Park, Stone, & Holloway, 2017; Tan & Goldberg, 2009). Jeynes (2005) finds that when parents assist children by reading to them, when they create a home environment that supports school learning, and share positive expectations about school achievement, it positively impacts the child's academic performance (see also Daniel, Wang, & Berthelsen, 2016; Loughlin-Presnal & Bierman, 2017).

Why does parental engagement have these positive academic effects? At a basic level, when parents do things at home that are also done at school, it lessens the separation between these two distant worlds. I mentioned earlier in the book the disconnect I felt when going from the elementary school environment back into a non-school environment. The school environment is unlike most cultures that one will find in the world. It is highly reflective, literate, and abstract. Recall from Chap. 7, it routinely engages in what Sigel (1970) calls "Level 3" communication strategies. Level 3 strategies make demands upon the child to engage in causal inferences, for example, "I wonder why that happened," to predict outcomes or employ hypothetical reasoning, for example, "I wonder what would happen if…," or to transform from one symbolic medium to another, "in what ways is the earth like a layer cake?" The more time children spend in discourse environments like these, the more likely they are to develop the abstract, representational structures that are prioritized in formal, Platonic, school settings.

But many studies show that family environments and the surrounding culture are not nearly as Platonic as our schools are. In fact, as I mentioned in Chap. 7, most non-school environments are "Epicurean" in that they are, "adapted to luxury and sensual pleasures." Recall, the Epicurean highlights the concrete, the immediate, and the particular. Think here of the images that endlessly dance across our children's (and our own) cell phones, tablets, or video game monitors. These Epicurean settings tend to engage in what Sigel calls "Level 1" communicative strategies. These practices make mental demands from the child to make visual observations, for example, "What is that?," associations, for example, "Where is the capital of Georgia?," routinized information, and direct commands, for example, "take that out of your mouth," "sit here." The point is you cannot raise a generation of Platonic philosopher kings and queens who swim all day at home in a sea of Epicureanism and then engage in high-level distancing for four to five hours, Monday to Friday, for 180 days a year.

The achievement of a Platonic set of learning outcomes requires more than just a few hours at school, rather it must be encased within a familial and social context that is driven constantly toward what Sigel (1970) calls *representational competence*. Our goal as a society should be that 75% of our exchanges with any child be at the "Level 3" level. The next time you are with adults and children outside of school, I urge you to do an experiment. Categorize the nature of the interactions the adult initiates with the child. Count how many are Level 1, 2, or 3. It is shocking! Some studies show that most children are lucky to have between 5% and 9% of their interactions with non-teacher adults be Level 3 in nature (McGillicuddy-De Lisi, Johnson, & Sigel, 1979; Sigel, Stinson, & Flaugher, 1991). The universal, Platonic educational project can only succeed with massive buy-in from other stakeholders, especially parents. To expect results from the school and teacher alone is unrealistic and irresponsible. Parental engagement is not simply about "pitching in" or "helping out" with the school a few times a year, but involves the daily engagement of the school's core intellectual activity at home.

I repeat here what I said in the Introduction, the American public school system is the most radical and just social project in the history of the world. I will say that again: *in the history of the world*. Our system is better, kinder, and fairer than any other country's school system on the planet. We should all be supremely proud of it. But our system is a work in progress, a bold idea that is trying to realize itself. It is succeeding in many areas, but failing in many others. For it to truly succeed for all, we all must involve ourselves much more in the life of the elementary school so that it is no longer that scary house on the corner that we have never visited. What needs to happen for parents, politicians, and citizens to feel a greater sense of ownership of the school system that they support?

What You Can Do
Breaking down the wall of separation will take some courage, but it starts with taking that first literal and figurative step from your car into the school building. Here are some practical suggestions on what might help lessen the distance between these two worlds.

1. Commit yourself to engaging in Level 3 communicative practices for as much time as possible when you are with children. It is the least you can do for their intellectual development. They are awash in a sea of images. They need your help to escape. (Perhaps first you must escape from the sea of images yourself.)
2. Make time for your kids' school. Get important dates at the beginning of the year and put them in your calendars early. Overcome any fear or hesitation that stem from your own days in school. School was not always pleasant for many of us, but we can still work to ensure that it is pleasant for our own children. Read to them each day. Help them with their homework. Get involved with the school in any way you can, and at the very least, attend all parent-teacher conferences. Ask your child's teacher about what you can do at home to support what she does in the classroom. Do what she says.
3. Parents should be on a report card system just like school children. Consider supporting such a proposal in your own school or district. Under this plan, the school would grade not only the child on his or her academic performance but also the parent on such dimensions as the following: regular attendance of parent-teacher conferences, responsiveness to teacher communication, promptness in returning permission slips and other paperwork, helpfulness in creating a quiet space and time at home for schoolwork, ability to ensure the child has adequate rest, and availability to the child for help with homework and practice studying for tests. Teachers and principals could assemble these data and grade communities, neighborhoods, townships, cities, and districts in terms of how well the community outside the school facilitates their work. Imagine if these results were as "high stakes" as student state standards assessments?

REFERENCES

Barbarin, O. A., Early, D., Clifford, R., Bryant, D., Frome, P., Burchinal, M., ... Pianta, R. (2008). Parental conceptions of school readiness: Relation to ethnicity, socioeconomic status, and children's skills. *Early Education and Development*, *19*(5), 671–701. https://doi.org/10.1080/10409280802375257

Common Sense Media. (2017). The common sense census: Media use by kids age zero to eight [PDF File]. Retrieved from https://www.commonsensemedia.org/sites/default/files/uploads/research/0-8_executivesummary_release_final_1.pdf

Daniel, G. R., Wang, C., & Berthelsen, D. (2016). Early school-based parent involvement, children's self-regulated learning and academic achievement: An Australian longitudinal study. *Early Childhood Research Quarterly*, *36*(3), 168–177. https://doi.org/10.1016/j.ecresq.2015.12.016

Fantuzzo, J., McWayne, C., Perry, M. A., & Childs, S. (2004). Multiple dimensions of family involvement and their relations to behavioral and learning competencies for urban, low-income children. *School Psychology Review*, *33*(4), 467–480.

Holliday, A. E. (1986). Home-high school communication and collaboration are plus factors—The question is "how?". *Journal of Educational Public Relations*, *8*(4), 4–7.

Jeynes, W. H. (2005). A meta-analysis of the relation of parental involvement to urban elementary school student academic achievement. *Urban Education*, *40*(3), 237–269.

Kohl, G. O., Lengua, L. J., & McMahon, R. J. (2000). Parent involvement in school: Conceptualizing multiple dimensions and their relations with family and demographic risk factors. *Journal of School Psychology*, *38*(6), 501–523.

Loughlin-Presnal, J. E., & Bierman, K. L. (2017). Promoting parent academic expectations predicts improved school outcomes for low-income children entering kindergarten. *Journal of School Psychology*, *62*, 67–80. https://doi.org/10.1016/j.jsp.2017.03.007

McGillicuddy-De Lisi, A. V., Johnson, J. E., & Sigel, I. E. (1979). The family as a system of mutual influences: Parental beliefs, distancing behaviors, and children's representational thinking. In M. Lewis & L. A. Rosenblum (Eds.), *Child and its family* (pp. 91–106). New York, NY: Plenum Press.

Mendez, J. L. (2010). How can parents get involved in preschool? Barriers and engagement in education by ethnic minority parents of children attending head start programs. *Cultural Diversity and Ethnic Minority Psychology*, *16*(1), 26–36.

National Center for Education Statistics. (1996a). Statistics in brief: Parent attendance at school events. Retrieved from National Center for Education Statistics Website: https://nces.ed.gov/surveys/frss/publications/96913/index.asp?sectionid=2

National Center for Education Statistics. (1996b). Statistics in brief: Parent attendance by school characteristics. Retrieved from National Center for Education Statistics Website: https://nces.ed.gov/surveys/frss/publications/96913/index.asp?sectionid=3

National Center for Education Statistics. (2017). *Parent and family involvement in education: Results from the national household education surveys program of 2016* [PDF File]. Retrieved from National Center for Education Statistics Website: https://nces.ed.gov/pubs2017/2017102.pdf.

National Center for Family Literacy. (2013). Half of parents have trouble helping their kids with homework [PDF File]. Retrieved from https://www.familieslearning.org/uploads/news_and_media/1388265133.4NBO.PR-Half-of-Parents-09-2013.pdf

Park, S., Stone, S. I., & Holloway, S. D. (2017). School-based parental involvement as a predictor of achievement and school learning environment: An elementary school-level analysis. *Children and Youth Services Review, 82*, 195–206. https://doi.org/10.1016/j.childyouth.2017.09.012

Reynolds, A. J., Mavrogenes, N. A., Bezruczko, N., & Hagemann, M. (1996). Cognitive and family-support mediators of preschool effectiveness: A confirmatory analysis. *Child Development, 67*(3), 1119–1140. https://doi.org/10.2307/1131883

Scholastic Publishing. (2018). Kids and family reading report [PDF File]. Retrieved from https://www.scholastic.com/content/dam/KFRR/Downloads/KFRReport_Finding%20Their%20Story.pdf

Sigel, I. E. (1970). The distance hypothesis: A causal hypothesis for the acquisition of representational thought. In M. R. Jones (Ed.), *Miami symposium on the prediction of behavior, 1968: Effect of early experience* (pp. 99–118). Coral Gables, FL: University of Miami Press.

Sigel, I., Stinson, E. T., & Flaugher, J. (1991). Socialization of representational competence in the family: The distancing paradigm. In L. Okagaki & R. J. Sternberg (Eds.), *Directors of development: Influences on the development of children's thinking* (pp. 121–144). Hillsdale, NJ: Lawrence Erlbaum Associates, Inc.

Spoth, R., & Redmond, C. (2000). Research on family engagement in preventive interventions: Toward improved use of scientific findings in primary prevention practice. *Journal of Primary Prevention, 21*(2), 267–284.

Tan, E. T., & Goldberg, W. A. (2009). Parental school involvement in relation to children's grades and adaptation to school. *Journal of Applied Developmental Psychology, 30*(4), 442–453. https://doi.org/10.1016/j.appdev.2008.12.023

The Nielsen Company. (2016, June 27). The total audience report: Q1 2016. Retrieved from https://www.nielsen.com/us/en/insights/reports/2016/the-total-audience-report-q1-2016.html

CHAPTER 13

What to Do About These Six Things

In Part II, I presented six additional worrisome things about today's elementary schools: the Platonic curriculum in an Epicurean society, the large amounts of wasted classroom time, the fact that far too many students are not achieving grade-level standards, the disturbing practice of differentiated instruction in an often unreasonably wide-ability-range classroom, the unsustainable number of non-academic and "special" services that schools provide, and the fact that the public is largely uninvolved with the academic mission of the schools. At bottom, these six things are all about *separation* and *diversion*. There is a huge wall that divides schools from the wider public, experts from laypeople/parents. There is also an excessively large number of services schools perform that dilute their educational effectiveness and endanger their financial health. In this chapter, I try to digest these six items and propose some practical solutions.

Wall of Separation

The wall of separation of which I speak exists both inside and outside the school. Inside, it expresses itself in the form of a vast achievement gap between the academically gifted and those who struggle, those destined for success in college, and those who will not make it to high school or college graduation. Outside the school, the divide expresses itself in the form of a chasm separating educational experts and the lay public. These two parties often work at cross-purposes. The experts run nearly everything in the schools and make most of the significant decisions. Our culture has developed a bad habit of relying on these experts to tend to all matters educational, even ceding the schools the task of feeding our children for us. Parents can (and do) complain about various things to the principal. They often get their way, but these issues are typically about the amount of homework or a grade their child gets. But parents have no real control or influence over what is taught, for how long, how tests are constructed, and the overall goals of education. This nearly unlimited power of educational experts and administrators has resulted in a one-sized college-for-all curriculum which is foisted upon all students (and teachers) with very little support from outside the school. I propose two different solutions to this problem of separation: a reimagined elementary curriculum and a renaissance in parental engagement.

A curriculum for all students (not just the academically gifted). A common theme that runs through most of the chapters of this book is the overwhelming impact of the difficult college prep curriculum schools introduce in Kindergarten and continue throughout high school. Our country expects (and legally requires) nearly every student to be proficient in this curriculum in the hopes that someday he or she will move onto college and/or a high-skilled career. The reasoning is that college will lead to good job prospects, financial security, social esteem, and perhaps even happiness. When students do not achieve proficiency in the Platonic curriculum, we worry and introduce legal and administrative pressure on teachers and special educators to achieve better results through improved instruction, special interventions, and/or formal accommodations. There are surely some cases where this response to student failure or underachievement is appropriate and/or effective, but it is mostly a well-intentioned mistake.

The whole situation changes once we let go of the alluring vision of college-for-all. Our nation and its educational system appear surprisingly unable to do this. We are like a dog with a bone. As well-meaning and noble-hearted as the college-for-all vision is, it does not work and is not based on a realistic assessment of what all students can or want to do. All of this causes more harm to children, teachers, and society than we fully appreciate.

College-for-all does not work for all. There are several reasons why I say the college prep curriculum is not working. We have doggedly pursued the college-for-all vision for nearly 30 years, and the results are dismal. As a college professor of 27 years, I have seen firsthand the folly of this overwhelming pressure to have everyone go to college. It has led to inflated grades in high school, poor high school guidance counseling, and crushing student loan debt. Despite graduating from high school with grade point averages (GPAs) of 3.0 or higher, more than half of my freshman and sophomore students cannot do college-level work or succeed academically. Most of these struggling students either do not want to be in college or are there because they do not know what else to do. Many are facing relentless pressure from their parents to attend. They have dutifully responded to the college-for-all battle cry, but at what cost? Only 40% of students at my university ever graduate. The other 60% often leave with a sense of personal failure and a weighty student loan debt that, by national averages, is nearly $14,000 for those who never graduate college.

These are not merely anecdotes. Many formal studies support my personal observations (e.g., Daniels, Zemelman, & Bizar, 2001; Gray & Herr, 2006; Hall & Handley, 2004; Kirst & Venezia, 2004; Moore et al., 2010). Test scores reported by the American College Testing (ACT) (2018) show that only 27% of U.S. high school students who took the American College Testing exam in 2018 were considered "college ready" on all four of its readiness scales. Only 11% of African American students and 22% of Hispanic students earned college ready scores on three or more of the four benchmarks on the ACT. Scores were 62% for Asian American students and 48% for white students. Gray and Herr (2006) broaden the definition of college readiness and note when we use a four-year high school grade point average, the type of courses completed in high school (honors, AP, and college prep), and College Board test results, 40% of (non-special education) high school students who graduate high school are prepared for college (p. 4). So, depending on the definition of readiness, between 27% and 40% of high school graduates are college ready.

The combined dropout rate of students who *do* attend two-year or four-year colleges is 50%. Because of poor readiness, most of the students who drop out are not prepared for the rigors of higher education. On top of this, one-third of all students drop out of high school, and of those who do graduate high school, some 30% go straight to work. *Only 10% of teens who graduate high school eventually graduate from college* (see Gray & Herr, 2006, p. 11; Moore et al., 2010). If our goal is to prepare all students to attend and graduate college, our K-12 schools are failing miserably.

College-for-all is not based on reality. There are three reasons why I say the college-for-all vision is not based on reality. First, a single curriculum foisted upon everyone does not reflect the vast human diversity that we see in each classroom and as parents in our own homes. I am not talking about racial or gender diversity, but diversity of interests, passions, capacities, and talents. The reason why only 27–40% of students are college ready by the end of high school is because only 27–40% of students are highly motivated academically, can perform college-level intellectual tasks, and enjoy schoolwork (Asch, 2010; Murray, 2008). Our current elementary curriculum is intellectually demanding, and college is even harder. This requires some considerable intelligence. Even more importantly, motivation, interest, attitude, character, discipline, habits, willingness to exert intellectual effort, and family support are as influential to college readiness and K-12 academic success as intelligence. Many students just hate school and would rather do almost anything else than sit in a classroom. But we force them year after year to do *what we want them to do*, believing we know what is good for them. Many of these students may be intellectually capable of college-level work in theory, but if the motivational and environmental impediments are at work over many years, students will do poorly in primary and secondary school and will not be ready for college. By fifth or sixth grade, students' dispositions, habits, and attitudes are as difficult to change as intelligence.

Second, the college-for-all vision is not based on reality because there are not nearly enough jobs that require a college degree, even for the limited number of students who graduate college. Gray and Herr (2006) note that throughout the 1960s, just one in five four-year college graduates was not able to find a degree-demanding job. By the 1990s, this figure jumped to one in three and is now two in five. In the professions like accounting or teaching, the number is as high as one in two college graduates who cannot find a degree-demanding job. Even with our low college graduation rates, there are currently nearly two times as many college graduates on the market as there are job openings requiring a college degree. More than 40% of college graduates wind up in employment that does not require college (Burning Glass Technologies and Strada Institute for the Future of Work, 2018). They are overqualified and in jobs with limited career development. Almost every family with a recent college graduate living at home can attest to this. These people are beginning to wake up from the hangover of the college-for-all party.

Third, the college-for-all focus has led to a serious shortage of skilled technical workers in the area of electronics production, building construction, information technology, precision manufacturing, and health care (National Academies of Sciences, 2017). The salary range in many of these jobs is comparable to degree-demanding jobs (Carnevale, Strohl, Ridley, & Gulish, 2018). These skilled technical jobs typically go overseas when companies cannot hire domestic workers to do them, or companies hire foreign-born workers. We have filled our students' heads with the false idea that there is simply no way to have a job that will support a decent life without a college degree. Many of my own academically struggling college students believe they cannot earn a good income without a college or graduate degree. I have them conduct a simple survey at the U.S. Department of Labor's *onetonline* site on the average yearly salaries, type of job, and overall job openings of each type that do not require a college degree. This convinces most that the college-or-bust story is just not accurate.

What is our response to the failure of the one-size-fits-all college prep curriculum? We reflexively blame teachers and assume they need to learn better techniques to engage students. We threaten teachers with sanctions or firing if their students continue to earn low test scores on tests that assess the college prep curriculum. Some even allege teachers' unconscious racial or gender bias plays a role in poor student performance (Cherng, 2017; Fitzpatrick, Côté-Lussier, Pagani, & Blair, 2015). Many school administrators and educational professionals assume if we just assess students earlier and get them the right kind of special interventions, they will get on the college prep path. They then take continued poor performance after such interventions as evidence the child may have a learning disability and so needs special education or formal accommodations. Once these poor performing students get this special assistance for their disability, we reason, they will hop on the Platonic path. Some do, of course, but most do not.

The one thing we never seem to do is *let go of the idea that college is for all*, that the Platonic curriculum somehow suits the interests, needs, and abilities of all students. I say with Elsa of Arendelle, "Let it go!" Once we do that, we begin to see our job as teachers (and parents) is not to force a single curriculum or career path on all children, to push them toward college (or a high-paying job), but to develop a curriculum that accords with their interests, needs, and abilities. Letting go of the college-for-all vision allows us to reject the universalist assumption behind our current educational project that insists "all students" can or should do one single thing. Even with our current college-for-all curriculum and all of our pushing, students still pursue many different paths after high school besides college. This is because people are different! Why not help and prepare these different people for the different life paths they eventually take? After more than 30 years of focused legislation and billions of dollars in funding, fully 80% of students either cannot or will not graduate from college. This is not a tragedy. There is dignity in all work and all career paths. The quicker we remove the prejudice toward people who do not attend college and provide them with an appropriate education and career plan, the better off we all will be.

My proposal is to have three to four different curricular "tracks" in middle and high school instead of just the one we have now (two, if you count the "AP/honors" college prep track and the regular college prep track as separate). The academic standards would be the same for all students in elementary school, but after fifth grade the standards would begin diverge into a variety of academic tracks with different curricula: one for four-year college preparation and university studies, one for high-skilled technical careers at two-year colleges or apprenticeships (information technology, precision manufacturing, electronics production, or health care), and one for artisans and students who will work with their hands (auto mechanics, masons, building construction, electricians, farmers). I will explore this idea in more detail in the next chapter.

Middle school would be the time to solidify academic gains made in elementary school, remediate any deficiencies, assess interest and ability for continued study, do serious guidance counseling and career exploration, and take tentative steps toward a formal curriculum track based on past academic performance, input from current and former teachers, families, and the student him or herself. There are currently "tracks" in middle and high school in the form of ability groups, but not a separate curriculum with different learning goals for each group as I am proposing. Having separate curricula will likely require additional legislation since the pattern of recent federal laws and court decisions has been to assert that all students have a "right" to succeed in the college prep curriculum no matter what.

We should redesign elementary school not to start an intensive Platonic curriculum, but to teach all students a basic package of numeracy, literacy, physical fitness, arts, and citizenship skills, all encased within the larger context of self-discovery, adventure, and high purpose. In many ways, this curriculum would be far less rigorous and difficult than it is now, so it is likely that most elementary students will be successful. At the same time, this curriculum would be much more interesting, practical, and relevant to real life than it is now. After all, the elementary curriculum should reflect what we want our kids to be as human beings, not the narrow vision of educational capitalism. Children do not live by bread alone, and there is much more to life than doing well on your SATs and going to college. What kind of adult do you want your Kindergartner to be when he or she leaves the educational system? I want my children to love learning, to enjoy reading, to be engaged in their community, to be able to work cooperatively with others and to solve real problems in the world, to be able to speak well, persuade others with words and make cogent arguments in writing, to be able to know who they are and what they believe, and to care for their bodies and the natural world around them.

What K-12 schools do in the classroom now is basically a 13-year SAT prep course. The curriculum consists of a set of decontextualized standards unrelated to any discernible real-world activities. Students practice these skills in isolation and are later tested on whether they can do them or not. This kind of learning is narrow, artificial, and boring. Academically successful students can "add up to four two-digit numbers using strategies based on place value and properties of operations," but they cannot necessarily reason logically or solve problems creatively. The successful ones can "describe the overall structure of a story including describing how the beginning introduces the story, the middle provides major events and challenges, and the ending concludes the action," but they cannot necessarily speak well in front of other people, write about their own or others' ideas, discuss ideas with each other, or formally debate points. Academically successful students have test knowledge, which is important for sure, but limited. What is more, most students do not know themselves, what they really think and believe, how to have healthy relationships, and how to constructively disagree with others. Many of these larger goals I speak of are already in state curricula of course, but they are rarely rigorously taught or formally assessed. This must change. Under my vision, the elementary school system would be redesigned not to push all students to college, *but to enable them to participate in democracy and a mature adult life*. States would therefore need to change their academic standards, to craft a much wider, more relevant and appropriate educational system than we have now. It is also imperative to *formally assess the whole curriculum*, not just Reading, Writing, and Math. My vision is bold, but it can be done.

Here are the academic subjects and general learning goals to be achieved by the end of elementary school:

1. *Individual and Group Problem-Solving.* This forms the main frame of the elementary curriculum within which all the other academic subjects are encased. It is based on the project-based (DuBois & Keller, 2016) and collaborative learning (Rutherford, 2014) initiatives that exist now. Students would be given (or choose) various real-world problems to solve, for example, How should cities dispose of trash? How should flood-prone areas deal with flooding? What is the wisdom that exists in people in today's nursing homes? How can we increase voter turnout? Since these would be interesting problems for children, this aspect of the curriculum establishes the primary connection to the important issues of adventure and high purpose described in Chap. 3. Students would learn to work individually and in groups on a project to deal with each issue. The teacher's role would be to facilitate the project development process. In turn, students would learn about group dynamics, procedures, committees, even Roberts Rules of Order. All other academic subjects would be brought into this problem-solving context. We would teach Math, for example, in the context of disposing trash or calculating the number of voters who participate in a certain region of the country. We would teach English in writing a letter to the City Council on trash disposal or composing the plan to increase voter turnout. Many public schools currently identify themselves as "Project-Based Learning" schools, but in the context of the many college prep state standards we have now, it is practically impossible to do it well.
2. *Citizenship and Democratic Character.* Preparation for capable citizenship has historically been more central to public education's mission than intellectual development. This aspect of the curriculum builds on work done by Damon (2011) and Noddings (2013) on making schools places that teach citizenship and embody healthy democratic procedures. The goal of this part of the curriculum is to develop "democratic character," which involves the set of virtues (e.g., courage, cooperation, self-restraint, and justice) necessary for healthy participation in a democracy. It is important to keep in mind this is not Social Studies as it is currently taught (e.g., "Identify the following elected officials of the executive branch and where they work: President, Governor, Mayor"). It is also not Character Development as currently taught. Under my vision, students learn about democracy and develop democratic virtues not so much by

learning about them, but by running the school and their classrooms as a functioning democracy. In the current climate of degraded public discourse and democratic engagement, we need to cultivate these skills in the students of tomorrow more than ever.
3. *Reading and Writing.* By the end of elementary school, students should love to read and write on their own. We forget this goal in our drive to teach reading and writing competence. Students should be able to comprehend grade-level literary and informational texts, as well as write both persuasive and factual essays, but this is less important than developing a real love of reading and writing. This part of the curriculum would be like what most states do with the English/Language Arts (ELA) curriculum, though there are currently far too many standards and technical operations at each grade level than is necessary. Current ELA standards are also often taught in isolation from real-world contexts, for example, "Take out your Reading book and turn to the story on page 13. Today we will analyze 'point of view.'" Many current ELA standards would be eliminated or scaled down because the goal of my curriculum is not college prep reading and writing, but the basic literacy, reasoning, and speaking skills needed to help children function as citizens who are able to read a book or news article, write a letter to the editor, intelligently vote, and competently serve on a jury.
4. *Public Speaking and Debate.* The goal here is for students to leave elementary school as excellent orators and critical thinkers. Students would practice writing and delivering coherent, evidence-based speeches using different formats. They would learn to adapt their presentations to their audience based on situational, cultural, and psychological factors. They would learn to listen, critically respond to, and discuss others' speeches as listeners. Students would get a great deal of practice in school sending and receiving messages, role-playing, sharing experiences, and translating nonverbal messages like gestures and facial expressions.
5. *Mathematics and Logical Reasoning.* The current elementary Math curriculum gives far too much attention to detailed mathematical operations and algorithms that have more to do with a career in mathematics and the SAT than with real-world problems and quantitative-logical reasoning. My proposed curriculum would facilitate numerical literacy, the ability to perform basic operations and computations, work with data, and conduct measurements, but

with the goal of developing abstract thinking and logical reasoning. Students also would learn to link premises to sound conclusions in a chain of logical and quantitative reasoning. My curriculum could be a greatly simplified version of the Common Core Math curriculum we have now but encased in the context of real-world problem-solving described in #2.

6. *Interpersonal and Intrapersonal Intelligence.* Interpersonal intelligence refers to the ability to understand the emotions, desires, and wishes of other people, and to interact with them in appropriate and effective ways. Intrapersonal intelligence concerns the ability to know one's own feelings, motivations, strengths, and weaknesses. Apart from democratic character, these "people skills" are perhaps the single most important skill that one can learn in school and life. They are central to making friends, maintaining healthy love relationships, parenting, career success, and happiness in adulthood. How many problems in the world are caused by people who do not know themselves and have poor people skills? This part of the curriculum is based on existing work in elementary schools on intrapersonal intelligence (Sellars, 2006) and interpersonal intelligence or "social emotional learning" (Dusenbury & Weissberg, 2017). There are also currently many fine standards in various state curricula (Pennsylvania Department of Education, 2012), but they are often taught just once or twice a month during a visit from the school counselor. For these standards to be meaningfully achieved, they need to be not only embodied and taught in class every day but also assessed in high-stakes tests at the end of the year.

7. *Physical Fitness.* Physical fitness is the ability to carry out tasks without undue fatigue. It includes muscle strength, muscle endurance, cardiovascular endurance, and flexibility. Physical fitness is not only about learning the rules of sports or nutrition but also *becoming physically fit*. As such, students would learn how to sleep in healthy ways, how to prepare the right foods, and they would train to meet certain physical fitness goals. There are several physical fitness programs designed for elementary schools (e.g., Kohl & Cook, 2013), but they are rarely assessed at the end of the year or taught in a systematic manner. The National Association of Sports and Physical Education (PE) standard is that children participate in 150 minutes of physical education per week, but only six states comply with that standard. To increase achievement in the Platonic curriculum, many

states have eliminated PE and recess entirely, contributing to a public health crisis. Imagine what the obesity rates would be if all students (save for those with disabilities) had to run a mile in 15 minutes to advance to the next grade level.

My model would not completely discard our current Platonic curriculum (Math and ELA), but would integrate it among other, equally important subjects and learning goals. All students should be reading, computing, problem-solving, and writing every day in multiple courses for hundreds of hours each school year, but the goal is basic literacy and numeracy, not test prep and college admission. In my estimation, we currently start college and high-skilled career preparation much too early in a child's life. By fifth grade, if not much earlier, the spirit of learning is crushed in far too many students. It is therefore not necessary to have as many different college prep subjects in elementary school as we do now. The Platonic part of my curriculum would be trimmed to just two subjects: Reading/Writing and Math. I would eliminate from the current curriculum Science, Social Studies, Health Education, and Physical Education as separate subjects. They are currently done very poorly in elementary school as to be almost educationally meaningless. Science would be part of Math and Problem-Solving; Social Studies would be part of Citizenship; Health and Physical Education would be part of Physical Fitness. It would be up to each school whether to continue the "Specials" of Art, Music, World Languages, and so on. To address the aforementioned problems with differentiated instruction (DI), some schools may wish to use separate tracks or tiered homogeneous groups for the Platonic part of the curriculum, but given the focus on group processes, public speaking, and citizenship, most classes under my proposal will only work if taught in whole group fashion.

I would scale back the Platonic component of our existing curriculum in both detail and intensity. My curriculum would not focus on isolated standards; rather, discrete Platonic operations would always be joined to real-world situations and abilities such as public speaking, debate, and group problem-solving. I believe this would increase student engagement and academic success. Student test performance on the Platonic and other parts of the curriculum would be carefully documented and monitored each year. Test data would also be disaggregated and publicly reported. We would take poor student academic performance, behavior problems, and/or lack of interest in school as indications during reviews or "conversations" that would take place in the third and fifth grades between students, parents, families, current and former teachers, and relevant administrators.

The fifth-grade conversation would be to prepare for one of the tracks that would begin on a preliminary basis in middle school. Schools would do everything possible to help all students achieve these reduced and greatly simplified academic standards in elementary school, but the goal would be to help prepare each student for what he or she is called to do rather than for what we think they should do. As I said in Chap. 8, these additional efforts may include getting more class time for students to practice tasks they cannot master, getting struggling students special help, separating some students for Math or Reading instruction, providing extra help/tutoring before or after school, extending the school day, week, or year for struggling students, investing heavily in early education, and insisting on academic support and changed discursive practices at home.

But it is important to keep in mind that if academically underperforming students do not perform well in the Platonic curriculum subjects (Math, Reading, Writing) by middle and late elementary school, they rarely change this performance in middle or high school (Beaudette, Chalasani, & Rauschenberg, 2017; Lloyd, 1978). Far better to get them on a track that suits their interests and abilities than to pummel them with the Platonic curriculum for seven more years after elementary school. I am aware of the controversy and tension with a proposal like mine, but I believe it will serve students much better than what we are doing for them now. Currently it is the Platonic curriculum or nothing. My proposal is to give middle and high school students more ways to succeed than just this one path.

The entire K-12 system would need to be reimagined for my proposal to become a reality. I realize that with the hold the Administration has on the various levers of educational power and the general passivity of the public, this scenario is unlikely. One can still dream. There are two major things that would need to change for my vision to be realized. First, millions of parents would need to get off the college-for-all bandwagon and let go of the seductive belief that the purpose of school is to train your child for college and a financially lucrative career. This will be incredibly difficult. Fifteen percent of parents with students in grades 6–12 expect them to attend two or more years of college; 29% expect them to earn a bachelor's degree; and 39% expect their children to earn a graduate or professional degree (National Center for Education Statistics, 2017).

Seventy percent of parents expect an outcome that only 10% of children attain. Only 25% of children ever even enroll in a college.

Second, many encrusted layers of the Administration would need to drop the total management mindset that casts schools as places to manage the successful transmission of the college prep curriculum to all students almost no matter what. Many special education, supervisory, assessment, support, and administrative posts have been created in our present system to help achieve these unrealistic goals when regular classroom instruction fails. There would be great resistance to eliminating these often better paid positions as the focus of the curriculum returned to having almost all employees teaching in regular classrooms rather than supervising, assessing, reporting on, or managing specialized educational problems.

Parental and neighborhood engagement. The second way to lower the current wall of separation between schools and the public is to increase parental engagement. All rights come with corresponding responsibilities. The constitutional right to express yourself is tempered by the responsibility to respect the rights and beliefs of others. The right to freely pursue life, liberty, and happiness is tempered by the responsibility to serve on a jury when called upon or to defend the country if the need should arise. In the same way, receiving specific government services requires certain responsibilities. Our nation has not quite enumerated the specific responsibilities it expects from families who receive the government service of a free education. Henderson (2018) notes, "A muscular debate is long overdue about the basic level of obligation parents owe the state, if any, for providing their child an education" (p. 122). This discussion will likely need to be initiated from the very highest levels of government with a Kennedyesque challenge, "ask not what your school can do for you…" I am not holding my breath, but it needs to happen. At present, given the fact that the courts have struck down many previous school requirements for parent participation, the consensus appears to be that there are absolutely no responsibilities we can demand of parents for receiving a public education. This situation needs to change.

What would it take for parents, politicians, and citizens to feel a greater sense of ownership in the school system that they support with their tax dollars and expect so much from? For any curriculum to succeed at a higher rate than the 10–20% of students it does now, it cannot work with below average levels of community and family engagement. A parent engagement program should be mandatory in each school. This will likely require new legislation to achieve. Increased parental engagement will not just happen on its own. My proposal is to require a commitment of parent/family time of 6–15 hours for the academic year. Some schools ask for as many as 30 hours, so my figure is quite modest. This service could be performed in several different ways: attending PTA meetings, school committee meetings, planning school events, participating in school improvement or maintenance projects, providing tutoring or classroom assistance. In addition, each parent would pledge to assist their child on homework, to read to their child, and complete all necessary classroom paperwork for a minimum of five hours per week.

Recall the barriers to parental engagement in education I discussed in Chap. 12. The main struggle parents say they have is lack of time. We could pass legislation similar to the Family and Medical Leave Act in which a parent would be free to leave work a certain number of hours each year for school-related activities. These hours could either be compensated or made up through a flexible scheduling arrangement with one's employer, but an employee could not be penalized for missing work for a school function. Schools, in cooperation with the PTA, could provide childcare to parents who had younger children and need to perform school service. Parents also say they do not always know how to help their children in school. There are several promising parent engagement programs that take it as their mission to build bridges between families and schools in culturally sensitive ways (Auerbach, 2009; Yull, Wilson, Murray, & Parham, 2018). These programs help teach parents who need it how to provide appropriate educational assistance, what the grade-level standards are, ways to support the standards at home, even parenting skills. Many parents may need this special help to become more involved in schools, but many others simply need to be asked. Other parents tell us they feel like they are overstepping their bounds by getting involved, or that their own children resist their efforts to become more involved. These issues could be addressed by slowly changing the school culture to one that is inviting to parents and lends itself to parent-school collaboration.

Multiplying Diversions

Schools are often saddled with legal regulations, complex curricula, and discipline policies that they did not choose themselves and which they must expend great time and effort to adhere to, often with limited benefit. In addition, for the noblest of reasons, many schools choose to get themselves involved in matters that divert them from their primary educational task. How can we help schools navigate through cumbersome laws, rules, political currents, fads, and programs to refocus on their main mission? In this section, I discuss six things that schools can do to regain focus on what they do best: educating students.

Stop non-academic services. The first thing that will help schools regain focus is to eliminate as many non-academic services as possible. This will obviously be a decision for each school, district, and state, but they currently do far too many non-academic things. They think they are being compassionate by doing these things, but they are really punishing students by diverting educational resources away from them and encouraging a passive dependency in parents and families. Schools will need to develop the courage to say "no" to many requests and to trust that someone else will do it. One major way to acquire additional assistance is to call upon parents, families, the community, and government stakeholders to do more for schools and children than they currently do.

Simplify the curriculum. I proposed a massively simplified elementary curriculum in the previous section of this chapter. The elimination of the relentless college-for-all vision will lower the pressure to have all students demonstrate mastery in what is often an extremely difficult, boring, and even irrelevant course of study. These changes will greatly reduce the need for educational specialists and special educators. More teachers would therefore return to the regular classroom, which will free money and resources to enable schools to focus on the general curriculum, hopefully engaging students more effectively. Simplifying the curriculum will also eliminate the need for the endless test preparation and assessment that currently go on all school year.

Fully fund IDEA. To achieve the educational goals required by *Individuals with Disabilities Education Act* (IDEA), what is required is full funding of IDEA. This will amount to more than $20 billion in yearly educational spending that can be used for the often time-consuming special initiatives, which take the regular classroom teacher away from the rest of her students (Litinov, 2015). The other cost-cutting measures I outline in this book will also free up additional funds that can be used to hire more teachers and create smaller classrooms where genuine differentiated instruction could be properly implemented. More individualized instruction will enable teachers to work with students in a way that is truly personal, developmentally appropriate, challenging, and relevant to the student's life (Pappano, 2011; Schmoker, 2010).

Zero tolerance discipline policies. When I talk to teachers about their struggles, the way the Administration handles (or does not handle) behavior problems is at the top of their list of complaints. Simply put, a classroom needs to be quiet for students to learn, and students need to listen to teachers' instructions for the system to work. We cannot tolerate anything less, and we often do. When I first returned to the elementary classroom after 20 years to begin my work on my doctoral dissertation, I could not believe how badly many students treated adults compared to when I was in school, and how many adults simply tolerated it. Teachers must deal with a host of disrespectful and disruptive behaviors that many parents would never put up with at home. Some classrooms do just fine, but many more do not. There is a national need to improve school discipline policies, but many teachers (and parents) are hamstrung because they have very limited autonomy over these matters. School discipline policy is typically in the hands of the Administration who often see student misbehavior as caused by the teacher's poor classroom management skills, frustrations of children's rights, student psychological problems, and even racial and social injustice (Skiba et al., 2011).

Teachers of all races and backgrounds tend to see the issue of student misbehavior and school discipline policy very differently from administrators and educational researchers. Teachers understand students' disruptive behavior as caused by a lack of interest in school, bad school climate, school and social permissiveness about misbehavior and violence, and most of all, *poor parenting* (Lopes & Santos, 2013; Riley, Lewis, & Wang, 2012). I tend to agree with the teachers. Most behavioral problems are choices children make, and very strategic ones at that. In my experience, I have rarely heard a teacher say student behavior problems are about psychological disorders, poor classroom management techniques, children not having enough rights, or the history of racial or economic injustice. A few surely involve these things, but most do not. Whatever the reason, no student has the right to monopolize a teacher's time with his or her misbehavior or to prevent other students from learning. It is that simple. Students who cannot behave despite multiple warnings must be removed from the general classroom for progressively longer periods if their behavior continues without being corrected. After many chances, if a student cannot behave at school, he or she should not be allowed to attend a typical school, but must attend an alternative program. Attendance at such programs could be reviewed every three months to monitor progress. It sounds harsh, and there is worry these policies will disproportionately affect minority student populations, but the damage disruptive students cause to themselves, other students, and the teacher is much harsher than the policy I propose.

Bring in the home to help with discipline and other school policies. No child should be able to hit teachers or other students, curse at them, spit at them, or generally be a disruptive menace all day long at school and then return home to enjoy an evening on his Xbox or cell phone. Parents and teachers must help each other and band together against this common foe: *student misbehavior and poor impulse control.* Many parents aim to support good behavior in their children at home and would likely be horrified to see how their kids behave at school. It is typically the administrators and educational researchers who make all the excuses and craft overly tolerant discipline policies. Many schools already do this, but students and parents should sign a clearly worded behavioral contract at the beginning of the year. This contract should explicitly define unacceptable behaviors and contain a sliding scale of increasingly severe penalties for infractions, leading ultimately to school reassignment to an alternative program. Parents and schools would then cooperate toward the realization of these behavioral goals.

Eliminate red tape and busy paperwork. Schools must renew their commitment to treating certified teachers as the trained professionals they are. As such, extra-duty assignments that take away from planning time and professional development must be kept to a bare minimum. They are burning teachers out (Fernet, Chanal, & Guay, 2017). In addition, the administration must realize that its various requirements for Response to Interventions, Individualized Education Programs, and other special interventions are stretching the regular classroom teacher beyond her ability to deliver effective instruction to the whole group. If the district or state requires data gathering, report-writing, meeting attendance, and special small-group teaching interventions for some students, those services should be separately funded and provided by someone other than the classroom teacher. She has quite enough on her plate already.

References

ACT. (2018). The condition of college and career readiness [PDF File]. Retrieved from https://www.act.org/content/dam/act/unsecured/documents/cccr2018/National-CCCR-2018.pdf

Asch, C. M. (2010). The inadvertent bigotry of inappropriate expectations. *Education Week, 29*(35), 35.

Auerbach, S. (2009). Walking the walk: Portraits in leadership for family engagement in urban schools. *School Community Journal, 19*(1), 9–32.

Beaudette, P., Chalasani, K., & Rauschenberg, S. (2017). How do students' 3rd grade reading levels relate to their ACT/SAT performance and chance of graduating from high school? [PDF File]. Retrieved from https://gosa.georgia.gov/sites/gosa.georgia.gov/files/related_files/press_release/3rd%20Grade%20Reading-Graduation-ACT-SAT%20Analysis%20Final%2003222017.pdf

Burning Glass Technologies and Strada Institute for the Future of Work. (2018). The permanent detour: Underemployment's long-term effects on the careers of college grads [PDF File]. Retrieved from https://www.burning-glass.com/wp-content/uploads/permanent_detour_underemployment_report.pdf

Carnevale, A. P., Strohl, J., Ridley, N., & Gulish, A. (2018). Three educational pathways to good jobs: High school, middle skills, and bachelor's degree [PDF File]. Retrieved from https://1gyhoq479ufd3yna29x7ubjn-wpengine.netdna-ssl.com/wp-content/uploads/3ways-FR.pdf

Cherng, H. Y. S. (2017). If they think I can: Teacher bias and youth of color expectations and achievement. *Social Science Research, 66,* 170–186.

Damon, W. (2011). *Failing liberty 101: How we are leaving young Americans unprepared for citizenship in a free society.* Palo Alto, CA: Hoover Institution Press.

Daniels, H., Zemelman, S., & Bizar, M. (2001). *Rethinking high school: Best practice in teaching, learning, and leadership.* Portsmouth, NH: Heinemann.

DuBois, A. L., & Keller, T. M. (2016). Curriculum weaving: Developing creative curricular opportunities for pre-service teachers and elementary students through project-based learning. *Journal of Curriculum and Teaching, 5*(2), 37–42.

Dusenbury, L., & Weissberg, R. P. (2017). Social emotional learning in elementary school: Preparation for success. *Education Digest, 83*(1), 36–43.

Fernet, C., Chanal, J., & Guay, F. (2017). What fuels the fire: Job- or task-specific motivation (or both)? On the hierarchical and multidimensional nature of teacher motivation in relation to job burnout. *Work & Stress, 31*(2), 145–163. https://doi.org/10.1080/02678373.2017.1303758

Fitzpatrick, C., Côté-Lussier, C., Pagani, L. S., & Blair, C. (2015). I don't think you like me very much: Child minority status and disadvantage predict relationship quality with teachers. *Youth & Society, 47*(5), 727–743.

Gray, K. C., & Herr, E. L. (2006). *Other ways to win: Creating alternatives for high school graduates.* Thousand Oaks, CA: Corwin.

Hall, E., & Handley, R. (2004). *High schools in crisis: What every parent should know.* Westport, CT: Praeger.

Henderson, C. (2018). *Sit down and shut up: How discipline can set students free.* New York, NY: St. Martin's.

Kirst, M. W., & Venezia, A. (Eds.). (2004). *From high school to college: Improving opportunities for success in postsecondary education.* San Francisco, CA: Jossey-Bass.

Kohl, H. W., & Cook, H. D. (2013). *Educating the student body: Taking physical activity and physical education to school.* Washington, DC: The National Academies Press.

Litinov, A. (2015, May 9). How Congress' underfunding of special education shortchanges us all. Retrieved from National Education Association Website: https://educationvotes.nea.org/2015/05/19/how-congress-underfunding-of-special-education-shortchanges-us-all/

Lloyd, D. N. (1978). Prediction of school failure from third-grade data. *Educational and Psychological Measurement, 38*(4), 1193–1200.

Lopes, J., & Santos, M. (2013). Teachers' beliefs, teachers' goals and teachers' classroom management: A study with primary teachers. *Journal of Psychodidactics, 18,* 5–24. https://doi.org/10.1387/RevPsicodidact.4615

Moore, G., Slate, J. R., Edmonson, S., Combs, J. P., Bustamante, R., & Onwuegbuzie, A. J. (2010). High school students and their lack of preparedness for college: A statewide study. *Education and Urban Society, 42*(7), 817–838. https://doi.org/10.1177/0013124510379619

Murray, C. (2008). *Real education: Four simple truths for bringing America's schools back to reality.* New York, NY: Three Rivers Press.

National Academies of Sciences Engineering and Medicine. (2017). *Building America's skilled technical workforce.* Washington, DC: National Academies Press.

National Center for Education Statistics. (2017). *Parent and family involvement in education: Results from the national household education surveys program of 2016* [PDF File]. Retrieved from National Center for Education Statistics Website: https://nces.ed.gov/pubs2017/2017102.pdf

Noddings, N. (2013). *Education and democracy in the 21st century.* New York, NY: Teachers College Press.

Pappano, L. (2011). Differentiated instruction reexamined. *Harvard Education Letter, 27*(3). Retrieved from http://hepg.org/hel/article/499#home

Pennsylvania Department of Education. (2012). Standards for student interpersonal skills [PDF File]. Retrieved from http://www.tulpehocken.org/Downloads/Student_Interpersonal_Skills_Standards.pdf

Riley, P., Lewis, R., & Wang, B. (2012). Investigating teachers' explanations for aggressive classroom discipline strategies in China and Australia. *Educational Psychology, 32*(3), 389–403. https://doi.org/10.1080/01443410.2012.662151

Rutherford, S. (2014). *Collaborative learning: Theory, strategies, and educational benefits.* New York, NY: Nova Science Publishers Inc.

Schmoker, M. (2010, September 27). When pedagogic fads trump priorities. *Education Week.* Retrieved from http://www.edweek.org/ew/articles/2010/09/29/05schmoker.h30.html

Sellars, M. (2006). The role of intrapersonal intelligence in self directed learning. *Issues in Educational Research, 16*(1), 95–119.

Skiba, R. J., Horner, R. H., Chung, C.-G., Rausch, M. K., May, S. L., & Tobin, T. (2011). Race is not neutral: A national investigation of African American and Latino disproportionality in school discipline. *School Psychology Review, 40*(1), 85–107.

Yull, D., Wilson, M., Murray, C., & Parham, L. (2018). Reversing the dehumanization of families of color in schools: Community-based research in a race-conscious parent engagement program. *School Community Journal, 28*(1), 319–347.

PART III

What to Do About All Ten Things

CHAPTER 14

A New Day

When I began writing this book, I did an exercise I conduct with my graduate students to help them when they have a big writing project due. In this exercise, you imagine your project as a person with a life of its own. Once you can envision this person, you have a conversation with him or her about what they want you to do, what they want the project look like, and be about. You can even ask the person questions weighing on your mind, for example, "What should I do about this issue?" or "How should I respond to that?" The exercise helps a writer see the larger goals and intentions of a project and experience why something needs to be written in the first place. My "person" turned out to be a happy little boy who had feelings about school I could only describe as enthusiastic and passionately curious. I realized right away these were very much like the feelings I had as a child growing up attending Red Oak Preschool and Fairview Elementary School. I recall those years as among the most exciting and fulfilling of my life. I loved to go to school, to learn, play, sing, build, draw, think, and be with friends.

Each morning when I sat down to write this book, I talked to this little boy first and asked him what he wanted me to do or say. Like me, this boy very much believes in the promise of public elementary education. It is hard for him to see so many children who do not feel good about school. When I talked with this little boy, he told me different things that would help him feel more excited about being in today's schools. These guided imagination exercises helped me conjure a vision of the elementary schools

© The Author(s) 2019
J. J. Dillon, *Inside Today's Elementary Schools*,
https://doi.org/10.1007/978-3-030-23347-1_14

that shepherded me through this book project and motivated me to work for positive educational change in the future.

The guiding vision that emerged from this imaginal dialogue is a picture of elementary schools where each of the Things described in this book is taken much more seriously than it is now. In this vision, schools are places filled with adventure and high purpose, with classrooms small and manageable enough to waste only a minimum of time, and built for the nature of both male and female students. They are places free from stifling levels of bureaucracy and regulation, supervised by rotating teacher administrators rather than career managers. They are places filled with scholarly, curious, and engaged teaching professionals dedicated to helping students live a life of the mind in a democracy rather than imposing a soul-killing, one-size-fits-all, furiously assessed college prep curriculum on everybody. They are places with classrooms of narrow ability ranges dedicated to teaching a single, coherent curriculum, all in a context of full buy-in and support from students' families and the wider community.

As we look forward to a "new day" in elementary education, it is clear to me that what stands in the way of this vision becoming a reality is each of the ten things I have described in this book (and probably a few more). Speaking as a psychologist, these obstacles really come down to just three things: fear, ideology, and an intense need to control.

Dealing with Fear

The first curriculum night at the beginning of the school year is filled with nervous parents. Most are secretly worried their child may not do well in school or will not "make it" as an adult in society. Many parent-teacher conferences are filled with anxious parents who wonder, and often ask, if there is "something wrong" with their child that will hobble their educational journey. As they hold their babies in their arms, most parents are filled with great expectations for their children. Maybe he will be a doctor, maybe she will be a lawyer, or maybe even the president of the United States. The idea of being "left behind" the promise of these dreams of the future fills many parents with dread. In the end, however, each of these hopes and fears only narrows the vision of success we have for our children and leads to the mistaken belief that college is the only way to a bright future. "Serious schools," people reason, begin the rigorous academic journey to college in Kindergarten, if not earlier.

Administrators share in this fear. They are terrified to have any students left out of this bright vision of the future. It leads them to implement all manner of inducements, threats, and policies to see to it that all students master the increasingly rigorous Platonic curriculum they have devised. They fear looking like they do not have a plan, that they are not "on top of" today's many educational problems. These fears lead them to burden teachers with impossible tasks that force them to cut corners on good teaching or even to cheat to play this results-oriented game.

Teachers and administrators both are often afraid to talk candidly with parents and students about ability, aptitude, and intelligence, about the fact that some students are just not good at or interested in certain academic things. Parents are afraid to have a child who is "just average," or worse, "below average." This fear leads them to ignore their children's actual gifts and focus instead on imagined ones they hope will someday appear with enough cajoling, discipline, and talented teachers.

Several things can happen to lessen these fears. First, our overall view of children and their nature needs to change. We should learn to accept that children vary widely in talent, disposition, and interests. Each child is called to do something very specific with his or her life and is given particular gifts to fulfill that calling. Each person's path is different from the other. Some are called to build with their hands, and some to design plans with their minds. Some are called to defend the territory, others to farm, and still others to attend to the sick. This great diversity is how it should be. Doing what one is called to do, following one's unique path, is *social justice* in the classical sense. It is *social injustice* to force everyone onto the same path. We adults must work hard to accept who children really are rather than what we want them to be, to help them discover their true path rather than impose it on them from the outside. Rather than fearing children will not do what we desire, our only fear should be that children grow up doing something he or she is not meant to do.

Second, there must be a grand social awakening from the intoxicating spell of educational capitalism. The purpose of elementary school is not to prepare children for college and a high-paying job, but to develop their intellects and character to prepare them for healthy adult living and democratic participation. These skills have also proven valuable in the marketplace, but that is not the reason why they are important. Given the true humanistic purpose of education, we must broaden the elementary curriculum beyond its current college prep focus toward a recovery of the liberal arts presented in Chap. 13. It is these liberal arts skills, not the isolated Platonic standards, which are ultimately valuable in the marketplace anyway. Such a shift will not only lead to the development of intellectual skills and character traits that will be good for students and the wider world, but it will also be an exciting invitation to the young child to begin the high adventure of physical, moral, and intellectual living.

Third, we must all work hard to create and celebrate multiple paths to success. Over the past 30 years, the educational experts have made major educational planning decisions based on an analysis of the "jobs of tomorrow." The conclusion is that the path to success in the jobs of the future will increasingly require a college degree. I believe this is greatly overstated and does not reflect a true picture, but in any case, far too many good noncollege jobs in agriculture, construction, manufacturing, and trades are going away. Tyre (2009) notes that well-paying manufacturing jobs comprised 32% of all jobs in 1959, 17% in 2003, and just 5.4% in 2014. This is an unsustainable course, but it is not a *fait accompli*. We can work together to transform the economy through political action into one that reflects the true diversity of interests, aptitudes, and abilities of the citizenry. We simply cannot become a nation whose only jobs are those requiring a college or graduate degree (along with a smattering of service and manual labor positions). We must trade goods, not just services. We should work together to make our economy one where we not only design but also make and assemble the products we use, where we not only import but also grow the food we consume (see Marglin, 2008; Schumacher, 1973). The "free trade" policies of the past 30 years, while adding some real economic gains, have also tilted the jobs of tomorrow toward an unnatural requirement for advanced degrees (Symonds, Schwartz, & Ferguson, 2011). This must stop.

Seeing Through Ideology

Henderson (2018) notes each classroom presents us with a miniature version of the same political, cultural, and economic dynamics that play out in the larger society. He writes, "the four walls of a nation's classroom are hothouse laboratories—chaotic, teeming, vibrant, tough—containing that nation's most vexing social issues" (p. 8). In educational settings in the United States, most everything is filtered through two big "lenses" or stories: race/class and social mobility. One story is about past and present barriers and the other about optimism and upward climbing. I look at the social mobility lens first. This is a modern story based largely on the work of the British philosopher John Locke (1974/1690) and the psychologist John Watson (1970). The basic idea is that children are born as a blank slate (*tabula rasa*). Development is the story of how our life experiences write on this blank page, forming us into what we become. We are, as it were, a "product of our environment." Any differences in older children or adults are therefore to be understood in terms of the influence of different social circumstances and life experiences. According to this story, if we want to reduce inequality and create a good life for all, we need to work hard to see that all children have supportive upbringings and useful resources provided to them. In the American educational context, the idea is if we can create quality schools and talented teachers, all children will be able to climb out of difficult circumstances and eventually "make it."

The social mobility story is behind the current one-size-fits-all Platonic curriculum. We want all children to achieve the result of "college and career-readiness" by the end of their K-12 experience. We reason if we design a rigorous curriculum based on science and best practices, train quality teachers, install effective managers, and have the right testing schemes, all children will rise to the top. If children fail in school, it is only because we have not tried hard enough, not funded the schools enough, trained the teachers well enough, or introduced special interventions to struggling students early enough. This is a powerful and seductive story, and it is true in many instances. Children surely are influenced by social inputs like schools, but this influence extends only so far. Schools can facilitate the development of what a child is by nature (and with a great deal of cooperation from other parties like parents and neighborhoods). But when the social mobility story is the only one we use to understand differences in student performance, it becomes an *ideology* that uncritically explains everything. We become unable to see when the story applies and when it does not.

The flip side of boundless optimism is the story of economic and racial injustice. This is also a modern story based largely on the "critical" work of the German philosopher Karl Marx (Marx & Engels, 1990/1867) and Russian psychologist Lev Vygotsky (Vygotsky & Cole, 1978). The idea is that the higher psychological functions are reflections of underlying class and socioeconomic conditions. One's socioeconomic station in life produces a certain kind of intellectual functioning and ability. Our history of racial, social, and economic oppression has created a rigid class system that then leads to different behaviors and competences in school children from each of these groups. Differences between older children are understood in terms of the influence of class and race. If we want to reduce inequality and create a good life for all, the injustice story tells us, we need to work hard to see that all children have adequate economic resources and are free from oppressive racial stereotypes and social structures. In the American educational context, the failure to achieve academically or to behave in the proscribed manner is understood to be caused by underlying social, economic, and racial conditions. The story tells us the way to address performance gaps between students of different socioeconomic classes or racial groups is for schools and teachers not to "perpetuate" these unjust conditions in the classroom and work instead to heal them.

The injustice story is behind landmark laws such as *Elementary and Secondary Education Act* and *No Child Left Behind Act*. It has also led to billions of dollars of additional school funding, learning support, special education, and other interventions for underserved schools in attempts to "equalize" them. As with the social mobility story, the belief is that all children can succeed academically if oppressive obstacles from the outside are removed. If children do not do well in school, it is only because we have not worked hard enough to remove the legacy of racial oppression, economic inequality, and social stratification that still plague our nation. This is another powerful and seductive story which is true in many instances. Slavery and racial oppression are tragic facts of our nation's history and current society. Social stratification and economic inequality still put a finger on the scale of who "makes it" in society and who does not. But as with social mobility, when we take this story to be the only valid account to explain academic differences in performance, it becomes an *ideology* uncritically used to explain absolutely everything. We become blind to see when the story applies and when it does not.

What is more, an inordinate amount of emotional energy is invested in these two stories in academic settings. People believe them with all their hearts. They come to comprise our professional identities, establish the professional groups we are part of, and build a powerful orthodoxy on certain questions that can lead to name-calling, shouting, firing, or professional ostracization if the stories are challenged or not rigidly followed. Holding firm to these stories forms what Jacobs (2017) calls an "inner ring" comprised of an "in group" of favored and powerful individuals who have the "right views" on educational matters and an "out group" of ostracized others not taken seriously and rarely hired. Educational experts, administrators, and many teachers are terrified to be viewed by their colleagues as "out of date," "behind the times," or worse, "privileged," "elitist," "sexist," or "racist" by not holding either of these two stories as ideologies. This fear often prevents people in education from clear thinking and common sense.

As partially true and helpful as each of these stories can be, each works together as ideology to make schools worse. The reason is that these explanations are empirical claims, not religious precepts. They are explanatory hypotheses that are actually true or false, applicable in a given case or not. The question is whether it is true that the struggling second-grader in Miss Thomas' class has difficulty drawing out the main idea of a four-paragraph essay on tortoises because of his economic circumstances, class consciousness, or the history and current experience of racial injustice. I imagine some economic circumstances, for example, would be so severe that they do account for the reading difficulty. In that case, the story is helpful and allows the school or the teacher to rectify the situation. This is the reason schools feed many students breakfast or send groceries home with them. Or, I imagine some internalized racial prejudices or effects of present discrimination are so severe that they account for the student's difficulties tackling the passage. In that case, the story is helpful and allows the school or the teacher to address and try to heal the injustice.

But in most cases, however, these explanations are unsound. When they are sound, it is often in the vaguest of ways. They provide the teacher no real help to deal with this student's current problems in learning. This is the reason why most teachers are not ideological. Teachers find ideologies do not work in the context of real classrooms which are always more complex and messier than these neat explanations allow. There is a reason why so many educational administrators and researchers are ideological. They do not have the accountability of an actual classroom full of students to convince them their story does not apply or is not useful. Ideology is, to return to the Picasso example at the beginning of the book, aesthetics and not turpentine. It is not that society is a bias-free zone or that economic equality has finally been achieved, but that these factors do not explain why this particular student is not listening to his teacher, is not interested in the four-paragraph essay, and wants to do almost anything else besides this lesson. Under the dominance of these two explanatory stories, failures and differences between students are explained in the same tired ways: past/present injustice, current teacher incompetence/managerial neglect, or inadequate school funding and resources. No matter what happens on the ground, these explanations tell us we need to work harder from the outside.

Letting Go of the Need to Control

Contrary to Locke, children are not blank slates. They do not become what we make them, but what *they are*. We are not really in control of their lives; they are. Yes, we shape, we guide, but we do not determine. Culture is the soil within which a child's nature grows. Cultures "cultivate" human nature, but they do not construct or determine it. True education is working to realize the child's inner nature rather than to form them into shapes of our own design. This is the classical understanding of education as *educare*, or "drawing out" a child's nature. Children will be themselves one way or another, sooner or later. The question is whether this self-realization process will be an easy or a hard one, whether we will end up causing so much damage in the end that the changes we manage to impose come at too high a price. As a psychologist, I see the casualties of this Lockean philosophy of parenting in the form of confused and depressed college students who are pressured by their parents into a career path they do not want, and miserable adults dealing with painful midlife crises when the energy of leading an inauthentic life chosen only to please their parents and teachers finally dissipates.

The current one-size-fits-all Platonic curriculum does not work well for many students. And this is not necessarily a problem. It may be that for these students, a different path with a different curriculum would be more fitting. Many of these struggling students are boys, and many others who falter are just called to other things. (Of course, some of these students are let down by poor schools and teachers, but this is vastly overstated. Many of these so-called failing schools are peppered with inspiring examples of educational success.) For example, the "boy problem" in schools outlined in Chap. 2 was not always with us. Boys fared much better in schools of the past. Their current decline closely tracks the educational reforms traced in Chap. 7 that started about 30 years ago and moved the curriculum toward more academic rigor and less play and movement.

Tyre (2009) notes we can see this shift even at the preschool level, where activities such as rhyming, sorting, and block-building have been replaced by formal school lessons and worksheets for two-, three-, and four-year-olds focused mainly on literacy and math. Consider also how most preschools have changed their names during this time from the whimsical "Children's Garden" to the serious "Whitmore Academy." Gone from elementary school is much of the free play, pretend games, toys, board games, and ball games of the past. Having seen most of these reforms up close, teachers I spoke with tell me with each new reform, the curriculum shifted down one to two years. In other words, what was covered in second grade under the old curriculum was now done in first grade under the new. What was done in first grade moved down to Kindergarten. As a result, two-thirds of elementary schools started spending more time on reading and math, the subjects assessed on state tests. Forty-four percent of schools reduced the time kids spend on social studies, science, art, music, lunch, Physical Education, and recess (Tyre, 2009, p. 84). Many students just have not done well with these changes. These changed schools make certain otherwise normal behaviors seem disabled or even pathological.

To stop this obsessive need to control and obtain a single educational outcome for every student, I suggest changing the curriculum in middle and high school to better accord with children's different callings, to truly differentiate the curriculum based on each child's competencies and interests. This book is not about middle and high school of course, but changing the nature of these levels in the ways I suggest would free elementary schools from the relentless pressure of the college prep curriculum beginning in Kindergarten. It would enable us to make the elementary curriculum much more practical, physical, exciting, and democratic than it currently is.

I outlined the elements of this renewed elementary curriculum in Chap. 13. That curriculum would only be possible if we shifted the goal of K-12 education from "college and career-readiness" to a multitude of different paths reflecting actual student differences. My model is loosely based on the German and Austrian public education system (Kolstad & Coker, 1996; Max-Planck-Institute for Education and Human Development, 1983; Rieble-Aubourg, 1996) that provides a general education in elementary, or what they call "primary school," and then differentiates the options as students move into middle and high school.

A renewed middle and high school. States and localities should be granted flexibility as to what their own arrangement would be, but the first years of middle school would be considered an *Orientation* level consisting of students of different abilities and interests all in the same school. The purpose of these years would be to continue the general education of primary school, but more importantly, to help each student (and their family) find their way within the options offered by different types of curriculum that would begin on a trial basis in seventh grade. Intense career exploration and guidance would be provided during sixth grade. There would be several formal conversations with students and families about which curricular option to take based on the student's prior and current academic performance, future interests, abilities, and goals. The Orientation level would keep the educational options open for students until the end of the sixth grade, when a provisional curriculum track choice would then be made. Different tracks would begin in seventh grade, but this decision would be subject to review at the end of the term and would therefore be somewhat tentative.

Instead of just one, there would be three to four curricular options after the Orientation level of middle school. These programs are designed not only to better accord with students' different intellectual abilities and life interests, but also line up with the actual career paths today's students take. This is not the "educational capitalism" described earlier in the book because the goal is not using education simply to get children a high-paying job, but to tailor the latter years of schooling to the various paths and interests of each student. Since students would not all be preparing for college, these paths would set them up for what they eventually decide to do in a much more thorough, proactive, and responsible way than we do now. I would leave it to states and districts to decide on descriptive names for each option, but I do not prefer graded names such as "Level 1" and "Level 2," nor do I like the European terms "High, Middle, and Low" schools. It is vital to keep in mind that each curricular option is different, but equally valid. One is not "higher" or "better" than the other. They are also not "levels" that sit atop one another, but separate tracks unique unto themselves.

The first curricular option would span from seventh through tenth grade. Its curriculum would provide a general education, building on prior learning in elementary school, but the final goal would be to get a job. This program option would serve the roughly 30% of students who graduate high school and get a job, and it would be much more effective in reaching the other 33% of students who currently drop out of high school entirely. These students, representing more than 60% of high schoolers, have struggled with Platonic curriculum their whole lives. The latter years of this level would be undertaken in close collaboration with companies, manufacturing firms, and other industries who could begin training these students for employment, or there could be internships and other field arrangements where a student could earn academic credit for apprenticeship or training work. Comprehensive guidance counseling would be provided to help the student select the best work option given their interests, talents, and abilities. Typical jobs would include ambulance drivers, millwrights, construction workers, auto mechanics, cabinet makers, landscape maintenance workers, electrical power-line installers, orderlies, wellhead pumpers, and restaurant cooks. Students would graduate high school after tenth grade and begin either formal vocational training or employment. It is not clear to me that there is any academic purpose to the latter two years of high school. Time could be better used for actual training and employment.

The second option is geared for those students who will not ultimately go to a four-year college, but who do seek employment requiring either a two-year Associate or technical degree. It would provide a general educational curriculum beginning in seventh grade, but the curriculum would be tilted more toward the aspects of the Platonic curriculum that are required to perform high- and semi-skilled operations as would be present in an Associates program, technical degree, or formal training for a highly skilled job. After intense guidance counseling and career exploration to ensure the proper path, students would graduate after 11th grade and then attend the relevant post-secondary program. Typical career paths would include medical sonographers, avionics technicians, electricians, web developers, machinists, plumbers, home health aides, computer network support specialists, dental hygienists, MRI technologists, and petroleum technicians

The last option is geared for those students bound for careers requiring a four-year college degree (or graduate school). It would provide a general education in sixth and seventh grade, but after that would begin an intensive four-year college prep program such as we have now in most high schools. This would be a heavily Platonic curriculum. This level might even be split into two tracks, one for applied studies, like medicine, psychology, law, and engineering, and another geared toward true university studies and academic research. Whether done as one track or two, after intense career exploration and guidance counseling, students would graduate in 12th grade to pursue college admission for their chosen career.

In addition to differentiating the middle and high school curriculum, schools might also consider eliminating age-based grades in fourth or fifth grade and replacing them with skill-based "gates." This would enable students who need more time to achieve grade-level standards the opportunity to catch up. The student would not be able to stay within a gate forever, but an extra year, two, or three within what is now just a single grade year could make a huge difference for some students. Children should not have to move to the next grade level with inadequate achievement merely because they had a birthday. Indeed, one of the most basic ways of organizing schools is putting students into groups by age. We assume that age is somehow an index of intellectual development, mastery, and skill. But this assumption is just not true. Surely, there are some abilities that come with age and physical maturation, but most do not. Every parent and teacher have witnessed often considerable developmental difference among children the exact same age. As I have indicated previously, in some single-age groups, ability differences can span four to five grade levels. Gate groupings would be based on abilities rather than ages. In addition, academic standards themselves could be grouped into various age clusters, rather than needing to be achieved by the end of a single grade year. This would take some of the pressure off underperforming students without compromising academic standards.

Replacing grades with gates would solve many problems at once. First, it would keep the ability range narrow within a single classroom and enable the teacher to effectively implement differentiated instruction the way it was meant to be done. Second, it would substantially eliminate the need for the furious testing and special interventions we administer to ensure students make adequate progress by the end of a single grading term or academic year. Third, gates would enable schools to provide academically underperforming kids the extra time they need and so would offer a real alternative to the often ineffective retention and social promotion policies we implement now to move students from one grade level to another (Hughes, West, Kim, & Bauer, 2018; Jimerson & Renshaw, 2012). And fourth, a class filled with students of different ages more faithfully reflects the actual groups children will eventually join in the adult world. One frequently hears the argument that we should keep all students of a certain grade in the same room rather than have separate rooms based on abilities because "there are no tracks in the real world" or "a mixed-ability group is what a real community is." But what group in the adult world is based on all members sharing the same birth year? An age-based group is a highly artificial arrangement. It resembles no community that a child will ever be a part of.

If the idea of gates sounds crazy, consider the Boy Scouts that I have been involved with for over ten years. We do not use age-based groups in our programing, but organize boys into groups of 8–14 members of ages that range from 11 to 17. This is called the *patrol method*. The idea is to build on the strength of age diversity and to enable scouts to be able to work together with different types of people (Baden-Powell & Boehmer,

2004). The various abilities present within the different-aged group members naturally organize themselves toward learning and solving problems. The older children learn from the younger, and the younger children learn from the older. Single-age groups tend to lead to rivalry and passivity among the members. The patrol method is not perfect, but has been working well for 105 years. It avoids many of the common problems you see in groups of dozens of children who are all the same age. I am fully aware that replacing age-based grades with gates would be controversial and potentially tricky to implement, but it its strengths far outweigh the limitations. This potential for controversy is the reason I suggest leaving this decision to each state or school district. For gates to succeed, there must be immense local buy-in and trust.

The likely objections to gates and curricular tracks. What are the objections to gates in elementary school and a split curriculum beginning in middle school? Many argue that proposals where we move away from the college-for-all vision mean we are "giving up" or "turning our backs" on certain students, relegating them to the difficult path of a life without a college degree (Giesinger, 2017). Others worry about the demographic composition of the groups who would need extra time in a gate or would not be on a track bound for college (Galster, Santiago, & Stack, 2016). Perhaps, it is feared, there will be a large percentage of African Americans, English-language learners, economically disadvantaged, or special education students in these groups, creating a sort of "academic ghetto" (Forman, 2012). These concerns are understandable and valid in many ways. If a split curriculum were ever implemented, it would require strict procedures to ensure everything was being done to address social, cultural, and economic barriers to educational progress and to make decisions based solely upon student academic achievement, interest, and ability.

The demographic composition of the noncollege tracks is such a difficult issue because it goes to the question of *why* a student does not do well in the Platonic curriculum or fails to attend college. Perhaps, many say, these reasons include past injustices, current racial or economic oppression, bias, or outright discrimination on the part of teachers or educational administrators, and/or unaccommodated disabilities. Absolutely none of these factors should be the reason why a student does not get on the college prep path. But the question is, after eight years of a K-7 formal schooling process which has been met with struggle, academic failure, behavioral problems, and even violence, whether it makes sense at that point to continue with the rigorous college prep curriculum for the remaining five or six years of middle and high school. I think it does not. The reason is because if students who underperform in the Platonic curriculum do not radically change their ways by fourth or fifth grade, most continue to struggle through middle and high school, even widening the low performance they showed in elementary school (Beaudette, Chalasani, & Rauschenberg, 2017; Lloyd, 1978). We should work with gates in the latter years of elementary school and the early years of middle school to get struggling students the extra help and time they need, but if that fails, we should help students and families craft the best possible academic option for each student rather than dragging out the same college prep curriculum they have struggled with for another five to six more years of adolescence.

Let me consider the fate of African American students, since this is the most frequently discussed population in the context of being "left behind" by tracked curriculum proposals like mine. Before talking about how bad things might be with any new changes, it is important to first consider how the current "college-and-career" ready public schools are serving many African American students now. Currently, just 69% of African American students graduate from high school, compared with 86% of white high school students (Governing the States and Localities, 2019). Some adjusted figures put the African American graduation rate at 78% and the white graduation rate at 89% (National Center for Education Statistics, 2019). Just 58% of those graduating African American students ever enroll in college before they turn 24, and only 42% of those ever graduate from college after they enroll (Bureau of Labor Statistics, 2017). Just 24% of African Americans graduating high school ever graduate from college. What does this mean in terms of real numbers of students? There are approximately 2 million high school students in the country who are African American. About 530,000 of these will drop out of high school, essentially rejecting the Platonic curriculum. My question is, could the middle and high schools be reformed to help these students find a path they would rather be on in school, or is the best solution to continue to implement the current college prep curriculum because we do not want to "give up" on them? Out of these 2 million African American students, 852,600 enroll in college, and just 358,092 of those ever graduate. And of these 358,092 students, 143,233 are employed in jobs that do not require a college degree. Out of 2 million students, we achieve our current college prep goals for 214,859 of them, just over 10% of all African American students. Could the middle and high schools have better prepared and guided those nearly 494,508 African American students who dropped out of college and the 143,233 who are overqualified for a future that did not require a college degree but did require some post-secondary education?

So, the question should not only be how will proposals like mine negatively affect African American, English-language learners, or other marginalized students, but will proposals like mine help students *more than the current system does?* I think they will. When I hear the fears that tracked curricula will "leave students behind," I must ask, "You mean leave them behind more than the current setup does?" We may feel good about ourselves, that we "believed in kids" and forced a Platonic curriculum upon them for 13 years, but what did this belief of ours get them? How many years have students who have underperformed in the Platonic curriculum wasted in middle and high school on a curriculum that is nearly useless to them? How much time did they lose not adequately preparing for the life path they eventually took anyway?

Further, my reformed elementary curriculum will be much more exciting, relevant to children's lives, and will hopefully promote more engagement in learning for all students, particularly boys and historically marginalized groups. With a more comprehensive and less college prep curriculum, students will have increased opportunities to achieve in elementary school, to learn about themselves, and to discover what they really enjoy and want to do. I also cannot reiterate enough how important it is to appreciate there is absolutely nothing wrong with pursuing a life path or a job that does not require college. Helping students prepare for what suits and interests them is far better than forcing them onto a track we choose "for their own good." This pressure toward college reflects an ugly prejudice against noncollege jobs and the people who do them.

In the end, all our pushing to have children do what we think is good for them only goes so far. This is the basic limitation of the Lockean view of the child. People are not infinitely malleable. Furthermore, schools cannot be institutions focused on initiating a vast social transformation from the classroom downward. Change does not work that way. Parents, communities, and other stakeholders, including the students themselves, need to be fully committed to this kind of educational project for it to have its intended effects. If schools simply try to do things "to" unwilling children and families, what schools do will fail no matter how much funding and talented teachers we pour into them.

Conclusion

I return to Sleepy Hollow Road, to the place where I began this book. There I hoped to crack open the intimidating gate that divides the public from our elementary schools and to take a good hard look inside. I hope I have succeeded in building a bridge between these two otherwise divided places. This book is only a start. Now that you have seen a little bit of the inside, go visit a local school for real. Volunteer, observe, tutor, and share whatever gifts you have with them. Perhaps it would be a good idea to put some formal programs in place that would ensure the gates of separation between the schools and the public never close again. What would our political discussion of education sound like, for example, if all our politicians and citizens were required to do a teaching internship at an elementary school for a semester or even a month in high school? It may take just an hour or two each week, but what a difference it could make. Why not require such a thing for most high schoolers? It would help the schools a great deal, it might attract many to enter the teaching ranks, and it would help ensure that a much larger percentage of the public was informed about what really goes on in a school each day.

Universal compulsory public education has been with us for a little over 100 years, hardly any time at all. It has also undergone several significant changes during its short history. We tend to see the public school system as a much more entrenched and stable entity than it really is. There have been three major chapters in public school history. The first chapter, which I call *the Founding*, begins in the 1820s with the establishment of the first public elementary schools. Massachusetts was the first state to make school attendance compulsory in 1852; Mississippi was the last state to do so in 1917. Some of the reasons for the founding of public elementary schools included a desire to weaken the power of Catholic parochial education and to protect children from labor exploitation, but most states believed more than anything else that free, common schools would help form disciplined and wise citizens who could effectively exercise the franchise of democracy (Groen, 2008). As such, the curriculum was focused on basic grammar and arithmetic until children left school, typically at age 14. It did not seek to send all children to college or to prepare people for a lucrative career.

As glorious as it was, this Founding also reflected the unjust social structures that existed at the time. Affluent students went to school with other affluent students (or had private tutors); poor students went to school with other poor students (or did not attend school at all). Whites in the north went to school with whites, blacks in the north with blacks. Many blacks in the South did not go to school at all. Girls were often not taught to write and given tasks in school such as sewing and needlework. After the Civil War, the regime of Jim Crow profoundly segregated all aspects of American life, leading to the landmark *Plessy v. Ferguson* case in 1896 which ruled that racially segregated public facilities were permissible so long as they were "equal in quality." This led to the creation of a separate and ostensibly equal system of education for African Americans that was far from equal in fact.

Many people during and after the Founding had the correct sense that access to a good school could change your life in a positive direction, while access to a poor school (or none at all) would keep you held down. In many ways, education has come to be seen as the ticket to the American Dream. The second chapter of public school history, which I call *the Welcoming*, is based on the idea that schools are a doorway to a better life which must not only be open to all children, but children of different backgrounds should all be together as they walk through it. The Welcoming began in earnest in 1954 after Brown v. Board of Education. The Welcoming holds that even if schools are all equal in quality, no longer should the affluent be educated only with the affluent, poor with poor, white with white, and black with black. Schools must be equal in quality and *integrated in diversity*.

We are still in this Welcoming phase now, and struggle to realize its vision of truly equal, high-quality, and fully integrated schools (Hochschild, 2003). We have made great progress, but still have a long way to go, particularly in the area of racial integration, school funding, and equal access to high-quality teachers. But this gradual equalization and integration will ultimately lead to a reckoning in a third chapter. Making all schools high quality and integrated will not guarantee the same educational outcomes for all students and it is not an educational panacea. Many of the same academic struggles students have in today's classrooms will be present even in highest quality and most integrated schools of the future. Students from the same circumstances, even kids from the same household, perform very differently in the same schools, often with the same teacher.

In 1953, just before the Welcoming started, U.S. education spending was 2.6% of gross domestic product (GDP). It is 5.5% of GDP now, more than a twofold increase (Chantrill, 2019). Despite this increased financial commitment and many special education interventions, on some measures like male high school graduation, male academic performance, and male college graduation, things are getting worse with time. The problem is not that we have not spent enough money, but that we have spent our money on just one thing—college prep for all—rather than on diversified things. The issue is not only about academic underperformance among certain students, but about whether we can widen our view to accommodate a world where there are different kinds of performance. Students are only "left behind" when there is one way forward.

Today's public schools are vast and clunky rather than nimble and tailored to the individual student. We are now at the threshold of a third phase of educational history which I call *the Reckoning*. In this chapter, we begin to appreciate the limits of our pushing and top-down social engineering. We recognize that children have their own nature, interests, and callings in life that may be quite different from our own. Instead of a single educational outcome, we work to create excellent, equally funded schools that prepare elementary students for democracy, healthy living, and a heroic future. We trust that later in middle and high school, with our help, they will discern the path in life that works for them. I hope this book will be a small contribution toward this emergent reckoning.

References

Baden-Powell, R., & Boehmer, E. (2004). *Scouting for boys: A handbook for instruction in good citizenship.* Oxford, UK: Oxford University Press.

Beaudette, P., Chalasani, K., & Rauschenberg, S. (2017). How do students' 3rd grade reading levels relate to their ACT/SAT performance and chance of graduating from high school? [PDF File]. Retrieved from https://gosa.georgia.gov/sites/gosa.georgia.gov/files/related_files/press_release/3rd%20Grade%20Reading-Graduation-ACT-SAT%20Analysis%20Final%2003222017.pdf

Bureau of Labor Statistics. (2017). 69.7 percent of 2016 high school graduates enrolled in college in October 2016. Retrieved from https://www.bls.gov/opub/ted/2017/69-point-7-percent-of-2016-high-school-graduates-enrolled-in-college-in-october-2016.htm

Chantrill, C. (2019). US education spending history from 1900. Retrieved from https://www.usgovernmentspending.com/education_spending

Forman, S. J. (2012). Ghetto education. *Washington University Journal of Law & Policy, 40,* 67–116.

Galster, G., Santiago, A. M., & Stack, L. (2016). Elementary school difficulties of low-income Latino and African American youth: The role of geographic context. *Journal of Urban Affairs, 38*(4), 477–502.

Giesinger, J. (2017). Educational justice, segregated schooling and vocational education. *Theory and Research in Education, 15*(1), 88–102.

Governing the States and Localities. (2019). State high school graduation rates by race, ethnicity. Retrieved from https://www.governing.com/gov-data/education-data/state-high-school-graduation-rates-by-race-ethnicity.html

Groen, M. (2008). The Whig Party and the rise of common schools, 1837–1854. *American Educational History Journal, 35*(1/2), 251–260.

Henderson, C. (2018). *Sit down and shut up: How discipline can set students free*. New York, NY: St. Martin's.

Hochschild, J. L. (2003). Social class in public schools. *Journal of Social Issues*, 59(4), 821–840.

Hughes, J. N., West, S. G., Kim, H., & Bauer, S. S. (2018). Effect of early grade retention on school completion: A prospective study. *Journal of Educational Psychology*, 110(7), 974–991.

Jacobs, A. (2017). *How to think: A survival guide for a world at odds*. Redfern, Australia: Currency.

Jimerson, S. R., & Renshaw, T. L. (2012). Retention and social promotion. *Principal Leadership*, 13(1), 12–16.

Kolstad, R. K., & Coker, D. R. (1996). Examining the excellence of German schools and their teacher preparation program. *Education*, 117(2), 280–284.

Lloyd, D. N. (1978). Prediction of school failure from third-grade data. *Educational and Psychological Measurement*, 38(4), 1193–1200.

Locke, J. (1974/1690). *An essay concerning human understanding*. New York: New American Library. Original work published 1690.

Marglin, S. A. (2008). *The dismal science: How thinking like an economist undermines community*. Cambridge, MA: Harvard University Press.

Marx, K., & Engels, F., (1990). *Capital: A critique of political economy* (B. Fowkes & D. Fernbach, Trans.). New York: Penguin Books. Original work published 1867.

Max-Planck-Institute for Education and Human Development. (1983). *Between elite and mass education: Education in the Federal Republic of Germany*. Albany, NY: State University of New York Press.

National Center for Education Statistics. (2019). Public high school graduation rates. Retrieved from https://nces.ed.gov/programs/coe/indicator_coi.asp

Rieble-Aubourg, S. (1996). Institutional arrangements of Germany's vocational education system. *International Journal of Comparative Sociology*, 37(1/2), 174–191.

Schumacher, E. F. (1973). *Small is beautiful: Economics as if people mattered*. New York, NY: Harper Perennial.

Symonds, W. C., Schwartz, R. B., & Ferguson, R. (2011). Pathways to prosperity: Meeting the challenge of preparing young Americans for the 21st century [PDF File]. Retrieved from https://www.gse.harvard.edu/sites/default/files/documents/Pathways_to_Prosperity_Feb2011-1.pdf

Tyre, P. (2009). *The trouble with boys: A surprising report card on our sons, their problems at school, and what parents and educators must do*. New York, NY: Harmony.

Vygotsky, L., & Cole, M. (1978). *Mind in society: The development of higher psychological processes*. Cambridge: Harvard University Press.

Watson, J. B. (1970). *Behaviorism*. New York, NY: W.W. Norton.

Index

A
Ability group, 171, 176–178, 220
Abstract, 35, 111, 112, 119–121, 138, 175, 210, 224
Academic ability, 173, 174
Accommodation, 153, 187–189, 197, 200, 201, 216, 219
Accountability, 6, 100, 119, 147–151, 158–160, 243
Achievement gap, 109, 117, 146–150, 153, 158–160, 177, 179, 180, 199, 215
Adequate yearly progress (AYP), 146, 147, 150, 153, 158
Administration, 47–62, 72, 81, 96–98, 100, 108, 135, 168, 188, 189, 192, 198, 226, 227, 230, 231
Adventure, 28, 29, 31, 35–41, 70, 80, 85, 88–91, 93, 94, 99, 121, 135, 220, 222, 238, 240
Adversarial posture, 55
Affluent, 5, 17, 148, 252, 253
African American, 17, 90, 116, 217, 249–251, 253
Aggregated data, 146, 147

American College Testing (ACT), 217
Assessment, 40, 46, 52, 58, 61, 72, 77, 81, 97, 99, 100, 107, 108, 112, 113, 117, 135, 136, 146, 147, 150, 153, 154, 159, 160, 167, 168, 172, 195, 212, 216, 227, 229
At-risk students, 59, 73, 132

B
Boredom, 27, 28, 41, 125
Boy problem, 17, 22, 244
Brown v. Board of Education, 148, 253
Burnout, 52, 55, 57, 58, 60, 136, 150, 178

C
Cafeteria, 45, 67, 105, 192, 193
Calling, 80, 117, 121, 122, 239, 245, 254
Centers, 19, 166, 186
Cheating, 151, 239
Citizenship, 111, 121, 220, 222, 225

Classroom management, 17, 46, 74, 76, 93, 94, 101, 131, 135, 230
College prep, 87, 110, 111, 114, 116, 119, 121, 135, 146, 151, 154, 158–161, 216, 217, 219, 220, 222, 223, 225, 227, 238, 239, 245, 247, 249–251, 253
College readiness, 173, 217, 218
College-for-all, 216–219, 226, 229, 249
Common Core, 76, 78, 101, 108–112, 114–116
Counseling, 93, 186, 188, 217, 220, 246, 247
Curriculum, 8, 27, 28, 33, 36, 40, 49–51, 58, 61, 72, 75–79, 81, 86, 88, 91, 97–102, 105–122, 126, 135, 145, 146, 148, 151, 154, 158–161, 171, 173, 174, 177, 180, 199, 215–227, 229, 238, 239, 241, 244–247, 249–252

D
Democracy, 23, 113, 116, 121, 221–223, 238, 252
Disability, 17, 22, 153, 181, 186–189, 194–197, 200, 201, 219
Disaggregated data, 158
Discrimination, 13, 14, 95, 243, 249
Disruptive behavior, 16–18, 133–135, 230
Distancing strategies, 119, 120, 122
Diversions, 215, 228–231
Drill-and-kill, 149

E
Educare, 244
Educational capitalism, 86, 87, 92, 94, 116–118, 122, 221, 239, 246

Education for All Handicapped Children Act (EHA), 194–196, 199
Elementary and Secondary Education Act (ESEA), 145–147, 159, 177, 199, 242
Engagement, 21, 39, 127, 133, 135, 160, 207–211, 223, 225, 227, 228, 251
English Language Arts (ELA), 27, 45, 89, 105, 106, 109, 111, 114, 119, 126, 167, 223, 225
Epicurean, 105–122, 210, 215
Every Student Succeeds Act (ESSA), 115, 146, 158, 159, 177
Expulsion, 170
Extra-duty assignments, 189, 192, 231

F
Fad, 8, 9, 169, 199, 229
Fear, 6, 21, 22, 53, 94, 201, 212, 238–240, 243, 251
Finland, 69, 74, 78, 99
Food insecurity, 190
Food service, 191
Founding, the, 252, 253
Free and Appropriate Education (FAPE), 195, 197, 200

G
Gates, 180, 247–250, 252
Gender, 14–22, 89–91, 95, 218, 219
Gender identification, 18, 21
Gender imbalance, 12, 14, 16–22, 85, 96
Germany, 245
Glass escalator, 14
Goals 2000, 108, 109, 146
Graduation, 51, 91, 148, 158, 160, 179, 215, 218, 253

H

Harry Potter, 29, 31–36, 40, 87, 92, 93
Heterogeneous group, 171
High purpose, 28, 29, 31, 34–41, 70, 79, 80, 85, 91, 93, 94, 99, 121, 220, 222, 238
High-stakes tests, 58, 59, 112, 180, 224

I

Ideology, 7, 8, 238, 240–243
Images, 12, 38–40, 86, 178, 187, 191, 210, 212
Index, 59, 248
Individualized Education Program (IEP), 186, 189, 195–201, 231
Individuals with Disabilities Education Act (IDEA), 194, 229
Industry, 36–38, 41, 76, 92, 116
Inferiority, 36–38, 92
Interpersonal intelligence, 173, 224
Intrapersonal intelligence, 224

L

Learning goals, 177, 194, 220, 221, 225
Learning style, 20, 101, 166, 167, 170, 172–175, 177, 178
Least restrictive environment (LRE), 194, 195, 197
Lesson plan, 46, 51, 106, 114, 136, 166
Literacy, 20, 75, 121, 159, 220, 223, 225, 244
Logical reasoning, 223, 224

M

Marginalized group, 18, 146, 147, 251
Math, 13, 18, 22, 28, 33, 36, 39, 45, 74, 86, 88, 89, 101, 105, 106, 108–110, 112, 114, 115, 118, 119, 125–127, 144–148, 150, 151, 153, 157–159, 166, 171, 174, 177, 186, 199, 221–226, 244, 245
Mini-lesson, 126, 130
Misbehavior, 134, 136, 160, 230, 231
Mother, the, 19, 34, 35, 50, 68–70, 78, 81
Muggles, 31, 38, 40, 94, 95
Multiple intelligence, 172–175
Myers Briggs Type Indicator (MBTI), 72
Myth of the great teacher, 118

N

National Assessment of Educational Progress (NAEP), 153, 178
National Defense Education Act (NDEA), 145
No Child Left Behind (NCLB) Act, 48, 108, 115, 143–162, 177, 242
Non-instructional time, 127
Nursing, 12, 188, 222

O

Oppression, 7, 8, 14, 91, 241, 242, 249
Orientation level, 245, 246

P

Parental engagement, 207–211, 216, 227, 228
Patrol method, 248, 249
Physical education (PE), 23, 36, 74, 106, 113, 126, 148, 149, 165, 224, 225, 245
Physical fitness, 116, 121, 220, 224, 225
Physical plant, 51, 96, 188

Planned instructional time, 130–133
Planning time, 46–48, 58, 61, 98, 192, 193, 231
Platonic, 105–122, 159–161, 173, 174, 210, 211, 215, 216, 219, 220, 224–226, 239–241, 244, 246, 247, 249–251
Potholes, 6–8, 22
Problem-solving, 88, 110, 111, 122, 173, 222, 224, 225
Proficiency, 94, 107, 108, 119, 147, 150, 151, 158, 159, 170, 216
Promotion, 56, 57, 179, 248
Public speaking, 116, 223, 225

R

Race, 17–19, 109, 148, 230, 240, 241
Reading, 18–20, 33, 36, 46, 67, 74, 75, 78, 88, 89, 93, 101, 106, 111–113, 118, 120–122, 125, 127, 130–132, 143, 144, 146, 153, 154, 156, 158, 159, 165, 167, 170–172, 174–179, 181, 185, 186, 188, 199, 205, 208, 210, 221, 223, 225, 226, 245
Recess, 16, 23, 38, 40, 51, 90, 125, 126, 128, 149, 225, 245
Reckoning, the, 253, 254
Representational competence, 211
Response to Intervention (RTI), 125, 131, 135, 186, 188, 195–199, 231
Retention, 47, 136, 179, 181, 248
Romantic stage, 35

S

Schedule, 13, 29, 46, 50, 51, 90, 112, 125, 126, 128–130, 133, 165, 209
School Breakfast Program, 190
School Lunch Program, 48
Sergeant, the, 68, 70–71, 78, 81
Sheep, the, 68, 72–73, 78
Social promotion, 179, 248
Special education, 52, 97, 132, 146, 150, 186–201, 219, 227, 242, 249, 253
Specific learning disability (SLD), 195, 199, 200
Standardized tests, 18, 47, 56, 100, 107, 109, 145–149, 152, 154, 157–159, 161, 175
Standards, 6, 13, 28, 29, 37, 40, 49, 61, 70, 73, 76–78, 89, 94, 99–101, 105–119, 145, 170, 188, 205, 215, 240
Standards movement, 107, 109, 113, 145
Story, 6, 21, 28, 31, 33–35, 37, 41, 87–91, 94, 119, 127, 130, 167, 175, 205, 219, 221, 223, 240–243
Supplemental Nutrition Assistance Program (SNAP), 190–192
Suspension, 17

T

Tabula rasa, 241
Teacher recruitment, 99
Teacher training, 74, 76–79, 81, 99–102
Testing, 6, 7, 9, 97, 102, 115, 145, 148, 151, 154, 158, 241, 248
Time-off-task, 132–135
Title 1, 132, 149
Title IX, 12
Total management mentality (TMM), 53–56, 58, 59, 61, 62, 72, 98, 100
Toxic culture, 57–60
Tracking, 168, 170, 176, 177
Transportation, 54, 97, 99, 185, 187, 188, 193, 209

U

Underachiever, the, 68, 73–76, 79, 81
Universal Design for Learning (UDL), 158

W

Wait-to-fail, 195
Waivers, 77, 101, 149–151, 158
Welcoming, the, 11, 206, 253
White, 17, 18, 148, 153, 159, 161, 217, 250, 252, 253

Women's work, 12, 13
Writing, 16, 19, 20, 74, 89, 112, 121, 122, 125, 126, 130–132, 136, 153, 155, 156, 167, 172, 175, 176, 198, 221–223, 225, 226, 237

Z

Zero tolerance, 21, 230
Zombie, 38–41, 94, 95

GPSR Compliance

The European Union's (EU) General Product Safety Regulation (GPSR) is a set of rules that requires consumer products to be safe and our obligations to ensure this.

If you have any concerns about our products, you can contact us on

ProductSafety@springernature.com

In case Publisher is established outside the EU, the EU authorized representative is:

Springer Nature Customer Service Center GmbH
Europaplatz 3
69115 Heidelberg, Germany

www.ingramcontent.com/pod-product-compliance
Lightning Source LLC
LaVergne TN
LVHW020343260326
834688LV00045B/1499